A HISTORY OF AMERICAN
POLITICAL THEORIES

A HISTORY

OF

AMERICAN POLITICAL THEORIES

BY

C. EDWARD MERRIAM, A.M., Ph.D.

ASSOCIATE IN POLITICAL SCIENCE
THE UNIVERSITY OF CHICAGO

New York
THE MACMILLAN COMPANY
LONDON: MACMILLAN AND CO., Ltd.
1903

Norwood Press
J. S. Cushing & Co. — Berwick & Smith Co.
Norwood Mass. U.S.A.

To

PROFESSOR WILLIAM ARCHIBALD DUNNING

MY TEACHER AND GUIDE IN THE STUDY

OF POLITICAL THEORIES

THIS VOLUME IS GRATEFULLY DEDICATED

PREFACE

THE development of American political theories has received surprisingly little attention from students of American history. Even the political ideas of the Revolutionary fathers and the tenets of such important schools as those represented by Jefferson and Adams have not been carefully analyzed or put in their proper perspective. The political theory of the controversies over slavery and the nature of the Union has generally been presented from the partisan point of view, while recent tendencies in political thought have received no adequate notice.

In explanation of this fact, it might be said that until very recent times but little interest has been manifested in systematic politics. But while it is true that Americans have never developed systems of politics after the philosophic fashion of the Germans, there has been no dearth of political theory from the days of the Puritans to the present time. Seldom worked out by political scientists or philosophers, American political ideas have generally taken shape in connection with some great question of national policy which has seemed to require a broad theoretical basis for either condemnation or approval. Conspicuous examples of this are found in the discussion over the Revolution, over slavery and secession. These political theories have played an important part in our national life, and are closely woven into the fabric of American history. Of particular significance are they in view of the fact that they represent the philosophy under which has been developed the mightiest democracy of modern times, or of any time.

It is, then, the purpose of this work to present a description and analysis of the characteristic types of political theory that have from time to time been dominant in American political life. An effort has been made throughout to discuss these theories in their relation to the peculiar conditions under which they were developed, and to keep in sight the intimate connection between the philosophy and the facts that condition it. Like all other political theory, American political ideas are of little importance aside from the great historical movements of which they are an organic part.

In the preparation of this volume, use has been made of several articles already published elsewhere. "Paine's Political Theory" appeared in *The Political Science Quarterly* for September, 1899, and "The Political Theory of Jefferson" in the same magazine for March, 1902. "The

Political Theory of Calhoun" was printed in *The American Journal of Sociology* for May, 1902; and the chapter on political theory in relation to the nature of the Union is an expansion of Chapter IX in my monograph on "The History of the Theory of Sovereignty since Rousseau" (in Columbia University Series in History, Economics, and Public Law, Vol. XII, No. 4, 1900).

This study is the outgrowth of investigations begun in the Seminar on American Political Philosophy given by Professor Dunning in Columbia University, 1896–1897; and the writer wishes to acknowledge his deep sense of obligation for the inspiration then given and for subsequent encouragement and assistance in the prosecution of this work. Acknowledgment is also due to Professor Judson, Professor Jameson, and Professor Freund of The University of Chicago, to Professor Hart of Harvard, Professor Willoughby of Johns Hopkins, Professor Macdonald of Brown, and others who have kindly read parts of the manuscript and offered invaluable suggestions.

SEPTEMBER, 1902.

CONTENTS

CHAPTER I

THE POLITICAL THEORY OF THE COLONIAL PERIOD

CHAPTER II

THE POLITICAL THEORY OF THE REVOLUTIONARY PERIOD

CHAPTER V

THE JACKSONIAN DEMOCRACY

CHAPTER VI

THE POLITICAL THEORY OF THE SLAVERY CONTROVERSY

The Anti-slavery Theory

The Pro-slavery Argument

CHAPTER VII

POLITICAL THEORY IN RELATION TO THE NATURE OF THE UNION

CHAPTER VIII

RECENT TENDENCIES

CHAPTER IX

A HISTORY OF AMERICAN POLITICAL THEORIES

CHAPTER I

THE POLITICAL THEORY OF THE COLONISTS

A STUDY of American political theories may appropriately begin with an examination of the ideas of the colonists who laid the foundations upon which the national structure now rests. In view of the fact that the Puritan ideals, political and moral, have been so potent a force in the development of American national characteristics, attention will first be directed to the Puritan political tenets.

Puritanism was primarily a religious and not a political movement.[1] Its central doctrine was that the spiritual element in worship is of far greater importance than the ceremonial element. The

[1] A complete discussion of the Puritan theory is given by H. L. Osgood in the *Political Science Quarterly*, Vol. VI, " The Political Ideas of the Puritans." See also *The Rise of Democracy in Old and New England*, by Charles Borgeaud; G. E. Ellis's *Puritan Age in Massachusetts;* and the standard histories of this period: in particular, Doyle's *Puritan Colonies* and J. G. Palfrey's *History of New England.*

Puritans condemned a ritualistic service as not only unnecessary and superfluous, but positively injurious and sinful; and they demanded a style of worship from which the ceremonial features were as nearly as possible eliminated. The Anglican Church they bitterly denounced for its failure to carry through the desired reforms, and its retention of so many of the features of the Roman worship. Theologically, Puritanism was closely allied to Calvinism, and it resembled Calvin's system on the political side also. In common with the other adherents of the Reformation, the Puritans denied the binding force of Church tradition, precedent, and law, asserting that the Scriptures are the only authoritative guide of human conduct. In a study of Puritan politics it is essential, therefore, to remember that the spirit and purpose of the Puritans' movement was only incidentally political. Their aim was to found a spiritual, not a political, organization — a church rather than a state. They were interested above all things in the true worship of God, which meant to them, of course, the Puritan style of worship.

It is important to observe at the outset the basis upon which the Puritans rested their commonwealth. Having rejected the authority of the Church and ecclesiastical law and precedent, they relied solely upon the Scriptures as a guide for all conduct, public as well as private, and considered the Bible as the only proper foundation upon which either a state or a church could rest. They attempted to deduce from the Old and New Testaments their whole system of public law, finding in these writings, expressly or by implication, authority for the government as organized and administered. As their theology and their form of church government rested upon a scriptural basis, so must their political theory and their state have the same foundation. This idea was well stated by John Eliot in his work on *The Christian Commonwealth ; or, The Civil Policy of the Rising Kingdom of Jesus Christ,*[1] when he said that "there is undoubtedly a form of Civil Government, instituted by God himself in the holy Scriptures, whereby any Nation may enjoy all the ends and effects of Government in the best manner, were they but perswaded to make trial of it. We should derogate from the sufficiency and perfection of the Scriptures, if we should deny it." In the establishment of New Haven Colony, one of the questions submitted to those participating was, "Whether the Scriptures doe holde forth a perfect rule for the direction and government of all men in all duties which they are to perform to God and men, as well in the government of families and in the Commonwealth, as in the matters of Church ?"[2] ; and to this all assented. This idea runs through the Puritan thought of that time. They devoutly believed that somewhere in

[1] *Mass. Historical Society Collections*, Third Series, Vol. 9, p. 134.
[2] *New Haven Records*, I, 12 (1639).

the Scriptures there must be a rule of public as well as of private conduct, and they further believed that they had discovered and were applying this rule in the development of their political institutions. The particular part of the Bible upon which they relied for this purpose was the Old Testament, with its frequent references to the political experiences of the Children of Israel. This was a rich mine of precedent, to which the Puritans frequently resorted when in need of such support to justify their conduct.[1]

It is not to be assumed, however, that the Puritans really constructed their entire political system from an interpretation of the Scriptures.[2] They brought with them to the New World the English common law, English political precedent and tradition of centuries' growth. This was beyond question the real basis of their system, and the additions to this from interpretation of the Scriptures were less important than the Puritans themselves thought. It would be near the truth to say that they did not begin with the Scriptures and build up a complete system, but that they attempted to justify a system already in existence

[1] For example, Cotton said that no instance could be given "of any capital Law of Moses, but is of moral (that is of general and perpetual) equity, in all Nations, in all Ages. Capitalia Mosis politica sunt aeterna." *The Bloudy Tenent*, Chap. LIII.

[2] O. S. Straus, in the *Origin of the Republican Form of Government in the United States of America*, maintains this proposition.

by finding for it a scriptural basis. In the general tendency to test all things by Scripture, it was only natural that the state should be subjected to the same treatment, and that an attempt should be made to find a scriptural model for political institutions.

The system of government adopted by the Puritans was what might perhaps be called theocratic in character. The most cursory view could not fail to reveal the predominant position of the clergy. From the beginning, the life of New England was largely under the influence of the ministers. In many cases men of marked learning and sagacity, whose Puritan morals and theology did not conflict with shrewd worldly wisdom, they dominated the political as well as the intellectual and religious life of the community. They were consulted upon all matters of public policy, such as Indian affairs or relations with the mother country; they frequently preached political sermons bearing directly on public questions; there was never, perhaps, a body of clergy that exercised greater influence on affairs of state than did these New England leaders. Especially in Massachusetts Bay, they established an ecclesiastico-political régime, recalling in many of its features the Geneva system of John Calvin. In two of the colonies membership in some approved church was essential to full citizenship. Only those who were church members could become "freemen" in Massachusetts Bay and in New Haven, and it is not likely that other than church members were actually received in Plymouth and Connecticut. As late as 1660 the General Court of Massachusetts Bay resolved that no person could become a "freeman" who was not in full communion with some orthodox church. The exclusive character of the Massachusetts Bay system is shown by the fact that down to 1674 only 2527 were admitted as freemen, one-fifth of the total number of adult males.[1] Of the other features in the theocratic régime it is not necessary to speak at length. The Sabbath Laws, taxation for purposes of church support, compulsory attendance on church services, the anti-heresy acts, — all were part of the general system in which the civil power was invoked to stimulate the religious sentiment and practice of the community. The same tendency is also shown by the attitude of the Puritans toward adherents of other religions. In the controversy with Roger Williams, with the Antinomians, with the Quakers and the Baptists, a determination was manifested to preserve the Puritan type of religion by force if necessary. Liberal use was made of fines, imprisonment, disfranchisement and banishment as means of grace for the spiritually perverse. The Puritans themselves were dissenters from dissenters, but they did not intend that the process of dissent should be carried farther.

[1] G. E. Ellis, *Puritan Age*, p. 203.

Their theory of the relation between church and state was clearly brought out in the famous controversy between Roger Williams and John Cotton, the spokesman for the Massachusetts theocracy.[1] An examination of this controversy may seem somewhat remote from the field of political theory, but only through such an inquiry is it possible to arrive at a satisfactory understanding of the political ideas of the Puritan. The gist of the Williams-Cotton debate is found in three pamphlets occasioned by the banishment of Williams. These were, *The Bloudy Tenent of Persecution for Cause of Conscience* (1644), by Williams; *The Bloudy Tenent washed, and made white in the Bloud of the Lambe* (1647), by Cotton; *The Bloudy Tenent yet more Bloudy* (1652), by Williams.[2]

Two of the most significant topics discussed may be considered here : first, the nature of the church and the state ; second, the extent of the civil power in religious affairs. First, then, the theory as to the nature of the church gives the key to the understanding of the entire dispute. Williams's contention was that the state is distinct from, and may

---

[1] See Doyle, *Puritan Colonies*, Vol. I, Chap. IV, for an account of this affair.

[2] See also the Cambridge Platform of 1648, Chap. 16. This was a statement of church doctrine made by a synod representing the four New England colonies. See also Cotton Mather, *Magnalia*, Vol. II, Book 5.

exist without, the church, as, for example, among heathen people. " The church," said Williams, " is like unto a corporation, society, or company of East India or Turkie merchants, or any other societie or companie in London, which may ... wholly breake up and dissolve into pieces and nothing, and yet the peace of the citie not be in the least measure impaired or disturbed."[1] This is true, because the " essence " of the church and the state is different, and consequently the religion may be radically changed, while the government of the city or state remains unchanged; or the government may be altered without affecting the character of the religion.   Ephesus may cease to worship Diana, and still be Ephesus; or it may happen that there are different religions in the same city, the aim of all these religions being distinct from that of the state.

Cotton, for his part, agreed that the church is a separate society, distinct from the state; but held that the church is the chief society in the state, and that the growth and welfare of the state are dependent on the purity of the church. The church, although not the " essence " of the state, nevertheless " pertains to the integrity of the city "; it is among the " conservant causes " of the state, and cannot be broken up without affecting profoundly the welfare of the body politic.[2]   Cotton conceded

---

[1] *The Bloudy Tenent*, Chap. VI.

[2] *Bloudy Tenent washed and made white*, Chap. VI.

that there are historical examples of states which have flourished under heathendom; but he declared that after the true church is once introduced, then this true worship must be protected by the state.

The crucial question in the controversy was that concerning the proper extent of the power of the civil magistrate in religious matters. Williams held that the true church is spiritual in nature, and, as such, has no need of the support of the civil magistrate in order to maintain its proper position. It does not require worldly means of defence, but should use only the spiritual weapons, such as "the breastplate of righteousness," "the helmet of salvation," "the sword of the spirit."[1] Civil magistrates had never been made defenders of the faith in the Scriptures, and the omission shows that there had been no intent to confer such authority on them. The civil officers should not proceed to organize churches; they should not inflict punishment on those adjudged heretics, or impose civil penalties or disabilities for any religious reason. Williams contended that if civil magistrates had rightful power in spiritual affairs, then even in a barbarous Indian tribe rightful jurisdiction over the church of Christ would be vested in the Indian civil authorities, and the Christian religion would be entirely at the mercy of rulers

[1] *The Bloudy Tenent of Persecution*, Chap. XLV.

with pagan consciences.[1] It is clearly evident, then, that Williams's view of the state was decidedly secular in character. He limited its activity in religious affairs to 'what were called at that time "breaches of the second table."[2] Transgression of any of the last six commandments might be punished by the state, but over violations of the commandments in the first table they should have no jurisdiction. "Scandalous (offence) against parents," he said, "against magistrates in the fifth command, and so against the life, chastity, goods, or good name in the rest, is properly transgression against the civil state and common weal, or the worldly state of men."[3] Such offences the government may rightfully punish, but those crimes which concern the relations of man to God it should not attempt to suppress. They are spiritual in nature, and civil penalties cannot properly affect them. On this ground Williams denounced in vigorous terms the treatment to which he and others had been subjected as wholly unwarranted and unjustifiable.

Cotton replied to these arguments that "it is a carnal and worldly, and, indeed, an ungodly imagination, to confine the magistrate's charge to the bodies and goods of the subjects, and to exclude

---

[1] *The Bloudy Tenent of Persecution*, Chap. XCII.

[2] The first four commandments, covering the duties of man to God, were called the "first table"; the last six, covering the relations of men to each other, constituted the "second table."

[3] *Ibid.* Chap. LVI.

them from the care of their soules." [1] He maintained that it is the evident duty of the magistrates to use all available means to prevent the
pollution and corruption of the church, and to
strive in every way to preserve its purity.[2] He
even attempted to show that laws about religion
are, strictly speaking, civil laws. "Whatsoever
concerneth the good of the city and the propuls-
ing of the contrary," is a civil law, said he. "Now
religion is the best good of the city, and therefore
laws about religion are truly called civil lawes." [3]
But Cotton's reasoning would have been inadequate and ineffective from the Puritan point of
view, unless supported by scriptural authority.
Unable to find any express warrant in the New
Testament, Cotton met the difficulty by showing
that there was not authority in that part of the
Bible, even for the punishment of such crimes as
adultery and murder, and that consequently it
must be assumed that a rule of action is elsewhere contained in the Scriptures. Such authority is found in the "Laws of Moses and the
Prophets who have expounded them in the Old
Testament."[4] He maintained that all the capital
laws of the Mosaic Code are of universal validity,
and that whatever the kings of Israel inflicted on
transgressors of either the first or the second table,

---

[1] *The Bloudy Tenent washed and made white*, Chap. XXXIII.
[2] *Ibid.* Chap. XXXV.   [3] *Ibid.* Chap. LXVII.
[4] *Ibid.* Chap. LXXIII.

was a pattern and example to Christian magistrates.[1]   Thus basing himself on the Mosaic
Law, Cotton found abundant sanction for any
measures required to preserve the peace and
purity of the church.   Such phrases as, "Thou
shalt surely kill him . . . because he hath sought
to thrust thee away from the Lord thy God,"
seemed to him to justify almost any means that
might be used.

It is evident, then, that Cotton was a thorough
believer in the doctrine that it is the right and duty
of the magistrates to punish transgressions against
the commandments contained in either of the
"tables."   In addition to the offences specified by
Williams, Cotton included many others.   He
declared that one who holds an "erroneous doctrine
or practise" is a violator of the civil law; "he who
refuseth to subject his spirit to the spirit of the
Prophets in a holy Church of Christ" comes under
the same category.   Even such offences as the
"censorious reproach" of one who rebukes our
spiritual error, or "rejecting communion" before
one is convicted, may be looked upon as a disturbance of the peace and hence as falling under the
jurisdiction of the civil magistrates.[2]   In short,
Cotton's theory was that the state should guarantee
the observance of church law and ceremony, just
as if they were its own enactment, and that to
accomplish this purpose any exercise of force

[1] *Ibid.* Chap. XXXV.   [2] *Ibid.* Chap. VII.

would be perfectly justifiable. As he phrased it on one occasion, "legall terrours are ordinary meanes blessed of God to prepare hard and stout hearts to conversion." [1]

He was far from admitting, however, that he justified persecution "for cause of conscience," as Williams alleged. On the contrary, he declared that the conscience is sacred and inviolable and not to be disturbed, whether it be conscience "rightly informed" or "conscience misinformed." [2] A significant exception was made, however, in case "it may appear that the erroneous party suffereth not for his conscience, but for his sinning against his conscience." [3] In other words, individuals are not punished because they follow conscience, but because they refuse to obey its dictates; not because they are blind, but because they wilfully shut their eyes. Of the same character is the argument that "to persecute is to punish an Innocent; but a heretic is a culpable and damnable person." [4] Cotton realized that the action of the magistrates might result in the production of hypocrites; but "better tolerate Hypocrites and Tares than Bryars and Thornes." [5] Or as elsewhere expressed: "Better a dead soule be dead in body, as well as in Spirit, than to live and be lively in the flesh." [6] Based on like logic was the argument that in reality men are never *compelled* to worship, for, "though teach-

---

[1] *Ibid.* Chap. IX.   [2] *Ibid.* Chap. X.   [3] *Ibid.*
[4] *Ibid.* Chap. LXV.   [5] *Ibid.* Chap. XXXIX.   [6] *Ibid.* Chap. XL.

ing and being taught in a Church estate be Church worship, yet it is not a Church worship but to such as are in a Church estate." [1]

Such was the character of Cotton's theory, and it was typical of Puritanism in the early days of settlement in America.   It was the theory of men to whom the preservation of the Puritan religion was an object of paramount importance — an end for which they had already given up much and for which they were ready to sacrifice still more. They were thoroughly convinced that it was the duty of the state to uphold and support the church at every possible point, and they acted on this conviction.[2]   In so doing they were neither in advance of nor behind the theory and practice of their time, but simply followed the custom of all the states of that day.   From one point of view it may seem strange that the Puritans, fleeing from persecution in England, should prove so ready to persecute in turn those who dissented from Puritanism.   What the Puritans objected to, however, was not the use of force to maintain a religion, but

[1] *Ibid.* Chap. LXX.

[2] In the Massachusetts Body of Liberties it was declared that "Civill Authoritie hath power and libertie to see the peace, ordinances and Rules of Christ observed in every church, according to his word, so it be done in a Civill and not in an Ecclesiastical way." Sec. 58.   The converse right was not given to the church, however. It was provided that, "No church censure shall degrade or depose any man from any Civill dignitie, office or Authoritie he shall have in the Commonwealth."   Sec. 60.

the use of force to support any other than the true religion. Regarding their own form of worship as the true one, they considered it perfectly just to call on the civil power to preserve it, even by force if necessary.

Having considered the Puritan theory of the relation between church and state, we now turn to an inquiry into the question how far Puritanism was democratic. It would be wide of the truth to assert that at the beginning there was any general enthusiasm for democracy as such. John Cotton on one occasion (1644) denounced democracy as "the meanest and worst of all forms of government," and on another occasion openly indorsed theocracy.[1] A proposition for the establishment of an aristocracy was made to Massachusetts Bay in 1634, and was rejected only because it involved the abandonment of the church-membership requirement for suffrage. "Two distinct ranks, we willingly acknowledge from the light of nature and scripture," they said, "the one of them called Princes or Nobles or Elders (amongst whom the gentlemen have their place); the other the people. Hereditary dignity or honors, we willingly allow to the former, unless by the scandalous and base con-

[1] Letter of Cotton to Lord Say and Seal, 1636, in Appendix to Hutchinson's *History of the Colony of Massachusetts Bay*, Vol. I. The Scriptures, he said, establish "theocracy as the best form of government in the commonwealth, as well as in the church." Pg. 498.

versation of any of them, they become degenerate." [1]
It is also notable that only a part of the inhabitants
of the colonies were made "freemen"; in the case
of Massachusetts, only about one-fifth. "Inhabitants" and "freemen" were sharply distinguished
and were accorded different degrees of political
privilege. All of these features were undemocratic.

Other parts of the Puritan system show more
democratic tendencies. Among these was the
emphasis on local self-government, finding expression in the town-government which has played so
conspicuous a part in American constitutional development. Furthermore, careful provision for
adequate protection of civil rights was made by the
colonies in such notable instruments as the Body
of Liberties in Massachusetts Bay (1641) and the
Fundamental Orders of Connecticut (1639). These
were largely, however, the guaranty of the ordinary
rights of Englishmen, and consequently cannot be
regarded as exclusively Puritan in character.

A democratic tendency is seen in the method
adopted in the formation of new communities by
the Puritans. The use of the contract as a basis
for the establishment of a "body politic" was a
widespread practice in the New England colonies.

---

[1] *Ibid.* I, 490 ff. This was somewhat qualified by the statement that, "Hereditary honors both nature and scripture doth
acknowledge (*Eccl.* xix. 17), but hereditary authority and power
standeth only by the civil laws of some commonwealths." *Ibid.*
493.

The first of these was the famous Mayflower covenant of 1620. Here it was declared that the undersigned, " Do by these Presents solemnly and mutually, in the Presence of God and one another, covenant and combine ourselves into a civil Body Politick, for our better Ordering and Preservation, and Furtherance of the Ends foresaid; and by Virtue hereof do enact, constitute and frame, such just and equal Laws, Ordinances, Acts, Constitutions, and Officers from time to time, as shall be thought most meet and convenient for the general Good of the Colony; unto which we promise all due Submission and Obedience." [1]

Another illustration of the same principle is afforded by the example of Connecticut in the adoption of the "Fundamental Orders." In this agreement it was stated that: "We, the Inhabitants and Residents of Windsor, Hartford, and Wethersfield . . . doe associate and conjoyne ourselves to be as one Publick State or Commonwealth and doe, for ourselves and our successors and such as shall be adjoyned to us att any time hereafter, enter into Combination and Confederation together to mayntayne and presearve the liberty and purity of the gospel of our Lord Jesus, which we now profess, as also the discipline of the Churches, which according to the truth of the

---

[1] Poore, *Constitutions and Charters*, I, 931. But they did not profess political independence. "We . . . the Loyal Subjects of our dread Sovereign Lord, King James, etc."

C

said gospel is now practised amongst us, as also in our Civell Affaires to be guided and governed according to such Lawes, Rules, Orders and decrees as shall be made, ordered and decreed, as followeth." [1]

In Rhode Island there were many similar contracts made, as, for instance, the agreement at Providence in 1636, and at Portsmouth in 1638. In the latter the form of the covenant was as follows: "We whose names are underwritten do here solemnly in the presence of Jehovah incorporate ourselves into a Bodie Politick and as He shall help, will submit our persons, lives and estates unto our Lord Jesus Christ." [2]

It is now necessary to inquire into the theory on which these contracts rested. The discussion of this question, however, involves an examination of the theory on which the New England churches were constructed. These ecclesiastical organizations, it appears, were formed on what is known

---

[1] *Connecticut Records*, I, 20.

[2] *R. I. Records*, I, 52. In the Newport Declaration of 1641 is found one of the boldest of democratic assertions. It is here proclaimed that "The Government which this Bodie Politick doth attend unto in this Island and the Jurisdiction thereof, in favour of our Prince is a Democracie or Popular Government; that is to say it is in the power of the Body of Freemen orderly assembled or the major part of them, to make or constitute just Lawes, by which they will be regulated, and to depute from among themselves such ministers as shall see them faithfully executed between man and man." *Ibid.* I, 112.

as the "Separatist" plan; namely, by voluntary agreement between a number of individuals to constitute themselves as a church. This was the method followed by the Separatists in England, who believed that the church is not formed by action of the state, or by virtue of apostolic succession, but is merely a number of believers under a covenant with God. Although the New England Puritans were not all Separatists while in England, they became so almost as soon as they reached this country,[1] and proceeded to adopt the covenant as the proper method of forming a church. Official recognition of this idea was given in the Cambridge Platform adopted in 1648, when reference was here made to the "visible Covenant, Agreement or Consent, whereby they give themselves unto the Lord, to the observing of the ordinances of Christ together in the same society, which is usually called the Church Covenant."[2] This covenant was described as the same as that which made Abraham and the Children of Israel the people of God, and was declared to have the force of constituting societies of believers as churches.

[1] See the case of the Salem church, 1629.

[2] Chap. IV, § 3. For a full discussion of these church covenants, see Williston Walker, *The Creeds and Platforms of Congregationalism* (1893); see also the classic work by H. M. Dexter, *Congregationalism as seen in its Literature*. The Cambridge Platform is given in Walker, pp. 194–237.

A remarkably clear and definite statement of the contract idea was made in a work by the famous Connecticut divine, Thomas Hooker, — *A Survey of the Summe of Church Discipline* (1648). The reasoning of Hooker, to which almost no attention has been given, is notable for its early exposition of the contract theory and the way in which it anticipates such classic writers as John Locke. Hooker urges that all men are ecclesiastically equal, and where every man remains uncontrolled there must follow the " distraction and desolation of the whole." " In the building," said he, " if the parts be neither mortised nor brased, as there will be little beauty, so there can be no strength. Its so in setting up the frames of societies among men, when their minds and hearts are not mortised by mutuall consent of subjection one to another, there is no expectation of any successful proceeding with the advantage to the public." [1] " Mutual subjection," he declares, " is as it were, the sinewes of society, by which it is sustained and supported." [2] He calls attention to two classes of covenant, the explicit and the implicit, and indicates a preference for the explicit agreement.[3] The effect of this contract is to make every part subject to the whole and bound by its orders. Nevertheless, the people still retain "the power of Judgment over each other " and hence they proceed against any officer "that

[1] *Survey*, p. 188.   [2] *Ibid.* Cf. p. 50.   [3] *Ibid.* 47.

goes aside." This they do, "though not by any power of office, for they are not officers, but by power of judgment which they do possess." [1] This is a striking anticipation of the theory of revolution, later developed by John Locke.[2] In the one case the theory is applied to the church, however, and in the other to the state.

The idea of the contract as the basis of associations was not peculiar to Hooker, but was common to the New England Puritans of his day. In defence of their form of church organization, government, and discipline, they asserted again and again that the contract is the method by which all associations are formed. "All voluntary relations," it was said in the *Apologie*,[3] "all relations which are neither natural nor violent are entered into by way of covenant." Hooker stated the idea with great clearness and force, but he spoke only as a representative of the general opinion in New England.[4] In the face of strong opposition from England, the Puritans defended the formation of churches through contract, the election of pastors and

---

[1] *Ibid.* 192. The Cambridge Platform declares that "If the Church have power to chuse their officers and ministers, then in case of manifest unworthiness and delinquency they have power also to depose them."

[2] In the second of his *Two Treatises of Government.*

[3] *An Apologie of the Churches in New England for Church Covenant* (1639), by Richard Mather.

[4] On this subject see John Cotton, *The Way of the Churches of Christ in New England* (1645); *The Way of Congregational*

teachers by the people, the rule of the majority in
church affairs, the right of the congregation to discipline or dismiss their ecclesiastical head.[1] Frequent reference was made to the contracts of Old
Testament days; for example, " Jehoiada made a
covenant between the Lord and the king and the
people; that they should be the Lord's people;
between the king also and the people " (II Kings
xi: 17). Another similar precedent was found in
Deuteronomy xxix: " Ye stand this day all of you
before the Lord your God . . . that thou should-
est enter into covenant with the Lord thy God . . .
that he may establish thee to-day for a people unto
himself and that he may be unto thee a God." It
seems to have been the prevailing idea that a con-

Churches Cleared (1648). Also Richard Mather, *Church Government and Church Covenant Discussed* (1643); *Model of Church
and Civil Power* (quoted by Osgood, *op. cit.*); John Davenport,
A Discourse about Civil Government (1663). A later exposition
is that of John Wise, *A Vindication of the Government of New
England Churches* (1772).

[1] Mather's explanation of majority rule is suggestive. It seems
that a vote was first taken and an effort made to secure unanimity.
But if the minority " still continue obstinate, they are admonished,
and so standing under censure, their vote is nullified." *Church
Government and Church Covenant Discussed*, p. 61.

It was explicitly denied that the form of church government was
purely democratic. Mather said, " our answer is neither thus nor
so, neither all to the People excluding the Presbytery, nor all to the
Presbytery excluding the People. For this were to make the government of the Church either meerly democratical, or meerly
aristocratical, neither of which we believe it ought to be."
Ibid. 57.

tract was the necessary basis for both the church and the state.[1] These two classes of covenants were known respectively as the " church covenant" and the "plantation covenant "; and there was an intimate relation between the democratic method of forming a church and the democratic method of forming a state.

Let us now consider briefly the Puritan ideas of liberty and equality from the political side. First, then, what was the Puritan conception of liberty? The common idea that the Puritans were enthusiasts for political freedom can hardly be sustained. What they were chiefly concerned about was moral rather than political liberty. This was shown by Winthrop when he divided liberty into two classes: natural liberty and civil or federal liberty. The first kind, natural liberty, is absolute and unlimited; it cannot be subjected to any restraint whatever from the side of authority. Civil or federal liberty, on the other hand, is constituted by the covenant between God and man, and by the political covenant. This liberty is freedom to do that which is " good, just, and

[1] This idea of the contract had been worked out by the controversialists of the sixteenth century. See the *Vindiciæ contra Tyrannos*, 1579, by an unknown author. This work contains a curious blending of arguments derived from the Bible, Roman law, and feudal custom. The rights, obligations, and other incidents of the contractual relation are taken from the Roman law. The contract theory was clearly stated by Richard Hooker in his famous work on *The Laws of Ecclesiastical Polity*, (*circa*) 1594.

honest." [1] "It is," says Winthrop, "the same kind
of liberty wherewith Christ hath made us free,"
that is to say, freedom from the bondage of sin,
and the restraints it involves.   Liberty was not
conceived as absolute and unqualified lack of restraint, but as freedom of motion in that particular
direction in which one should go in accordance
with the covenant made with God.   The Puritans
brought with them the undoubted liberties of Englishmen, and these they were careful to preserve.
The political liberty, however, about which they
were most anxious was the independence of their
corporation or society.   This they were always
ready to defend against any other authority, especially the rule or attempted rule of the home government in England.   But they were not so eager
in behalf of the individual within the corporation.
The corporate conscience and the corporate conduct
must be free and untrammelled, but not necessarily
the conduct and conscience of the individual.   The
Puritans did not preach or practice religious toleration, nor did they become enthusiastic about the
inherent rights of man.   They jealously guarded
their traditional English liberties, they were ear-
nestly desirous of moral and spiritual freedom, but
their great end and aim politically was to secure a
kind of civil government under which their religious system could best be maintained.

Nor were the Puritans given to assertions about

[1] *History of New England*, II, 280–81.

the innate equality of all men. Particularly in Massachusetts Bay, there were manifest in the early period decidedly aristocratic tendencies. The equality upon which the Puritans laid greatest stress, and which was to them most significant, was the equality of all men before God. Before Him, all men were regarded as sinners, hopelessly lost, so far as their own efforts could avail, and no one more worthy than another. In the doctrine of the Fall there is no room for rank or preëminence, but all are reduced to one common level. Thus it appears that the Puritans were believers in what is sometimes termed "spiritual equality," as distinguished from other types; and even in this connection, as has been suggested, they held to "democracy in the Fall, but aristocracy in the Redemption," for only the elect were regarded as saved.

Nor did they grant religious equality to all, for, as already indicated, they were intolerant of other religions than their own. The idea of full and complete freedom to choose whatever religion the individual might prefer, they were not prepared to accept, as the controversy between Williams and Cotton indicates. They did not entertain doctrinaire ideas about equality of any kind. They granted equality in civil rights, but did not include equality of political rights even among the adult males. This was true not only of the earlier period of the Puritan age, but of the later as well; for the religious requirements at first exacted were succeeded in the latter part of the seventeenth century by property qualifications for office-holding and for suffrage. The conclusion must be, then, that for political equality as such there was no great enthusiasm among the Puritans.

From this discussion it is evident that Puritanism in New England, and particularly in Massachusetts Bay, may fairly be characterized as theocratic. The dominant class was the clergy; church-membership was a prerequisite to full citizenship; the civil power was invoked to insure to the church financial support, to enforce church discipline, to suppress and root out heresy.

From a consideration of these tendencies of Puritanism it might perhaps be assumed that there was no democratic element in the system worth considering. It would, however, be just as far from the truth to conclude that there was no democratic element in Puritanism, as to assume that its adherents came to the New World for the express purpose of establishing political and religious liberty for all men. Neither claim is borne out by a consideration of the Puritan theory and practice. Of greatest significance from the standpoint of democratic political theory is the Puritan idea of the contract. Primarily applied to ecclesiastical relations, to the formation of a congregation through the instrumentality of a church covenant, the same theory of the contract was carried over into political relations. The church covenant and the plantation covenant went hand in hand. This theory of contract necessarily emphasized the importance of the individual as the unit in both the ecclesiastical and the political society, for it was voluntary consent and not divine right or long-established custom that was the basis of both church and state. This individualistic idea contained a germ of democracy which could not fail to develop under favorable conditions. In New England the early tendencies toward aristocracy or theocracy soon began to disappear, and the process of democratizing social and political institutions began a course which is not yet completed.

This result cannot all be attributed to Puritanism as such, however. The Puritans inherited from English ancestors and brought with them to the New World the political capacity characteristic of a highly developed political people. There was also a highly favorable environment, inviting if not compelling the growth of a democratic society and state. In estimating the democratic value of Puritanism these facts cannot be ignored.

Next in importance and interest to the political ideas of the Puritans were those of the Friends in Pennsylvania. Here was worked out a system differing from that of the Puritans in respect to religious tenets and upon many political

principles.[1]   In the religious teachings of the
Friends, the sternness and severity of the Puritan
theology was in many ways modified.   In place of
the doctrine of election, it was taught that the
grace of God is universal in its application, and
that there is an immediate revelation of the spirit
of God to each individual soul in the form of an
"inner light." [2]   In this respect the doctrine of the
Friends was the antithesis of Puritanism.   In other
ways, however, the Friends were more Puritan than
the Puritans themselves.   They not only denounced
ceremonialism as fiercely as did the Puritans, but
further abandoned all sacraments, denied the necessity for any special priesthood, denounced church
tithes, and refused to take an oath or have anything to do with war.   They emphasized plainness
of dress, and directness of speech, and refused
to uncover the head or bow to any man.   But
at the same time the Quakers possessed practical characteristics that enabled them to achieve
great worldly success.   Of this the establishment
of the colony of Pennsylvania was a signal proof.

The government of Pennsylvania was on the
whole about as democratic as that of the Puritan
colonies.   The emphasis on the contract was lack-

[1] A. C. and R. M. Thomas, *A History of the Society of Friends
in America ;* Isaac Sharpless, *A Quaker Experiment in Government,* 1902.

[2] See William Penn, *The Rise and Progress of the People called
Quakers* (1695); Robert Barclay, *Theologiæ veræ Christianæ
Apologia* (1676).

ing, but the theocratic element found in New England was also wanting. Religious toleration was granted to all deists, and there was no religious qualification for office except the belief in Christianity.[1] The ecclesiastical organization of the Friends was more democratic than that of the Puritans. There was no special body of ministers exercising authority over the people, women were granted equal rights with men, and the meetings whether for business or worship were conducted with the greatest informality, not even a presiding officer being regarded as necessary.

An interesting fragment of Quaker theory is contained in the Frame of Government drawn up by Penn for the colony.[2] In this document attention is called to the great ends of government, which are said to be two, namely, to terrify evil-doers and to cherish those that do well. Particular emphasis is laid on this double character of governmental activity. " They weakly err," it is said, "that think there is no other use of government than correction, which is the coarsest part of it." Of the forms of government three are suggested as being most commonly discussed, but the conclusion is drawn that, "any government is free to the people under it . . . where the laws rule and the

[1] After 1705, Roman Catholics were disqualified from holding office.

[2] Poore's *Constitutions*, Vol. II, p. 1518. Compare with this The Fundamental Constitutions of Carolina, 1669, *Ibid*. II, 1397.

people are a party to those laws." Any government will work in the proper hands; for like clocks they go from the motion communicated to them, and in general depend on men rather than men on governments. Good men will always have good laws, whereas good laws may lack good men for their enforcement. The great end of the Frame of Government was declared to be "to support power in reverence with the people and to secure the people from the abuse of power."

The opposition of the Quakers to taking the oath and to participation in war involved them at times in difficult situations. It was charged by their enemies that their unwillingness to take an oath frequently resulted in failure to convict criminals, since in some communities no sworn jury could be secured. This seems, however, to have occasioned no serious difficulty, and the matter was finally settled by granting the Quakers the privilege of affirming instead of taking the oath.[1]

The refusal of the Friends to take up arms was a matter of greater importance. During the intercolonial wars, frequent requisitions were made upon them for a quota of troops. All such requests were refused, however, even when the colony was itself threatened with invasion by the enemy. They steadfastly declined to send any soldiers, or to grant any money for the conduct of the military opera-

[1] Cf. Sharpless, *op. cit.*, Chap. V.

tions. It was urged that if they could maintain a
local police force and take human life in punishment for crime, they might properly take up arms,
at least in self-defence. But the Quakers maintained that a distinction must be drawn here. It
was one thing, they said, to kill a soldier fighting in
obedience to the commands of his sovereign, and
another to kill a burglar who maliciously steals
one's goods in wilful violation of laws human and
divine.[1] Although they declined to send troops
or vote money for the war, the Quakers did not
put themselves in the position of absolutely refusing
assistance to the government to which they owed
allegiance. They were willing to contribute money
to the home government, provided it was not used
for military purposes, but for other governmental
needs. For example, in 1709 the Assembly voted
£500, "as a present for the Queen."[2] In 1745
they voted £4000 for "bread, beef, pork, flour,
wheat, and other grain." "We have ever held it
our duty," they said, "to render tribute to Cæsar,"[3]
and therefore made the contribution. Their attitude
occasioned earnest remonstrance and bitter criticism, but the Quakers remained unmoved, and uni-
formly refused to appropriate men or money for
the war, except in the indirect way just described.
When no other alternative seemed possible, the

---

[1] *Minutes of the Provincial Council*, IV, 371 (1739).
[2] *Ibid.* II, 466.
[3] *Ibid.* IV, 769.

strict Quakers refused to try for seats in the Assembly, and allowed that body to pass under the control of those who had no scruples against military operations.

The rapid growth of the democratic spirit was not peculiar, however, to the Puritan and Quaker colonies. The conditions did not favor aristocracy, and the experiments made in that direction showed conclusively that its establishment was impracticable. The resources of the colonies would not support the necessary expenditure, nor was the temper of the people favorable in any greater degree. Something in the environment seemed to arouse the spirit of liberty and inspire the assertion of individual and colonial rights in the most aggressive fashion.

To this there are many witnesses whose testimony, biased though it was, shows unmistakably the nature of the new movement. Take, for example, the indignant references of Governor Spotswood of Virginia to the election of " representatives, persons of narrow fortunes and mean understandings," and to the general opinion "that he is the best patriot that most violently opposes all overtures for raising money, let the occasion be what it will" and to the "mobish candidates" who "always outbid the Gentlemen of sence and principles, for they stick not to vow to their electors that no consideration whatever shall engage them to raise money."[1] He was particularly aggrieved because "some of them have so little shame, as publicly to declare that if, in Assembly, anything should be proposed which they judged might be disagreeable to their constituents, they would oppose it, though they knew in their conscience, it would be for the good of the country."[2] He denounced those who "inflame the common people with notions of the ruin of their Libertys," and charged that "the liberty of doing wrong is none of ye least contended for here."

In Pennsylvania the same leaven was at work, even under the proprietorship of one so little disposed to arbitrary rule as was William Penn. In 1704 it was said that the people think "all that can be grasped to be their native right." It was alleged that "some people's brains are as soon intoxicated with power as the natives are with their beloved liquor, and as little to be trusted with it."[3] Significant was the denunciation of one Guest, because "a desire to be somebody, and an unjust method of craving and getting, seems to be the rule of his life." Penn himself observed this "excess of vanity" on the part of the Americans. "Having got

[1] Spotswood Letters, in *Virginia Historical Collections*, New Series, Vol. II, 134 (1715).

[2] *Ibid.*

[3] Penn-Logan Correspondence, in *Memoirs of the Historical Society of Pennsylvania*, Vol. IX, 299.

D

out of the crowd in which they were lost here,"
said he, "upon every little eminencey there, (they)
think nothing taller than themselves but the
trees."[1]

What the governors or royal agents characterized as stubbornness or stinginess, or quibbling
over technicalities, or playing into the hands of
upstarts and demagogues was, however, merely
the expression, often indeed very crude, of the
widespread democratic sentiment slowly gaining
strength for the outburst in the Revolution.

The storm centre of the democratic movement
during the colonial period was the conflict between the governors and the colonial legislatures or
assemblies.[2]   For this contest there was English
precedent in the action of Parliament during the
seventeenth century, and local reason in the colonial desire to escape administrative control by
the home government.   Especially in Massachusetts and New York the conflict was hard-fought,
bitter, and long protracted, but the difficulty was
by no means confined to these provinces.   In the
course of this battle, the assembly constantly
gained on the governor, and steadily enlarged

[1] Penn-Logan Correspondence, in *Memoirs of the Historical
Society of Pennsylvania,* Vol. IX, 374.   Cf. *Maryland Archives,* IX,
177–178 (1758);   Carroll, *Historical Collections of South Carolina,*
II, 164.

[2] On this point see E. B. Green, *The Provincial Governor,* in the
Harvard Historical Studies, Vol. VII, 1898.   In this connection
see Jeremiah Dummer, *Defence of the New England Charters,* 1745.

its power at the expense of his. The control of
the finances, especially, gave them the opportunity
to direct or influence the governor's activity in
many ways. Appropriations might be withheld
to the embarrassment of the administration, or,
if granted, might be made for specific and de-
tailed purposes. The salary of the governor was
determined by the assembly, and voted by that
body at its pleasure, thus making it master
of the governor's financial situation, — an advantage more than once used to extort his assent to
measures favored by the assembly. The appointing power was also in many cases wrested from
the governor and assumed by the representatives
of the people. This was especially true as to the
treasurer, who, as financial agent of the colony,
was exposed to attack. The movement was not
confined, however, to this officer, but the assembly
appointed in some cases nearly all of the agents
of administration, as in Pennsylvania and South
Carolina.

In other ways the assembly asserted its
power by assuming the direction of matters of
public policy which had generally been considered a part of the prerogative of the executive.
Indian affairs, for example, it sometimes man-
aged by means of commissions appointed for that
purpose; intercolonial relations were also treated
in the same fashion; military affairs the legislature sometimes controlled by granting supplies,

prescribing the operations to be undertaken, appointing and removing officers, and even interfering with the discipline of the troops. So far had these encroachments gone, that in 1757 it could be said of Massachusetts that "almost every act of executive and legislative power, whether it be political, judicial or military, is ordered and directed by the votes and resolves of the General Court, in most cases originating in the House of Representatives."[1] More than anything else, this conflict served to bring out the spirit of democracy which was everywhere ready for action. It was a rallying point around which tendencies favorable to independence and popular government could gather, and as the intercolonial wars helped to teach the colonists military science, so these political battles afforded them indispensable training in the art of statecraft.

On the whole, it may be said that during the colonial period the democratic spirit made remarkable progress. The colonies passed out of the stage in which they were religious experiments or industrial ventures of a rather hazardous character, and became prosperous communities eager for governmental autonomy. The individuals within these colonies were filled with a democratic enthusiasm, and ready for an advance in the direction of popular government. Until the decade

[1] Board of Trade to Governor Pownall, cited by Green, *op. cit.* 194.

preceding the Revolution there was, however, little systematic discussion of the problems of political theory, with the exception of the indirect contribution made by the Puritans. A steady democratizing process was going on under the influence of the new conditions, but there was little conscious reflection accompanying this process. With the agitation preliminary to the Revolution came a group of leaders who sought a philosophical basis for their policies, and accordingly made frequent use of the formulæ of political theory in their great struggle for independence.

CHAPTER II

THE POLITICAL THEORY OF THE REVOLUTIONARY
PERIOD

THE most important and significant statement of
American political theory is that made at the time
when the United States asserted the right to an
independent existence. The Declaration of Independence has been generally regarded as the
corner-stone of the American political system, and
the ideas of the "Fathers" of 1776 as a correct
statement of the typical American political philosophy. These doctrines have undoubtedly exerted a profound influence in determining the
course of American political thought. Even down
to the present day, they are the standards by
which must be measured all that is attempted in
the world of politics. No study of American political ideas, or of American political institutions,
would be complete without a careful analysis of
the characteristic doctrines of 1776.

It is, then, the purpose of this chapter to examine carefully the nature and origin of the political
ideas prevalent during the score of years covering
the Revolutionary period; that is, from about 1763
to about 1783. The exposition of the doctrines of

this period is rendered somewhat difficult by the fact that there was no systematic presentation of political theory made during this time. There was an unlimited amount of discussion from platform and pulpit, in pamphlets, resolutions, addresses, and newspapers, but a scientific statement of the popular beliefs was not made. It was natural that under the conditions no scientific shape could be given to any body of doctrine. Men wrote and spoke with eloquence and force, and they were men of intellectual keenness and power; they spoke, however, not as philosophers, but as partisans and promoters of a concrete revolutionary program.

Among the most important sources of information for this period, despite their unsystematic form, are the speeches and writings of such men as Otis, John and Samuel Adams, Dickinson, Paine, Jefferson, and Hamilton. Many indications of the Patriot theory are also found in the various declarations of colonial rights that were made on numerous occasions by legislatures or other less formal public assemblages. Finally, in the Revolutionary state constitutions are expressed, in legal form, the principles that were dominant among the people. From this material the ideas of this time may be reconstructed, and a fairly adequate and comprehensive view of its political theory obtained.

At the outset a few words may be said in regard to the historical situation under which was developed the theory to be considered. The result of the French and Indian wars removed a great obstacle to American independence, and from 1763 on the drift of political conditions was steadily in the direction of separation from the mother country. The long experience of the colonies in the art of self-government, their remoteness from England, and the difficulties of successful administration from so distant a base, the clash of colonial interest with Britain's nationalist policy,—all were conditions likely to find expression at a favorable opportunity, in terms of political independence. The crisis came when the home government in England endeavored to tighten the long-relaxed bonds of union and to establish over the colonies a more complete administrative control.[1]

The immediate occasion of the conflict was a question of colonial taxation. In 1764 came the Declaratory Resolves, indicating the intention of the ministry to levy a tax on America. This was followed in 1765 by the famous Stamp Act, which aroused the opposition that found best expression in the Stamp Act Congress. This act was re-

[1] The following works are especially useful in the study of this period: Richard Frothingham, *Rise of the Republic of the United States;* George Bancroft, *United States*, Vols. III and IV ; W. E. H. Lecky, *England in the Eighteenth Century;* M. C. Tyler, *Literary History of the American Revolution;* W. M. Sloane, *The French War and the Revolution.*

pealed the next year, but at the same time the significant declaration was made that Parliament possessed the undoubted power to bind the colonies "in all cases whatsoever." The excitement over this assertion of Parliamentary authority had not died away before the Townsend Act was passed (1767), imposing taxes on such commodities as glass and tea, and providing means for the enforcement of the same. Though this act also was repealed (1770), with the exception of the duty on tea, the resistance continued to be as bitter as before. In 1773 the colonists instituted what proved to be a powerful agency in the development of their organization, namely, the Committees of Correspondence between the colonies. In the meantime fuel was added to the flames of colonial discontent by the instructions sent to the royal governors and by the Regulating Act for Massachusetts. The Boston Port Bill, passed in 1774, aroused universal indignation and sympathy, and led up to the first Continental Congress of 1774. In the following spring came the clash of arms at Lexington; in May, 1775, the Continental Congress made its declaration on taking up arms against Great Britain; and finally, all hope of reconciliation having been destroyed, the Declaration of Independence was issued. During this period of thirteen years there was incessant debate upon questions of colonial policy, of constitutional law, and of political theory. These were topics of absorbing interest among the colonists, and occupied the minds of the ablest thinkers of that day. In 1776 began the work of constitution-making in the various states, and opportunity was given for the development or application of constructive theory. This process was completed by 1784, and with this date the epoch of the Revolutionary theory may be said to have closed.

The argument with which the colonists began their resistance was constitutional in nature, involving the legal relations between the home government and the colonies. To this doctrine brief notice must now be given, in order that the full significance of the Revolutionary political theory may appear. The contention of the Patriots was that the course of the British Parliament, in taxing the American colonies, was not merely inexpedient and unjust, but actually contrary to the principles of the British Constitution. Consequently they affirmed that the government, in attempting to enforce such legislation, was wholly outside of legal and constitutional right. The basis for this claim was not always clearly stated, and was sometimes shifted, but the main features of it may be noted here.

It was asserted, on the one hand, that the colonists owed their allegiance, not to Parliament, but to the king. From him they had received their charters, and to him, and not to Parliament, they were accountable. Britain and the colonies, it was said, are distinct states, as were England and Scotland before the union; they are bound together only by their common allegiance to a common king. "The fealty and allegiance of the Americans," said John Adams, "is undoubtedly due to the person of the King George III, whom God long preserve and prosper."[1] In accordance with the charters received from him and of other express or implied contracts, the colonists owe obedience to the king, although not to Parliament. This body has no authority to tax, it was urged, except for the regulation of colonial trade, and this is not strictly a right, but exists "merely by the consent of the colonies, founded on the obvious necessity of a case which was never in contemplation of that law, nor provided for by it."[2] The various Acts of Trade were even compared to commercial treaties between the colonies and Great Britain.

By some of the Patriots a distinction was drawn between acts of Parliament levying external taxes

---

[1] See John Adams, *Works*, IV, 146; Answer of the Massachusetts House of Representatives to the Speech of the Governor, 1773, in Niles, *Principles and Acts of the Revolution in America*, 287–294; Stephen Hopkins, *The Rights of the Colonies Examined* (1764), reprinted in *R. I. Records*, VI, 416; Richard Bland, *An Inquiry into the Rights of the British Colonies* (1766); Jefferson, *Summary View of the Rights of the Colonists* (1774). See Adams's reply to the argument that the king owed his position to an act of Parliament, *Works*, IV, 114.

[2] Adams, IV, 33. Cf. Hopkins, *R. I. Records*, VI, 420.

for the purpose of general regulation of the trade of the kingdom, and on the other hand acts levying internal taxes on the colonies.[1] The authority of Parliament to levy the former was conceded on the ground of necessity for the general interest, but it was denied that the imposition of an internal tax was a constitutional exercise of power.

Another line of reasoning was that by the terms of the charters the colonists were entitled to all the rights and privileges of native-born English citizens. They were to be as free in America as if they had remained in England. As Hopkins said, "There would be found very few people in the world, willing to leave their native country and go through the fatigue and hardship of planting in a new and uncultivated one for the sake of losing their freedom." On this basis the assertion was made that the colonists possessed the right of Englishmen to be taxed only in case they were represented. This, they held, was the most fundamental of all the rights of Englishmen, and one of which they could not be deprived by any act of Parliament. Inasmuch as the colonists were not represented in Parliament, it followed they were not liable to internal taxation by that body.

It was also argued that, owing to the local conditions, American representation was impracticable or impossible, and consequently that such taxes

[1] This idea was developed most clearly by Pitt in the House of Commons.

must be levied through the colonial legislatures, — the only channel through which consent could legitimately be given.[1] Formal recognition of this doctrine was embodied in the resolutions of the Stamp Act Congress in 1765, which declared that "it is inseparably essential to the freedom of a people and the undoubted right of Englishmen, that no taxes be imposed on them without their consent, given personally or through their representatives." Later this doctrine assumed a still bolder form in the Declaration of the Congress of 1774, to the effect that the colonists "are entitled to life, liberty and property, and they have never ceded to any sovereign power whatever a right to dispose of either without their consent."

Such was the constitutional argument upon which resistance was at first based. This line of attack proved to be vulnerable, however, in at least two points. First, the contention that the colonies were dependent upon the crown alone and independent of Parliament, so far as internal taxation was concerned, was not in harmony with the opinion of the ablest jurists of the time, notably Mansfield. Again, the doctrine that no Englishman could be taxed when unrepresented in Parliament was not in accord with the system of that day, which left totally unrepresented such popu-

---

[1] John Adams enumerated the objections to colonial representation, *Works*, IV, 139. Cf. Samuel Adams, *Natural Rights of the Colonists*, Wells, I, 507 ; also Bland, *op. cit.*

lous and important communities as Sheffield, Bir-
mingham, and Leeds.   From this point of view it
appears that the colonists were advocating a new
theory and practice of representation, and not defending an old and well-established one.[1]   They
had in short an antiquated theory as to the position
and power of Parliament, and a premature theory
of Parliamentary representation.   Doubtless the
colonists were influenced by certain seventeenth
century opinions that the courts had the power to
declare void an act of Parliament contrary to the
common law.[2]   But in the eighteenth century, the
opinion of crown lawyers was undoubtedly to
the effect that Parliament did have the power to
bind the colonies "in all cases whatsoever."   The
earlier idea crept into the law books, however, and
hence came to be used for political purposes, after
it had ceased to have any real value as a legal
principle.

Such was the nature of the constitutional argument which gave legal color and character to the
first resistance against the British government.[3]
Concurrently with this reasoning appeared much

[1] Mansfield's argument in favor of Parliamentary supremacy is
sketched by Bancroft, Vol. III, 190 ff. (last revision, 1891).

[2] See Bonham's Case, 8 Rep. 118 a.

[3] On this subject see an article by H. L. Osgood, "England and
the Colonies," in the *Political Science Quarterly*, II, 440–69; also
Sir Frederick Pollock on "Sovereignty in English Law," in the
Harvard Law Review, Vol. VIII, 243 ff.

that was based on more abstract doctrines. The fundamental principles of the political theory of the "Fathers" were similar to those of the English revolutionists in the seventeenth century. The leading propositions in this philosophy were these. Before the establishment of civil government, men exist in a "state of nature," are subject only to the "law of nature," and possess a number of so-called "natural rights." How far these rights extend every man determines for himself, and each enforces his own judgment. Government is created by means of a contract in which every one surrenders enough of his natural rights to permit the establishment of an organized authority, — "a common umpire." But in case the government becomes oppressive, the people may then exercise the reserved right of resistance and overthrow the established authority.

The colonists believed, then, in a pre-governmental state of nature. In this condition no man is subject to another, but each protects and defends himself — is perfectly free and independent. In the state of nature, moreover, all men are equal, not in the physical or intellectual sense, but so far as concerns jurisdiction or authority. No man is born ruler or governor of others, but all are created free to rule themselves, and equal in the right to rule themselves.

All men possess, it was further maintained, a group of what were called "natural rights." No subject was more frequently a topic of discussion than the rights of the colonists. These were to a great extent regarded as legal or constitutional rights against Parliament or against the crown, and elaborate arguments were made from this point of view. The colonists were not content, however, to stop with this kind of reasoning, but carried the discussion beyond the boundary line of public law. They declared that there exists a body of natural rights antedating the existence of government and superior to it in authority. These natural rights, it was held, are the real basis of political rights, and hence the action of the Britis 1 government, even if strictly legal, was still regarded as contrary to the inherent rights of man. This idea was boldly and forcibly expressed by many of the Patriot leaders. Dickinson declared that "our liberties do not come from charters; for these are only the declaration of preëxisting rights. They do not depend on parchments or seals; but come from the King of Kings and Lord of all the earth." John Adams said that rights do not come from princes or parliaments; but are coæval with these. They are founded "in the frame of human nature, rooted in the constitution of the intellectual and moral world," derived from "the Great Legislator of the universe." Even more vividly the youthful Hamilton asserted that "the sacred rights of mankind are not to be rummaged for among old parchments or musty records. They are written as with a sunbeam in the whole volume of human nature, by the hand of the Divinity itself and can never be erased or obscured by mortal power."

What constitutes these rights was best stated in the Declaration of Independence, where it was asserted that all men are " endowed with certain inalienable rights ; among these are life, liberty, and the pursuit of happiness." In the state constitutions the same idea appeared, clothed in different phraseology. For example New Hampshire stated that there are " certain natural, essential, and inherent rights, among which are the enjoying and defending life and liberty ; acquiring, possessing and protecting property ; and in a word, of seeking and obtaining happiness." These are rights which belong to every man by virtue of his existence. They are antecedent to the formation of political society, and the necessary basis of all just government. The colonists proposed, therefore, to base their claim on the rights of British subjects, but if these were not recognized, then they would go deeper down and rest their contention on the natural rights of man.

The belief in the state of nature, and in the freedom, equality, and natural rights of man, was accompanied by the theory of contract as the necessary basis of all legitimate government. If men are born free and equal, then no government can claim allegiance and obedience from them,

E

unless they agree to it. It appeared to the men of this time as indisputably true that a just and free political society could rest on no other basis than the consent of the individuals to be ruled. This seemed the only rational way to explain the existence of government with coercive power over individuals who might otherwise live as independent sovereigns. Hence some form of contract was regarded as a necessary step in the establishment of all legitimate government. This idea was taken up the more readily by Americans, because of the prominence it had enjoyed when the early New England settlements were formed. Hence it is not surprising to find in the Declaration of Independence the statement that " governments derive their just powers from the consent of the governed " ; or in the Massachusetts Bill of Rights that, " the body politic is formed by a voluntary association of individuals; it is a social compact by which the whole people covenants with each citizen and each citizen with the whole people, that all shall be governed by certain laws for the common good."

The exact nature of this contract was little discussed. Thomas Paine in his *Common Sense* gave a fanciful sketch of early patriarchs assembling to form a government. Another authority agreed with Locke that the contract dates back so far that we have no record of it. "What eye," he said, "could penetrate through gothic night and barbarous fable to that remote period?"[1] In general, however, there was a wise indifference to the details of the original contract. The Patriots were content with the understanding that governments derive their just powers from the consent of the governed, as a working hypothesis. This was accepted as one of the axioms in political philosophy, which no one in his political senses would question.

Closely connected with the theory of the social contract, was the proposition of the Americans, that "taxation without representation is tyranny," and the more general idea into which this was often merged; namely, that all legitimate legislation must rest upon representation or consent. This was discussed from the point of view of Parliamentary authority and the rights of Englishmen; but this was not the only angle from which the question was approached. The right to be represented was regarded not only as the right of Englishmen, but as the right of all men existing under a free government;[2] indeed it seemed to be considered as the most fundamental of all rights, the *sine qua non* of political liberty. The principle was looked upon as one of general application, and not peculiar

[1] *Boston Orations*, in Niles's *Principles and Acts of the Revolution in America*, pp. 51–52. Cf. Samuel Adams, in Wells, I, 429; Hopkins, in *R. I. Records*, VI, 416. Otis's idea of the contract was somewhat different.

[2] Adams said that "English liberties are but certain rights of nature reserved to the citizen by the English constitution." IV, 124.

to English constitutional law. John Adams maintained that "the very definition of a freeman is one who is bound by no law to which he has not consented."[1] Dickinson repudiated in strong terms the right to levy taxes, where the taxpayers are not represented. "Craft and cruelty," he said, "are striving to brand us with marks infamously denoting us to be their property as absolutely as their cattle."[2] In accordance with this line of argument was Hamilton's assertion that "civil liberty cannot possibly have any existence, where the society for whom laws are made have no share in making them."

The principle of consent to taxation and lawmaking in general was the strategic point, which the Patriots defended with all the resources of constitutional law and political theory at their command. If natural rights and the social contract have any vital force at all, they reasoned, they must be capable of use in the defence of a man's own property. If all that one has can be taken away by laws passed by a distant legislature in which one has no voice, then there is an end of natural right and the subversion of the social contract. This question of taxation appeared to the Patriots as the central point in the whole controversy, theoretically as well as practically. It mattered not what the amount of the tax was, nor

[1] *Works*, IV, 28.
[2] *Ibid.*, XIV, 495. Cf. S. Adams, in Wells, I, 154 ff.

how easily it might be paid; the principle was essentially the same. Hopkins declared[1] that "one who is bound to obey the will of another is as really a slave, though he have a good master, as if he had a bad one." The men of the Revolution saw only the two alternatives: freedom or slavery; taxation and representation, or taxation without representation.[2] They recognized no middle ground either in constitutional law or in political theory: they must be either wholly slave or wholly free, and the test of this was whether they were or were not afforded an opportunity to consent to taxes levied upon them. This was the theoretical point upon which the Revolution turned.

Related to the theory of natural rights and the "consent of the governed," was the doctrine of popular sovereignty. That the people are the basis of all legitimate political authority was a proposi-

[1] *R. I. Records*, VI, 423. Cf. Dickinson, XIV, 356 ff.

[2] Dickinson evolved an elaborate syllogism to prove that taxation without representation is tyranny.

(1) God gave no one a right to make others miserable; hence the right to be happy.

(2) There can be no happiness without freedom; hence the right to freedom.

(3) There can be no freedom without security of property; hence the right to such security.

(4) Property is not secure if it can be taken without one's consent; hence the right to be taxed only when consenting, personally or through representatives. *Memoirs of the Historical Society of Pennsylvania*, Vol. XIV, 262.

tion which was little disputed at this time. Since all men are born with the same natural rights, and inasmuch as all legitimate government must be based upon the consent of these individuals, it is evident that the great mass of the people are the foundation of the state. No sovereignty can come into existence or continue to exist, unless the people consent to and authorize it. The inherent and inalienable sovereignty of the people was therefore assumed as a political principle of incontestable validity, — a premise which could not be assailed. Although frequent reference was made to this doctrine, there was little attempt at scientific discussion of the idea : it seemed, indeed, to be so generally recognized that elaborate argument upon the question was superfluous.

In the Declaration of Independence the doctrine was stated in the familiar form, "governments derive their just powers from the consent of the governed." A more explicit statement was that contained in the Massachusetts Proclamation (1776),[1] to the effect that the sovereign power "resides, always, in the body of the people ; and it never was, or can be, delegated to one man or a few, the great Creator having never given to men a right to vest others with authority over them, unlimited either in duration or degree." Similar declarations found their way into the state constitutions. Thus North Carolina said that "all political power is vested in

[1] Force's *American Archives*, Fourth Series, Vol. IV, p. 834.

and derived from the people only"; New Hampshire, that "all government of right originates from the people"; and the same sentiment was expressed elsewhere with slight variation in the phraseology. The constructive applications of this doctrine will be considered later. The destructive application of the doctrine took the form of the right of resistance, — naturally one of the most conspicuous of the doctrines of 1776. The Revolutionary movement rested upon a theoretical basis which served as a justification for the necessarily illegal conduct of the Patriots. In the preceding century two revolutions had occurred in England, and the theory of revolution had received classic formulation in the treatise of John Locke. The Americans were thus supplied with ample precedent from England in both historical events and philosophic formulæ.

Even before the conflict with England had begun, a decidedly independent spirit had been manifested in many of the colonies, and there were not lacking corresponding expressions of opinion. A bold statement of the right of resistance was made by Rev. Jonathan Mayhew on the anniversary of the execution of King Charles (1749). Mayhew referred to the experience of England and to the theory of Locke. He denounced unjust and tyrannical magistrates in the most unsparing terms, declaring that when they cease to perform their functions properly, they " cease to be the ordinance

and ministers of God, and no more deserve that
glorious character than common pirates and high-
way-men." [1]   Mayhew admitted that this principle
might be perverted to bad ends, but maintained
that this is true of all principles, including that of
passive obedience.

When the opposition to the English policy
became widespread, and it seemed that open resistance must be made, arguments in favor of the
right of revolution appeared upon every hand.   A
general belief in such a right was vital to the success of the Revolutionary movement, for nothing
could be done if it was believed that government
was something too sacred to be touched.   History
and philosophy were therefore drawn upon, to
support the justice of resistance to government in
extreme cases.   All of the Patriot leaders defended
the right of revolution with earnestness and vigor.
Samuel Adams turned the argument against rulers,
by asserting that kings and magistrates may also
be guilty of treason and rebellion, and on the whole
have been guilty more often than their subjects.[2]
Dickinson took strong ground against the doctrine
of passive obedience, urging that Parliament might
sometimes do wrong, and in such cases resistance
was advisable.   Although praising the king and the
royal line, he showed that even a father may do

[1] Sermon at the West Meeting House in Boston, 1749–1750, contained in *The Pulpit of the American Revolution*, by J. W. Thornton.
[2] Wells, I, 433 (1771).

injury to his child :—"If my father, deceived and urged on by bad or weak men, said he, should offer me a draught of poison and tell me it would be of service to me, should I be undutiful, if, knowing what it is, I refuse to drink it ?"[1] Samuel Langdon, President of Harvard, declared before the Congress of Massachusetts (1775) that if magistrates forget their duty, "reason and justice require that they should be discarded and others appointed in their room, without any regard to formal resignations of their forfeited power."[2] Seldom was there dispute as to the right of revolution ; the greatest difference was in the form of statement, or, on the part of others, in regard to the expediency of resort to it at that particular time.

As might be expected, the Revolutionary idea found at times rather radical expression. An example of this type is the following statement made in one of the annual Boston orations. The speaker here defined civil liberty as "a power existing in the people at large, at any time, for any cause, or for no cause but their sovereign pleasure, to alter or annihilate both the mode and essence of any former government and adopt a new one in its stead." Benjamin Church declared that "where a degrading servitude is the detestable alternative, who can shudder at the reluctant poignard of a Brutus, the crimsoned axe of a Cromwell, or the

---

[1] Cf. Hamilton, *Works*, edited by J. C. Hamilton, II, 95.
[2] Thornton, *op. cit.*, 250.

reeking dagger of a Ravillac?"[1]   The more
moderate form of the Declaration of Independence
is familiar to all: "Whenever any form of government becomes destructive of these ends, it is the
right of the people to alter or to abolish it, and to
institute new government, laying its foundations on
such principles and organizing its powers in such
form, as shall seem most likely to effect their safety
and happiness."

Frequently this philosophy found a channel of
expression in the constitutions of the states.   New
Hampshire asserted that the doctrine of non-resistance is "slavish, absurd, and destructive of the
good and happiness of mankind."   Pennsylvania
said that "the community hath an indubitable, inalienable and indefeasible right to alter, reform or
abolish government in such manner as shall by
that community be judged most conducive to the
common weal."   Delaware stated that "persons
entrusted with the Legislative and Executive power
are the trustees and servants of the publick, and as
such are accountable for their conduct; wherefore,
whenever the ends of Government are perverted
and publick liberty manifestly endangered by the
Legislative singly or a treacherous combination of
both, the people may and of right ought to establish a new or reform the old Government."

The theory of the state of nature, natural rights,
and the contract were all steps leading up to the

1 Niles, *op. cit.*, 10.

right of revolution. If all these premises were accepted, as they generally were, the conclusion was easy. One might doubt the expediency or advantage of revolution; but that it was logically justifiable in theory was hardly questioned. The right of resistance was one of the "fundamentals" over which there was but little dispute. The colonists firmly believed that their natural rights had been violated, and that they were wholly justified in the best self-defence possible. These rights were not to be infringed by the government, but to be protected; if, on the contrary, these inherent and inalienable rights were attacked and abused by government, then there was undoubted justification for armed defence of them. Such defence was not only a right, but even a duty for all free men or those who loved freedom.

This argument was of course closely related to the constitutional plea made in behalf of the Patriots. There was thus a twofold justification for their resistance; first, that the action of Parliament in regard to the colonies was unconstitutional; and second, that even if constitutional, this action was in violation of the natural rights of the colonists. In the early period of the struggle the constitutional defence was most conspicuous; in the later period the plea of natural rights was more prominent. If their rights as British subjects could not be maintained, they could at least defend their rights as men. The argument from the constitution was not abandoned, but the doctrine of natural right was less open to attack and was consequently more effective. Hence the increasing complaints of the colonists that their inalienable rights as men were being attacked, and that they were in danger of being reduced to abject slavery. In some cases it was claimed, following the precedent set by the House of Commons in 1689, that the king had broken the contract with the people.[1] In others it was asserted that the social contract had been broken, and the state of nature restored.[2] To all, however, it was plain that their sacred rights were being assailed, and that they had a counter-right to resist to the last extremity.

In an examination of the revolutionary theory, some attention must be given to the prevailing

[1] Judge Drayton's charge to the grand jury (Charleston, S.C.), in Niles, 75 ; James Wilson in the Philadelphia Convention of 1775.

[2] Thacher, in *Boston Orations*, Niles, 23. In the first Congress, the theory was advanced that after the disavowal of allegiance to Great Britain, in 1776, the people were reduced to a state of nature and formed an entirely new social compact. The seat of one Smith, of South Carolina, who was abroad at that time, 1776, was contested on the ground that he had not taken part in their compact and hence was not a citizen. Mr. Jackson said that "many of the states were a considerable period without establishing constitutions of government, and during that period we were in a little better state than that of nature ; and then it was that every man made his election for an original compact, or tie, which by his own act, or that of his father for him, he became bound to submit to." *Annals of Congress*, I, 407. See Madison's argument to the contrary, I, 404.

conception as to the purpose of government. There is not to be discerned, however, any careful analysis of this idea, for the men of this day were concerned with the purpose of government only in so far as they could use it to show that England was perverting this purpose. So far as they reasoned at all about the function of government in general, their theory was in line with the individualistic and democratic character of their other philosophy.

The chief end of government was considered to be the welfare of the people, by whom and for whom it is instituted and maintained. Massachusetts said that "the end of the institution, maintenance, and administration of government, is to secure the existence of the body politic, to protect and furnish the individuals who compose it with the power of enjoying in safety and tranquillity their natural rights and the blessings of life." Again, the function of the government as the guardian of the general interest is contrasted with the "special privilege" idea. Thus it was urged in the constitution of Vermont that "the common benefit, protection, and security of the people, nation, or community, and not the particular emolument or advantage of any single man, family, or set of men who are a part only of that community," is the proper end of government.

The "good of the people," if more closely examined, was found to consist in the protection of person and property. The prevalent idea was forcibly expressed by John Hancock when he said: "Security to the persons and properties of the governed is so obviously the design and end of civil government, that to attempt a logical proof of it, would be like burning tapers at noonday to assist the sun in enlightening the world."[1] Samuel Adams asserted that "the security of right and property is the great end of government. . . . Such measures as tend to render right and property precarious tend to destroy both property and government."[2] That such were the great purposes for which government was instituted appeared self-evident, and extended defence of the propositions was deemed unnecessary and superfluous. Government must on the one hand protect the individual from the danger of foreign attack, and on the other maintain the security of his property and the safety of his person.

On the whole, there was a much more definite idea as to what the government should not do than as to what it should do. This is evident from the denunciation of the arbitrary conduct of English officials on certain occasions, and from the limitations placed upon the power of the state govern-

---

[1] Niles, 13.

[2] Wells, I, 154. In the theory of Paine, a distinction was made between society and government. Society is regarded as a blessing, government as an evil; society is a "patron"; government a "punisher." *Works*, I, 69.

ments in the state constitutions. Interference with freedom of person, security of property, free speech, freedom of religion, equality before the law, — these were things which were expressly forbidden to the government. It was the negative side of government with which the Patriots were most concerned. They did not reason about the purpose of government further than to assert that whatever the state does, a large measure of civil liberty should be left to the individual.

It is not to be presumed, however, that there was entire unanimity of opinion among the people upon these questions of political science. Loyalist feeling was strong among the colonists and with many was predominant. The number of Tories is of course difficult to estimate, but it must have been large. In some localities the Tory element was in the majority and in others constituted a strong minority. Many of the Loyalists were opposed to the Revolution on grounds of expediency, others from personal reasons, but still others on political principle. A striking type of this latter class was Jonathan Boucher,[1] a clergyman in Virginia and Maryland from 1759 to 1775, and finally driven out for his too decided expression of Loyalist sentiment. His ideas are contained in a collection of

[1] Born in England, 1738; removed to America, 1759; rector in Virginia and Maryland to 1775; died in England, 1804.

his addresses under the title, *A View of the Cause and Consequences of the American Revolution* (1797).

Boucher's opposition to the colonial theory was clear-cut and distinct. There was no attempt to evade the issue or to conceal his true sentiments on the political questions of the day. He was squarely opposed to the doctrines of the Revolutionary leaders, and his boldly enunciated ideas stand in striking contrast to those defended by the Patriots.

Boucher had little love for the people, and saw nothing to admire in the prevailing democratic tendencies. Never was there a time, he declared, when there was a greater lack of steady and fixed principles than now. The irreverence of the children, the infidelity to the marriage relation, the attitude of the rich toward the poor, afforded him evidence of a sad decline in general virtue.

The doctrine that government rests on the consent of the governed, he regarded as wholly unfounded. If there were such consent given, it could be withdrawn at the option of the one who had given it. Consent, therefore, is an utterly impracticable basis for the existence and maintenance of any settled government. If the principle were logically carried out, no authority of any permanent character would be possible. The contract theory, as he saw it, involved assumptions which could not legitimately be made. "The supposition," said he, "that a large concourse of people, in a rude and imperfect state of society, or even a majority of them, should thus rationally and unanimously concur to subject themselves to various restrictions, many of them irksome and unpleasant and all of them contrary to their former habits, is to suppose them possessed of more wisdom and virtue than multitudes in any instance in real life have shown."

That men are in any sense equal he also denied. Individuals are not equal, as is often presumed, but differ from each other in everything that can be supposed to lead to supremacy and subjection — "as one star differs from another star in glory." The foundation principle of government is not any such alleged natural equality of men, but, on the contrary, the very fact that there are inequalities among them makes possible the superiorities and inferiorities implied in any governmental system.

Boucher's theory was that government is from God. "It would be unreasonable," he said, "to suppose that God, having created men, should turn them loose in the world with no other guide than their own passions ; that like so many wild beasts, they might tear and worry one another in their mad contest for preëminence." He therefore rejected emphatically any such theory of governmental genesis, and declared that the power of government was given by God to the first man. The first father, therefore, was the first king, and

F

all kings and princes derive their power from God,
the source and centre of all power. Though they
govern for the benefit of the people, they are not
created by the people. Their tenure of office they
owe to God, and they reign independently of the
people.[1]   Nor did Boucher agree that government
is an evil, as alleged by some of the democratic
writers. Government, he declared, is no more an
evil than is medicine. The evil is not in the government, but in the conditions which are such as
to render the coercive action of government necessary. To political authority, men owe some of the
greatest blessings they enjoy. It has brought
them out of the original state of sin, misery, and
barbarity, and enabled them to reach the high
position they now occupy. Lawful government is
the greatest blessing that mankind enjoy, and is
the very life and soul of society.

All government, according to Boucher, is essentially absolute and irresistible. It is not within the
competence of the supreme power to limit itself;
for such limitation must come, if at all, from a
higher source, i.e., from a superior. The government which ceases to be absolute, ceases to be
government by elimination of the very element
upon which its governmental character depends.
This theory Boucher would apply to government
by the many as well as by one. He does not limit

[1] For the English origin of Boucher's theory, see Sir Robert
Filmer's *Patriarcha*, the classic defence of divine rights in England.

the doctrine to any particular form of rule, but maintains it as true of any and all government, as such.

The obvious corollary of these fundamentals in Boucher's theory is the denial of all right of resistance to authority. Government being based, not upon natural right, nor upon popular consent, but upon the will and the ordinance of God, every man is consequently bound to render to the government under which he lives an obedience either active or passive, — active obedience in all cases where not forbidden by God and passive wherever forbidden by God's command; for no governmental order has any force against the express word of God.

Resistance to government Boucher held in the deepest abhorrence. Lucifer, he declared, was the author and founder of rebellion. He condemned in set terms "the damnable doctrine and position that any government, lawfully established, may be denounced or resisted by any self-commissioned persons invested with no authority by law, on any pretence whatsoever." Government was to him something sacred and inviolable, deserving the respect and obedience of all citizens. The character and the acts of rulers should not be defamed and decried, for such conduct is unbecoming toward the divinely sanctioned authorities. Every citizen owes and should pay strict obedience, except in the case already cited. Kings are not infallible; rulers may on occasions do wrong, but even in such rare instances, obedience is better than revolt against the law and against the rulers. " A non-resisting spirit," he declared, "never made any man a bad subject." For one to rebel against an insignificant, unimportant tax on tea, is entirely unjustifiable on legal grounds and on the theory of the church, as well as on considerations of general expediency.

Boucher could not see that any substantial benefit could arise from opposition to the government's policy. He did not even concede that the opposition party in Parliament afforded any real advantage to the state as a whole. While some good might result from this opposition in a Parliamentary way, yet, on the whole, more evil than good was likely to issue from it. The policy of opposition is in general unwise, as it leads to a low opinion of government, and tends in that way to destroy the prestige and power of the rulers. Moreover, people are seldom competent to criticise the acts of those who are over them. Even if flaws are discovered in the administration's policy, it is better not to make violent complaint against those in authority.[1]

Of any popular participation in government he was profoundly distrustful. Democracy was, in his eyes, almost the equivalent of anarchy. It signified to him a desire for equality of possessions, a destruction of all motives to industry, and an

[1] Cf. Samuel Johnson, *Taxation no Tyranny* (1775).

end to all security. His attitude toward the people is well summed up in his sermon on Absalom, in which he declared: " Mankind have seldom been assembled in great numbers for any useful purpose. Whenever we see a vast multitude, we may well exclaim with Jacob, O my soul, come not thou into their secret; unto their assembly, mine honor, be not thou united." [1]

Further light on the ideas of '76 is given by an examination of the attitude of the colonists toward monarchy and the hereditary principle. In the early days of resistance there was no show of contempt for monarchy or for the British constitution. On the contrary, there was frequent expression of admiration for this type of political organization. Otis accurately voiced this popular feeling when he said that the British constitution was the best in the world, its king the best, and his subjects the happiest. John Adams pointed out the strong features of the British constitution and praised its many excellencies. Even Samuel Adams was on record as having strongly indorsed the English system: " In none that I have ever met with is the power of the governors and the rights of the governed more nicely ad-

---

[1] In the preface to his volume Boucher suggested that the people of Great Britain remove to the East, where " undisturbed by republican projects, so abhorrent to the genius of Asia," they might live at peace with all the world.

justed, or the power which is necessary in the very nature of government to be intrusted in the hands of some, by wiser checks prevented from growing exorbitant." [1] The colonists wished to show that they were not at all in opposition to the British constitution, but only to its abuse by unscrupulous and designing men. Their position was, that if the constitution were only properly interpreted and applied, there would be no ground for complaint.

But when once the war had actually begun, the latent democratic sentiment appeared, and it then became evident that the British model was no longer to be regarded as the most perfect instrument of government in the world. By far the most striking expression of this democratic idea was Thomas Paine's remarkable pamphlet *Common Sense*, which appeared in 1776. [2] This was a bitter and violent criticism of the British constitution, of monarchy, and everything connected therewith; and it was indicative of a striking change of sentiment in America.

In the institution of monarchy, Paine could discern nothing whatever that was worthy of approval, much less of imitation. Every king was

[1] Wells, I, 21.

[2] See the discussion of "Paine's Political Theories," *Political Science Quarterly*, September, 1899. Cf. also Paine's *The Forester's Letters* (1776), and *The American Crisis* (1776–1783). References are to Conway's edition of Paine's writings.

to him a George III and a George III at his
worst. The whole vocabulary of abuse he ex-
hausted in the effort to render monarchy odious
and ridiculous. "Sceptred savage," "royal brute,"
"breathing automaton," are his attempts at accurate characterization of kings. Monarchs, in his
estimation, are really only useless and expensive
figureheads, the sooner dispensed with the better.
In an absolute monarchy a king may possibly
have some function to perform, even though it be
an odious one; but in the so-called constitutional
monarchy the king is neither judge nor general;
he is only a superfluous figurehead. His duties
consist in giving away places for £800,000 a year,
and being worshipped in the bargain. Paine ridiculed the idea of the divine right of kings, holding
up, as an example of the absurdity of this, William
the Conqueror. Kings are chosen in general, he
thought, because of their "ruffianly preëminence,"
rather than by divine approval. Paine's opinion
of monarchy may be summed up in the one brief
statement: "Of more worth is one honest man to
society, and in the sight of God, than all the
crowned ruffians that ever lived." [1]

For the principle of hereditary succession, Paine
had an unconquerable antipathy. In *Common
Sense* he discussed and refuted three alleged
methods of its origin, — namely, lot, election, and
usurpation. If the first ruler were chosen by lot,

[1] *Works*, I, 84.

said Paine, then this establishes a precedent for such a method of choice, and the next one should be chosen in the same way. The fact that the first was chosen by lot is also an argument that the second should also be so selected. If by election, then this does not destroy the right of the succeeding generation; for, if the first generation had the right to choose, then the second must have the same right. The only parallel to the doctrine that after the first election the element of choice disappears, is the theological tenet of original sin: "In Adam all sinned, and in the first electors all men obeyed; in the one all mankind were subjected to Satan, and in the other to sovereignty; our innocence was lost in the first and our authority in the last."[1] Usurpation, as a basis for hereditary succession, he refused to consider seriously, declaring it beneath the dignity of a refutation.

Specific arguments were also made against the system in question. Such an institution is unwise, it was urged, because of the training of the prospective ruler in idleness and luxury; because of the danger involved in the accession of an infant monarch; and again because of the likelihood of wars to determine who is the proper heir. Nor was Paine able to see any justification for the system in utility. He was blind to all elements of strength it might contain, and could find scarcely

[1] *Works*, I, 81.

anything good in hereditary descent; it seemed to him an absurd method of selecting officials. The plan is contrary to nature and reason; and it is, in fact, hardly conceivable how apparently sensible people ever came to adopt it. We do not think of attempting to establish an hereditary wise man, or an hereditary mathematician, or an hereditary poet. Why, then, an hereditary ruler, who is no more certain of possessing the necessary governing qualities than the hereditary wise man of possessing the proper amount of knowledge?

Even the much lauded checks and balances found in the British constitution did not elicit any praise from Paine. He inquired why such a device as balances should be necessary at all. If the king is trustworthy, why need he be checked? if not trustworthy, why should he be king at all? In any event the heaviest weight will always be the governing power, and in the British constitution this is the crown. The other departments may check or retard its motion, but cannot prevent its ultimate action. The strongest power will finally prevail, and what it wants in speed is supplied by time. Paine was therefore unwilling to join in the general worship of the English check and balance system. In fact, he maintained that the security and happiness of the English are not due to the form of the constitution, but to the characteristics of the people. So far as the government alone is concerned, it might be as despotic as in Turkey.

The essential and fundamental fact is the habit and custom of the people, and this it is that makes England a free country.

Paine's reasoning, however, presented a style of argument new to the colonists. There was now displayed no love of, or even respect for the king, or for the institution of monarchy; no praise was bestowed on the English constitution. It was no longer intimated that the old institution with some modification would prove perfectly acceptable, but there was a bold demand for separation from government by the mother country and from the form of government in the mother country. The *Common Sense* seemed to mark the turning-point in American policy. From that time on, the advocates of independence triumphed; the " Fathers " turned against George III, and from the institution of monarchy as well, and at about the same time.

More light on the political ideas of the " Fathers " is given by a further study of the extension and application of the doctrines already considered. The fundamentals of the revolutionary theory were almost altogether reproductions of the English political philosophy of the preceding century, but the founders of the Republic did not halt at the point reached by their fore-fathers. They advanced the line of democratic theory and practice in accordance with the more democratic conditions. The English movement of the seventeenth century culminated in the establishment of a constitutional monarchy; the American movement went far beyond this in a democratic direction. To these changes our attention will now be directed.

In the construction of state constitutions, the monarchic and many of the aristocratic elements found in the British constitution were omitted. The frame of government became more democratic in nature. Privileged aristocracy had never been able to obtain a foothold in the colonies, and 1776 was no time to gain one. Monarchy was identified with George III and the English system of administration, and consequently no place was made for such a governmental feature.

Many expressions of dislike for special privilege and hereditary rank are found in the first constitutions adopted in the states, and no stronger evidence as to the nature of the prevailing sentiment could be given than is offered by these early declarations. Massachusetts, for example, asserted that government is instituted for the common good and happiness of the whole people; — " not for the profit, honor or private interest of any one man, family or class of men." Virginia declared that " no man or set of men, are entitled to exclusive or separate emoluments or privileges from the community, but in consideration of public services; which, not being descendible, neither ought the offices of magistrate, legislator, or judge to be hereditary."

The democratic environment had rendered special privilege unwelcome, and the legislators were anxious to give the prevailing sentiment constitutional recognition. There still remained a controlling class of gentry, but they possessed no hereditary title, office, or privilege. There had never been anything more than a theory of nobility in America; with the Revolution, even this was swept away and the overwhelming sentiment declared against the institution.[1]

In the formation of state governments, the doctrine of delegated powers was everywhere prevalent. Assuming that the people were, originally, and continue to be the only source of political power, it follows that all governmental authority is only delegated by the people and is held in trust for them. Governmental authority has no inherent force in itself; it is not the creator, but the creature; it is not the master, nor even the partner of the people, but their agent or servant; it acts in the name of and in behalf of some one else and not for itself. Not only is government the servant of the people, but it is an untrustworthy and unreliable servant. It cannot be given a free hand in caring for the affairs of its master, on the contrary, it must be limited in many ways; it must be checked at every possible point; it must be at all times under suspicion. Otherwise it will cease to

[1] Ga., N.C., S.C., Penn., declared against the entailment of estates.

be servant and take the place of the master. Too much emphasis cannot well be laid upon the fear which the "Fathers" had of government. To them the great lesson of history was, that government always tends to become oppressive, and that it is the greatest foe of individual liberty.

To the end that government may be properly held in check, the "Fathers" developed an elaborate system which it was thought would adequately safeguard the rights of the people. In the first place, government should not be granted much power; in the next place, such powers as were given should be balanced and played against each other; and finally even these powers should be held for short terms only. By these means it was thought that political authority might be kept close to the people from whom it emanates, and by whose grace it stands.

More specifically, it was an opinion of Revolutionary times that government should not be too strongly organized, lest its strength be turned against the people. Hence a large military force was always under suspicion. A standing army was looked upon as a constant temptation to the ruler and a perpetual menace to the citizen. It was necessary for the government to have at its disposal a certain amount of military strength, but this should be kept within strict limits, and in subordination to the civil power. Again, every kind of centralized government was steadily opposed.

It was believed that liberty was safer in the care of the local communities, where it could be kept under the eye of the people, and any attempt at usurpation be instantly detected and checked. The idea was that the farther the government is removed from the community, the more likely it is to tyrannize over that community. The classic illustration of this would be, of course, the conduct of England toward the colonies. There was, consequently, great jealousy of centralized government within the states, especially in New England, and everywhere there was opposition to a strong government *over* the states. A perfect expression of this latter feeling was the organization of the central government effected under the Articles of Confederation. Following out the principle of limiting the government as much as possible, there were many restrictions on its action in the state constitutions. In long and eloquent bills of rights notice was served on government not to trespass on certain fields of individual activity. Government must not interfere with freedom of speech, freedom of religion, freedom of assembly and petition, or freedom of person and property, except through the recognized and prescribed forms of law.

In these various ways, then, a strong effort was made to restrict the government to the minimum of strength : by the subordination of military to civil power, by the decentralization of political authority, and by the enumeration of specific guaranties against invasion of personal liberty and property.

In the same connection comes another theory widely entertained by the "Fathers," namely, that of the separation and balance of governmental powers. This doctrine had been formulated by Montesquieu in the *Spirit of Laws* (1748),[1] basing his reasoning, however, on observation of English conditions; both the theory, therefore, and the facts were well known among the Americans. They valued highly the division and balance of powers among king, lords, and commons, and saw in this piece of mechanism the strongest support of English liberty. Consequently they readily accepted and acted upon Montesquieu's theory. They firmly believed that unless the three classes of governmental power — the legislative, the executive, and the judicial — were separated and a distinct organ of government provided for each class, there could be no certainty of political liberty.

In the state constitutions the idea of the separation of powers found the clearest expression. Massachusetts asserted that "in the government of this commonwealth, the legislative department shall never exercise the executive and judicial powers or either of them; the executive shall never exercise the legislative and judicial powers or either of them; the judicial shall never exercise the legislative and executive powers or either of them — to

[1] Book XI.

the end that it may be a government of laws and not of men." A less doctrinaire statement was that of New Hampshire, to the effect that there should be such a separation of powers "as the nature of free government will admit, or as is consistent with that chain of connection that binds the whole fabric of the constitution in an indissoluble bond of union and security."

Though the separation and balance of governmental powers, was accepted in theory there was in practice no such equilibrium established as the theory called for.[1] On the contrary, there was an exaltation of the function and position of the legislature and a corresponding depression of the others, particularly the executive. Everywhere there was manifested great jealousy of the state executive, and numerous restrictions were thrown around his tenure, term, and prerogatives. In many cases the governor was elected by the legislature,[2] his term of office was limited to one year,[3] restrictions were placed upon his appointing power, and in only a few cases was the veto allowed.[4] The judiciary was declared independent by some states, but was generally dependent in respect to appoint-

[1] On the Revolutionary State Constitutions see "The First State Constitutions," by W. C. Morey, in *Annals of the American Academy of Political and Social Science*, Vol. IV ; also, in Vol. IX, " Revolutionary State Constitutions," by W. C. Webster.

[2] N.J., Del., Md., Va., N.C., S.C., Penn., Ga.

[3] N.H., N.C., Va., Mass., N.J., Penn., Ga., Conn., R.I., Md.

[4] Mass., S.C. (1776), N.Y. (with Council of Revision).

ment and salary upon the governor and council, or even directly upon the legislature.[1] When it is further considered that in many states almost all of the important officers were appointed by the legislature; that in two states there was a unicameral legislature;[2] and that the constitution-amending power was often vested in the ordinary legislature,[3]—it becomes evident that the predominant position was held by that body. The strong dislike of the English crown and of the royal governors had led to a reaction against executive authority in general that resulted in the practical supremacy of another of the three coördinate branches of government, namely, the legislature. There was naturally greater readiness to intrust the necessary governmental powers to this body, inasmuch as the legislators were regarded as the immediate representatives of the sovereign people. In the long and bitter struggles of colonial days, the Americans had learned to trust and rely upon the legislature, and to suspect and antagonize the executive. They, therefore, reduced to a minimum the powers of the executive and intrusted such authority as seemed necessary for the establishment of government to the legislature. They

[1] Va., N.H. ('76), N.C., S.C., N.J., Del., R.I., Conn.

[2] Penn., Ga., Vt.

[3] In Ga., Mass., and Penn. provision was made for amendment by a convention ; in the other states where mention was made of amendment, the power was vested in the legislature.

G

did what the English Parliament had done and
was yet to do still more emphatically, — asserted the
superiority of the legislature over the executive.

In addition to the separation of powers, another
method used for the purpose of holding in check
the government was the grant of power for a
short term only.   To guarantee security, it was
thought that power must be kept close to its true
basis, the people.   In this way the rise of arbitrary rulers could be prevented and the officers
intrusted with power be made responsible to the
people.   As John Adams once said, "where annual
elections end, there tyranny begins." [1]   This idea
was conspicuous in the constitutions of the states,
where frequency of election received both theoretical and practical support.   Maryland declared
"a long continuance in the first executive departments of power or trust is dangerous to liberty;
a rotation, therefore, in those departments is one
of the best securities of permanent freedom."   Of
like import was the statement of Massachusetts:
"In order to prevent those who are vested with
authority from becoming oppressors, the people
have a right . . . to cause their public officers to
return to private life."   In general, officers were
allowed short terms only.   Governors were in
many cases annually elected, legislatures for the
same period, and other officers, with the exception of
judges, followed the same rule.   This requirement

[1] Cf. the Pennsylvania Constitution, Sec. 19.

was made still more rigid by the provision in many instances that the office-holder should be ineligible to the same office for a certain period of years, as one in three, two in four, or some like ratio. Thus the officer was not only limited to a short term, but was forbidden continued reëlection, and constitutionally forced to retire, even though his administration had been of the ablest kind. The evils arising from the existence of a permanent or hereditary office-holding class, it was determined to prevent even at the cost of administrative efficiency.

In these different ways, then, the attempt was made to keep alive the principle of popular sovereignty, and to prevent the development of a tyrannical government. What was feared at that day was not the incapacity or inefficiency of those conducting the administration, but the tendency of the ruling class to oppress in some way or other the class to be ruled. To the theorist of that time, every officer appeared to be a possible foe to the security of the individual and his property. The great guaranty of liberty was, therefore, to give the rulers as little power as possible and then to surround them with numerous restrictions, to balance power against power, to compel a frequent return to the people for renewal of the tenure of authority. This was the mechanism devised to carry out the democratic theory, and to prevent the recurrence of governmental tyranny.

It is essential to notice, however, that while the

revolutionary theory was democratic on its destructive side, and to a certain extent on the constructive side, there were also present aristocratic tendencies of a pronounced character. Democracy had by no means reached the degree of development that was attained in the following century.

The most marked of these aristocratic features in the government of the "Fathers" was the limitation upon the suffrage. In actual practice the basis of their democracy was not very broad, or, at least, was relatively narrow when compared with that of the present day. The principle was laid down in some of the state constitutions that those were entitled to the suffrage who showed "sufficient evidence of attachment to the community." This evidence, however, generally consisted in the possession of a certain amount of property, preferably real estate. In discussing the subject of representation, Franklin said that "as to those who have no landed property, . . . the allowing them to vote for legislators is an impropriety." [1] Hamilton considered that those who possessed no property could not properly be regarded as having a will of their own.[2]

In drawing up the state constitutions the property qualification was adopted, as a guide for determining who should be entitled to participate in the choice of officers. The accepted idea was that

[1] *Works*, IV, 221, 1766.
[2] *Ibid*, II, 62 ff., *The Farmer Refuted.*

the political people were the land-holding class. The states either required the possession of a free-hold, or accepted a property equivalent of some kind. All the states agreed in requiring some evidence that the voter had a financial interest in the community, — either a free-hold of a certain value, or other estate, or the payment of some public tax. The man who was not able to qualify in this way could not cast a vote under the laws of any of the states. He was not regarded as sufficiently attached to the community to justify participation in its political life. In this way the voting constituency was limited to a fraction of the adult male population, much less than half.

The same tendency is evident in the requirements for office-holding. Here also the property-holding class has the privileged position. It was provided in many states that the governor must be a freeholder, thus showing a preference not only for property in general, but for landed property in particular. In some instances the value of the freehold was fixed at a very considerable figure; in Massachusetts, for example, at £1000, in Maryland at £5000, and in South Carolina at £10,000. High property qualifications were also required for many other offices, although not for all.[1] Generally speaking, therefore, participation in political

[1] An interesting discussion of legal qualifications for office in America is given by F. H. Miller in the *Annual Report of the American Historical Association for 1899*, Vol. I.

life was limited to the most prosperous element in the population, and the government of that day was a government of and by the propertied classes.

In addition to these limitations upon the political people of 1776, there were also important religious restrictions. Notwithstanding the rationalistic tendencies of such leaders as Benjamin Franklin, Thomas Jefferson, and Thomas Paine, religious qualifications held a conspicuous place in the state constitutions. The principle of toleration for all sects was generally recognized, but the requirement of some religious test for public officers was not condemned by public sentiment. In certain states it was necessary that the governor be a Protestant,[1] in others that he be a Christian.[2] It was often specified that a member of the legislature must be a Protestant,[3] in some cases he must be a Christian.[4]

Freedom of worship was recognized in strong terms, with the qualification that the exercise of the right should not disturb the public peace. For example, in Maryland freedom of worship was granted, " unless under color of religion any man shall disturb the good order, peace or safety of the state, or shall infringe the laws of morality, or injure others in their natural, civil, or religious rights."

---

[1] N.H., N.J., N.C., S.C. ('78).   [2] Md., Mass.

[3] Ga., N.H., N.C., S.C., N.J.

[4] Mass., Md. Pennsylvania required belief in God, future rewards and punishments, inspiration of Scriptures. In Delaware there was a similar requirement.

This grant of general toleration was not construed, however, as prohibiting the financial assistance of the church by the state. In some cases the legislature was allowed to levy a tax for religious purposes, allowing the taxpayer to designate the religion to which he wished his contribution to be given.[1] This did not establish any one religion in preference to another, but was a political recognition of all the accepted religions. On the whole, there were but two states in which no religious qualifications or tests of any kind were required for office, namely, New York and Rhode Island.

On the other hand, however, there was inserted in the constitution of almost every state a clause forbidding the clergy to hold office under the state. This disqualification was sometimes absolute, extending to all civil offices, or it was sometimes applicable only to a seat in the legislature. The limitation was imposed for the benefit of both church and state, that there might arise no difficulties for either from too intimate a union.

It appears, then, that despite the assertion that all men are equal, the "Fathers" in framing their constitutions felt no reluctance about conditioning political rights upon certain financial and religious considerations. These restrictions operated to throw the control of political affairs into the hands of the freeholders who were at the same time

[1] Religious establishments were constitutional in Conn., Mass., Md., N.H., S.C., Va. during the Revolutionary period.

Christians and preferably Protestants. This was the contemporary interpretation of the Declaration of Independence. The field of political privilege appears narrower still, when it is considered that the negro element of the population was held in slavery and had no political recognition at all. Evidently the "Fathers" themselves did not regard property, religious, or racial limitations as inconsistent with the rights of man or those principles of political philosophy to which such frequent reference was made.

It is necessary to turn now to a brief consideration of the source of the theory of this time. The origin of the dominant ideas during the Revolution is not difficult to find. As the Patriots were guided by the historical precedents established by England in the seventeenth century, so they followed the political theory developed at that time by the revolutionary party. The rejection of two kings within half a century was sufficient warrant for the refusal to obey George III. The colonists were not striking out upon a new and wholly untried path, but were following in the way broken by their ancestors of a few generations before. If revolution were wrong, then the House of Hanover had no legitimate claim to rule, and resistance to its members could not constitute rebellion. The same kind of reasoning used in justification of the revolution that drove out the Stuarts, might fairly be applied to the successors of the Stuarts. The *jure divino* theory had been repudiated in England, leaving only the argument from expediency, as the support of an existing constitution, and in accordance with this argument the colonists decided that independence from Britain was better than union with her.

The advanced stage of development of English political speculation from the democratic point of view is often overlooked.[1] The doctrines of natural rights, the contract, popular sovereignty, the right of resistance, had been worked over and over by the popular leaders of the seventeenth century. The contract theory was advanced and defended by many able writers, conspicuous among whom were: Milton, in his *Areopagitica* (1644), *Tenure of Kings and Magistrates* (1649), and first and second *Defence* of the English people (1650–1654); Sydney, *Discourses concerning Government* (1698); and above all John Locke in his *Two Treatises of Government* (1689). These men stated the revolutionary doctrines in the boldest form.

The Patriots were familiar with this philosophy of their English predecessors and they followed it closely. They referred to these writers, quoted from them, and adopted the substance of their argument, and in some cases the form as well.

[1] This theory is analyzed by G. P. Gooch, in *English Democratic Ideas in the Seventeenth Century*, in Cambridge Historical Series, Vol. X, 1898.

Locke, in particular, was the authority to whom the Patriots paid greatest deference. He was the most famous of seventeenth century democratic theorists, and his ideas had their due weight with the colonists. Almost every writer seems to have been influenced by him, many quoted his words, and the argument of others shows the unmistakable imprint of his philosophy. The first great speech of Otis was wholly based upon Locke's ideas; Samuel Adams, on the "Rights of the Colonists as Men and as British Subjects," followed the same model. Many of the phrases of the Declaration of Independence may be found in Locke's *Treatise;* [1] there is hardly any important writer of this time who does not openly refer to Locke, or tacitly follow the lead he had taken. The argument in regard to the limitations upon Parliament was taken from Locke's reflections on the "supreme legislature" and the necessary restrictions upon its authority.[2] No one stated more strongly than did he the basis for the doctrine that "taxation without representation is tyranny." No better epitome of the Revolutionary theory could be found than in John Locke on civil government. The colonists claimed no origi-

[1] See Secs. 220, 222, 225, 230.

[2] See Sec. 135 ff. The four limitations upon the legislature, named by Locke were: 1. It cannot be absolutely arbitrary. 2. It must rule by standing laws. 3. "Cannot take from any man part of his property without his own consent." 4. Cannot transfer the power of making laws.

nality for the fundamental doctrines they preached;
in fact they declared that these ideas were at least
as old as the days of Greece and Rome. John
Adams said: "These are what are called Revolution principles. They are the principles of Aristotle and Plato; of Livy and Cicero, and Sydney,
Harrington and Locke; the principles of nature
and eternal reason; the principles on which the
whole government over us now stands."[1] The
Patriots did not profess to have discovered a
hitherto unknown system of political theory; on
the contrary, they appealed to an old and long
accepted theory, — a theory indeed upon which
rested the legitimacy of the English political system of that day.

The French radical influence upon the Revolution
was comparatively small. Montesquieu's *Spirit of
Laws* (1748) was known to the colonists, and the
doctrines therein contained were frequently quoted.
But many of the features admired in Montesquieu
were derived from his study of the English constitution and the English political system. This was
eminently true of his celebrated doctrine of the
tripartite division of governmental powers, which
he had found or thought he found in the English
constitution. Many of the other projects advocated
by him were also derived from his study of English
institutions. The greatest of the revolutionary
philosophers of France, Rousseau, did not write

[1] *Works*, IV, 15.

his classic work, *The Social Contract*, until 1762, whereas the revolutionary doctrines of Otis were uttered in 1761. The general philosophy of the colonists shows little likeness to that of Rousseau, and but infrequent reference to his theory is made. Indeed, the fundamental ideas of the French writer were very similar to those of Locke.[1] There is little evidence to show that the bent of the revolutionary theory in America was determined by the great apostle of the French Revolution; but on the other hand very much to prove that the theory of Locke and the English school was predominant.

On the whole, the theory of the Revolution was in direct line with English political precedent and philosophy. In their destructive or revolutionary doctrine the "Fathers" of 1776 simply followed their "Fathers" of the preceding century. But in their constructive theory, notably in their substitution for monarchy and nobility of the many democratic features embodied in their state constitutions, they were striking out on new lines of political experiment. Many of these ideas, perhaps all of them, had been already suggested in the seventeenth century; but they had been unable to win a definite place for themselves in the English system

[1] Cf. D. G. Ritchie, "Contributions to the History of the Social Contract Theory," in *Political Science Quarterly*, VI, 664. In this connection see Georg Jellinek, *Die Erklärung der Menschen- und Bürgerrechte*, Leipzig, 1895.

of that day,[1] and were left to be realized in practice by the American democracy of the next century.

In conclusion, then, it appears that the fundamental political ideas in vogue among the Patriots were not the product of American soil, and were not original with the men of the Revolutionary day, but were the inheritance of English political experience and philosophy in the preceding century. The form in which they were expressed was striking and dramatic, but the ideas themselves were not new ; on the contrary they were, from the viewpoint of political theory, doctrines long familiar. The teaching that all men are by nature equal is found in the Roman law,[2] while the idea that governments derive their just powers from the consent of the governed, is a long accepted maxim. Professor Gierke, the distinguished German authority, says that "from the end of the thirteenth century it was an axiom of political theory that the legal basis of all authority lay in the voluntary subjection through contract of the community ruled."[3] The doctrine of the right of resistance was stated with greatest emphasis by the political theorists of the revolutionary type in the sixteenth

[1] Cf. "The Agreement of the People," 1647, in Gardiner's *Constitutional Documents of the Puritan Revolution*, p. 270.

[2] *Digest*, L, 17, 32.   Quod ad jus naturale attinet, omnes homines æquales sunt; from Ulpian, who died *circa* 328 A.D.

[3] Otto Gierke, *Johannes Althusius und die Entwicklung der naturrechtlichen Staatstheorien*, Breslau, 1880.

and seventeenth centuries.[1]   To attribute the orig-
ination of these ideas to the men of 1776 is, therefore, simply to ignore the historical development of
political theory.   But in respect to the practical
application of these doctrines, what has just been
said does not apply; for a set of principles like
those involved in the construction of state constitutions had never before received such public recognition.   The destructive democratic theory of
the day was old, but the constructive democratic
theory as worked out in the state governments
was the product of new conditions.

By way of summary, it may be said that the
leading doctrines of the Revolutionary period were
those of what is known as the *Naturrecht* school
of political theory.   They included the idea of an
original state of nature, in which all men are born
politically free and equal, the contractual origin
of government, the sovereignty of the people, and
the right of revolution against a government
regarded as oppressive.   The latter doctrine, in
particular, was stated in the boldest and most
uncompromising form, since this was the ultimate
argument upon which the Revolution rested for its
justification.

On the constructive side, an elective executive
was substituted for hereditary monarchy, and the
institution of hereditary aristocracy abolished.

[1] Cf. Rudolph Treumann, *Die Monarchomachen*, Leipzig, 1895.

The greatest danger feared was an oppressive government, hence numerous restrictions were placed on the action of its organs. Many rights were expressly reserved to the people, the tripartite separation of governmental powers was accepted, officers were made responsible to the people directly or through the legislature at frequent intervals, and often constitutionally disqualified for a term of years. Distrust of centralized government was shown at every point, with the exception of the legislature, which escaped popular suspicion.

It will be observed that the spirit of this reasoning was decidedly individualistic. The starting-point was the independent and sovereign individual, endowed with a full set of natural rights. He consents to give up a part of these natural rights to form a government by means of a contract. On this basis, political society and the state are constructed, and in this spirit political institutions are interpreted throughout. This was the general character of the revolutionary theories of the seventeenth and eighteenth centuries, and from this tendency America was no exception.

CHAPTER III

THE REACTIONARY MOVEMENT

AFTER independence from Great Britain had been won and formally recognized, two broad tendencies appeared during the formative period of the Union, — the reactionary and the radical. The theory of the first party is well expressed in the Constitution itself, in the *Federalist*, and in the writings of John Adams and Alexander Hamilton. The theory of the radical element is best stated by Thomas Jefferson, the central figure in the practical politics as well as in the political philosophy of the democratic school.

What may be called the reactionary theory was the outgrowth of certain conditions which must now be briefly noticed. The eleven years that intervened between the Declaration of Independence and the Constitutional Convention witnessed rapid and extensive changes in the political conditions of America.[1] The Declaration of Independence was followed by seven years of war, resulting in the recognition of the independence of the American states. The common danger which had bound

[1] On this period see such standard histories as Schouler, Hildreth, McMaster, Curtis.

the colonies in a united whole was thus removed and the forces of disintegration and disunion began their fatal work. The Articles of Confederation, adopted in 1781, signally failed to express the sentiment of nationality evident at the outset of the war, and resulted in a federal government which was so hampered and crippled at every turn that its power and prestige soon disappeared.

With a constitutional requirement of unanimity for amendment and of an overwhelming majority for the passage of any measure of importance, and at the same time with the actual existence of discord upon almost every subject of common interest, the Congress was soon reduced to a condition of pitiful impotence. Most of the states refused to pay the requisitions levied on them. There were serious difficulties with foreign powers, involving the fulfilment of treaty obligations to England, the attitude of Spain toward the Mississippi, and the payment of the debt to France. By 1785 the central government had literally fallen to pieces, shattered by the blows received from the jealousy and particularism of the individual states. Between the states themselves there was a feeling of hostility that resulted in the restriction of trade by the imposition of unfriendly tariffs.

Moreover, there was widespread financial distress throughout the various states of the confederacy. The long strain of the eight years' war had left a large and clamorous debtor class ready

H

for any measures to relieve their sufferings, while an epidemic of paper money added to the general distress. Massachusetts had felt the force of social disorder in the proceedings of the malcontents who followed Shays; and in the suppression of courts, plundering of towns, and armed intimidation of officers, the commonwealth came face to face with the problems of anarchy and social revolution. By 1786 it was apparent that the Articles of Confederation, as an instrument of government, was utterly ineffective. It was seen that it must be supplanted by some other and more effective form of political organization; but the shape which the government was to take could be foretold by none. The wisest statesmen and leaders feared for the safety and security of the country and looked with the very gravest fears upon the impending crisis. Under these circumstances the movement for a constitutional convention forced itself into acceptance, and in May, 1787, the ablest political thinkers in America met to amend the old form of government. The result of their deliberations was the Constitution.

Accompanying these changes in political conditions, there were also pronounced differences in the tendency of political thought. The period of the Revolution had been largely one of destruction; the new era was one of constructive effort. The period of 1776 required a philosophy of politics to justify rebellion against the mother country; that from 1783 on was guided by the great purpose of establishing a firm national government on the ruins of a feeble confederacy. In response to the necessities of the case, there were consequently modifications of the old theory; emphasis on points before passed lightly over; failure to emphasize points upon which the greatest stress had been laid.

In the Constitutional Convention there were clear-cut expressions of the change in sentiment since the days of 1776. These utterances present a striking contrast to the democratic enthusiasm of a few years before. For example, Gerry asserted that "the evils we experience flow from the excess of democracy,"[1] and expressed a belief that the people were the "dupes of pretended patriots." He confessed that "he had been too republican heretofore; he was still, however, republican, but had been taught by experience the danger of the levelling spirit."[2] Randolph said that in tracing the evils of the day to their origin, every man had found it "in the turbulence and follies of democracy."[3] Mason could only say that "notwithstanding the oppression and injustice experienced among us from democracy, the genius of the people is in favor of it, and the genius of the people must be consulted."[4] These statements are significant of the change in attitude among the promi-

---

[1] The *Madison Papers*, II, 753.
[2] *Ibid*.
[3] *Ibid*. 758.
[4] *Ibid*. 788.

nent men of the time.   They had not abandoned
their belief in the ultimate sovereignty of the
people, but their faith in popular administration
of the government had received a severe shock.

Evidence of the change of sentiment is given by
the Constitution itself.   Its structure was in many
respects less democratic than that of the states.
The judiciary received broader powers and a life
tenure of office; the executive was clothed with
far more ample powers than those given to the
state governor, was assured of a four-year term
and made reëligible indefinitely; the senate was
based on a six-year term; there was not even a bill
of rights, such as was found in the state constitutions.   Although there were no religious or property qualifications, the general tendency of the new
instrument of government was decidedly conservative, and even reactionary, in its leading features.

The submission of the Constitution for ratification or rejection was the signal for a discussion
of the principles of political theory and of government, in which the ablest minds in the states
participated.[1]   Of all the defences of the proposed
Constitution, the *Federalist* is universally conceded
to be the ablest and the most important.   The
eighty-five numbers of this series were published
between October 27, 1787 and August 15, 1788,
above the signature of "Publius."   The authorship

[1] Cf. *Pamphlets on the Constitution*, edited by P. L. Ford.

of the papers was divided among Hamilton, Madison, and Jay; but the number produced by each is still a subject of some controversy.

In considering the political theory of the *Federalist*, allowance must be made for the fact that it makes no pretence to the dignity of a carefully developed, well-matured treatise on the science of politics. On the contrary, the papers were prepared in haste and were written in defence of a particular system of government at that time before the people of New York for their consideration. The *Federalist* was an advocate's plea for the Constitution, not the dispassionate system wrought out by some thinker upon the general principles of politics. Such references as are made to political science in the general sense, are incidental to the discussion and subordinate to the main purpose, which was the persuasion of the popular mind to the adoption of the Constitution.

In examining the *Federalist* one soon notices that the revolutionary tone of unrestrained democratic enthusiasm has disappeared. The dominant note is that sounded by the statesman, not the alarm bell of the revolutionist. The experience of the past ten years has taught that even where it is recognized that all men are created equal, and endowed with certain inalienable rights, there may be difficulties of the most perplexing character in actual administration. Unmistakable is the meaning of the statement that "the citizens of America have too much discernment to be argued into anarchy; . . . experience has wrought a deep and solemn conviction in the public mind that greater energy of government is essential to the welfare and prosperity of the community."[1]   A government of law alone and without any coercive power would be good, but such a system has "no place but in the reveries of those political doctors, whose sagacity disdains the admonitions of experimental science."[2]

Proceeding to the more systematic doctrines of the *Federalist*, that of the origin and basis of government may be first noted.   Here it is discovered that the *Federalist* indorses the same views as were prevalent during the Revolutionary times. It suggests an original state of nature in which every man is endowed with a full equipment of natural rights; and finds the institution of government arising from the cession of certain of these natural rights through the familiar form of the social contract.[3]

The basis of government is the consent of the people, "that pure, original fountain of all legitimate authority."[4]   The nature of government receives the same Revolutionary characterization already noticed, especially in the theory of Paine. Government is necessary, because the passions of men are so unruly as to require restraint.   Pure

---

[1] No. 26, Dawson's edition.   [2] No. 28.
[3] Nos. 2, 43, 50.   [4] No. 22.

reason must be reënforced by a coercive authority.[1]
And again it is announced that " government is the
greatest of all reflections on human nature. If men
were angels, no government would be necessary."

In short the *Federalist* accepts the fundamentals
of contemporary political theory without much protest. The original state of nature, the social compact, the necessary-evil theory of government —
the staple of eighteenth century political science —
none of these doctrines was openly called in question. In fact it could hardly have controverted
these ideas, even if so disposed, so deeply were
such notions impressed upon the public mind, and
so universally were they recognized in the political
instruments of the time. So far, however, as the
main argument of the *Federalist* is concerned, it
rests in no way on these ideas, and is but little
related to the political theory embodied in them.
There is not very much said, after all, about the
rights of man, the natural equality of men, the
tyranny of kings, and the other doctrines of
the philosophy that characterized the Revolution.
The proportion of Revolutionary theory has notice-
ably declined.

It is now proposed to examine the theory of the
Federalist at those points where it showed more or
less deviation from the lines of the revolutionary
argument. The doctrine first discussed concerns

[1] No. 15.

the relation between the territorial extent of a country and democratic government. One of the most frequent, and, indeed, one of the most troublesome, objections, that the supporters of the Constitution were obliged to meet, was the contention that a republican form of government could not be successfully operated over so large a territory as would be included in the United States. The only form of government capable of administering the affairs of so vast a country, would necessarily be a despotic one. In support of this doctrine the eminent authority, Montesquieu, was quoted to the effect that "it is the nature of a republic to have only a small territory; without this it could scarcely exist." [1] Exceedingly jealous of their local liberties, many of the citizens of the various states regarded the establishment of a strong central government as practically equivalent to the erection of a despotism over them. To consent to such a government as that proposed by the Philadelphia convention, they considered as simply fastening the chains of slavery around them. Historical precedent was against the proposed government, for the great democracies of the past had been confined to limited areas of territory. Greece, Rome, the Italian Republics, so called, were all of small extent. It was necessary, therefore, for the defenders of the Constitution to present

[1] *Esprit des Lois*, Book VIII, 16. But he expressly indorsed the federation composed of small republics, IX, 1.

an explanation and justification of the new conditions.

The *Federalist's* argument in defence of the
Constitution was directed along the following lines.
It was urged that the modern system of representation enables government to extend over far
wider limits than would otherwise be practicable.
While in ancient times it was true that the limit
of a democracy was that size which would allow
all the citizens to assemble in order to exercise the
necessary public functions, by the modern plan
the limit is that extent which will allow the *representatives* of the citizens to assemble.[1] Again, as
between large and small republics, the larger state
has the advantage in this respect, that its officers
are chosen from larger numbers, and hence the opportunities are greater for the selection of able men.
The broader the field or range of choice, the greater
the chance for a good selection, is the argument.[2]
A third reason in favor of a large state is that increased size will afford a wider variety of interests.
Now, the larger the number of these, the greater
the difficulty of forming such a combination as will
lead to the tyrannical rule of any one faction.[3] Hence
the greatest possible security for the rights of the
individual is found where there is a large number
of different interests in the given community ;
and the larger the number, the greater the difficulty of forming a dangerous combination. In

[1] Nos. 14, 62.　　　　[2] No. 10.　　　　[3] No. 50.

Rhode Island, for example, there is only a small extent of territory to be ruled and only a few groups to be considered. Under these conditions it seems that any particular interest is in the highest degree insecure. But in the United States, with its vast area and great variety of occupations, there must of necessity be such a balancing of claims as will render the domination of any one, or even of a few interests, impossible.[1]

The *Federalist's* discussion of forms of government is interesting and suggestive, particularly in respect to the "Republic."[2] This is defined as "a government which derives all its powers, directly or indirectly, from the great body of the people, and is administered by persons holding their offices during pleasure, for a limited period, or during good behaviour."[3] The essential fact is that the government derives its authority from the great body of the society and not from any particular class. The method of election may be indirect, the tenure of office may be almost permanent, but these facts do not detract from the republican character of the government, provided the ultimate responsibility rests with the great body of the people. The distinction between a pure democracy and a "republic" consists, according to the *Federalist*, mainly in two points : first,

[1] This was a favorite idea of Madison.

[2] The discussion of the federal-national character of the new Union is given in Chap. VII, *infra*.   [3] No. 38,

in the more complete development, in the republic, of the representative idea; and, secondly, in the greater territorial extent of the republic.

The common division of governmental powers into legislative, executive, and judicial was adopted by the *Federalist* as one of the axioms of political science.[1] The advocates of the pending constitution were forced to meet, nevertheless, the objection made by certain jealous admirers of liberty, that the proposed plan of government did not respect this fundamental principle—that, on the contrary, the three classes of power were dangerously confused. It was pointed out that the legislature might impeach and convict the executive, that the executive would appoint the judiciary, and that the senate would confirm appointments and ratify treaties. To these plausible arguments the *Federalist* replied by a closer examination of the theory of the tripartite division of powers. This doctrine, it was held, does not imply or require that each of the several departments is to be absolutely and entirely isolated from the others; or that one department is to have no influence whatever on the determinations of another. The only danger to be averted is that the whole power of any two or more departments might pass into the same hands, as would be the case if one governmental organ should obtain both the law-making and the law-executing power, or the executive and the

[1] No. 46.

judicial power. This, it was claimed, was the proper interpretation of the doctrine, and the view actually taken by the states in framing the Revolutionary constitutions. Not only was the radical theory deemed incorrect, but it was regarded as wholly impracticable and even dangerous. It is not possible, so argued the *Federalist*, to separate governmental organs in any measure whatever unless they are so connected and related as to give each one a certain control over the others. It is entirely insufficient to delineate "parchment barriers" against the encroachments of one department upon another. There must be provided some constitutional means by which each department may exercise a certain restraint on the encroaching tendencies of the others. It is well enough to write down in the Constitution the declaration that the three sets of powers must be distinct and independent, but unless the departments are interrelated there will be no separation whatever.[1] In other words, the greatest and strongest barrier against consolidation and concentration of power is the mutual interrelation and interdependence of the various departments. The *Federalist* abandoned the doctrinaire theory of the absolute separation of the functions of government, as it was stated, for example, in the Massachusetts constitution. In fact, it was definitely admitted that it was wholly impossible accurately to

[1] Nos. 46–50. Cf. James Wilson, *Works*, I, 368.

define the boundary lines between the various departments, and consequently the true policy was to devise such a balance of interests and motives as would insure, not an absolute separation, but a substantial and enduring interdependence of the three classes of powers.

In addition to the threefold division of powers, the *Federalist* called attention to another method of securing a constitutional equilibrium. The new theory now advanced was that the states and the Federal government would be balanced against each other, while within both state and Federal governments there would be a balance of legislative, executive, and judicial organs. The different governments would control each other, and at the same time each would be controlled by a division of powers within itself. This unique arrangement, it was urged, afforded additional guaranty that the government would not easily become an instrument of tyranny.[1]

The discussion in detail of each of the three classes of power—the legislative, the executive, and the judicial—is a masterly treatment from the side of constitutional law, and also reveals many deviations from the radical political theory of the preceding decade. In the Revolutionary constitutions, as already seen, the executive power was in disrepute, and the legislative the object of popular confidence. The executive authority suggested

[1] No. 50.

both the provincial governor and the English crown, and consequently an effort was made to get as far as possible from the establishment of a powerful head of the administration. The legislatures, however, had been left almost entirely free from restraint. Independence from England having been gained, it appeared that the greatest danger was not the undue predominance of the executive, but the aggressive disposition of the legislature. This view the *Federalist* adopts and expounds in the discussion of the three classes of powers.

It was made clear that in republican governments the greatest danger to liberty arises from the expanding power of the legislative body. The legislature, being chosen directly by the people, seems to fancy itself the people, and to consider itself as the superior of the other branches of government. The legislators come to believe that the "exercise of rights by either the executive or judiciary, is a breach of their prerogative and an outrage to their dignity."[1] Hence it is exceedingly difficult for the other powers to maintain the constitutional and governmental equilibrium desired. Instances of this are given, notably the case of Pennsylvania. The testimony of Jefferson is cited to the effect that in Virginia "all the powers of government result to the legislative body," and that "173 despots would surely be as oppressive as one."

[1] No. 70. Cf. James Wilson, II, 286, 393.

This dangerous superiority of the legislature is attributed, first to the fact that its constitutional power is generally more extensive and also is less susceptible of precise limitation than that of the other departments ; secondly, to the fact that the legislature has access to the pockets of the people, on the one hand, and on the other exerts an influence on the pecuniary rewards of the other departments.

The *Federalist's* observations on some other features of the legislative power are also worthy of note; for example, on the subject of the bicameral system. All single legislative bodies, it is said, are apt to be impulsive, passionate, violent.[1] They are liable to be drawn by unscrupulous leaders into hasty and intemperate measures, which on more mature reflection would never have been indorsed, and of which they will afterward repent.[2] On such occasions as this, when the assembly is carried away by its passions and led to the verge of unwise action, we require the influence of "some temperate and respectable body of citizens to check the misguided career . . . until reason, justice, and truth, can regain their authority over the public mind."[3] Such a body the United States Senate was to be.

The basis of representation in the lower House, it was said, is not individuals, or even all interests.[4] The representation of every class is impossible;

[1] No. 61.   [2] No. 62.   [3] *Ibid.*   [4] No. 33.

but that of certain general interests is both practicable and prudent.   The *Federalist* holds that
this representation will be included under three
classes: (1) merchants, (2) landed interests, (3)
learned professions.   The merchants will naturally represent the artisans and manufacturers, as
their interests are to a great extent identical.   The
mercantile class will be opposed by the landed
interests, while the learned professions will hold
the balance between the two.   Thus the *Federalist*
outlines an equilibrium of interests, on the basis of
the natural antagonism between the mercantile
and agrarian groups, and the assumption that the
learned and professional classes have the power to
mediate between them.

Another interesting argument employed at this
time was that in regard to the proper size of the
legislature.   It was frequently urged against the
Constitution that the number of representatives,
particularly in the lower House of Congress, was by
far too small.   It was pointed out that in a house
of 65 members, 33 would form a quorum, and 17
might then pass a bill; and that in the Senate, 8
members might pass a bill.   The constitutional
provision was consequently denounced as utterly
inadequate for the purposes of effective representation of the people and security of their interests.
There was only the shadow of representation, it
was said, not its substance.

The *Federalist* replied to this criticism by calling

attention to the fact that a large legislature may be less faithfully representative of the people than a small one. After reaching a certain number in the assembly, — that is, a number sufficient " for the purposes of safety, of local information, and of diffusive sympathy with the whole society," [1] — the addition of other members will defeat the attainment of the very ends desired. It will be found true that the greater the number of legislators, the fewer will be the number of those who actually direct the proceedings ; and furthermore that the greater will be the ascendency of passion over reason. Or, as the *Federalist* sums up the situation : " The countenance of the government may become more democratic, but the soul that animates it will be more oligarchic. The machine will be enlarged, but the fewer, and often the more secret, will be the springs by which its motions are directed." [2]

Passing from the discussion of the legislature, it is important to observe the *Federalist's* theory of the executive. While the burden of suspicion, in the minds of many leaders at least, had been largely transferred from the executive to the legislature, there was still a lively anxiety on the part of others lest the President of the Union might acquire powers that would in time become equivalent to those of a monarch. Both the amount of authority vested in the chief executive and the

[1] No. 57. Cf. 55, 56.   [2] No. 58.

I

tenure upon which it was held were objects of pronounced hostility.[1]

The *Federalist*, however, contended boldly for an energetic executive, maintaining that this is essential to any efficient government.[2] A vigorous executive, it was said, is by no means contrary to the genius of republican government. There is nothing in the nature of free institutions making it necessary that the executive should be subject to every impulse that sways the popular mind.[3] Republican government, the argument continued, does not and should not signify a political system in which the popular voice is to be obeyed *instanter*. It is right that the will of the people should prevail, not immediately, however, but ultimately; for while the people are generally desirous of the public good, it is not true that they always reason

---

[1] This is vividly illustrated by a quotation from the *Federalist*: "The authorities of a magistrate, it is said, in a few instances greater, in some instances less, than those of a governor of New York, have been magnified into more than royal prerogatives. He has been decorated with attributes, superior in dignity and splendor to those of a king of Great Britain. He has been shown to us with a diadem sparkling on his brow and the imperial purple flowing in his train. He has been seated on a throne surrounded with minions and mistresses, giving audience to the envoys of foreign potentates, in all the supercilious pomp of majesty. The images of Asiatic despotism and voluptuousness have scarcely been wanting to crown the exaggerated scene. We have been taught to tremble at the terrific visages of murdering janizaries, and to blush at the unveiled mysteries of a future seraglio." No. 66.

[2] No. 70.   [3] No. 70.

correctly about the means of obtaining that good.[1] In the construction of a governmental system we ought, therefore, so to dispose the organs of government as to enable us to consult the reason of the people; not their temporary, transient emotions, but their deliberate judgment. And there should be certain persons whose duty it is to stem the tide of popular passion, and give cooler judgment opportunity to assert itself. One of the most important organs for the accomplishment of this purpose is the executive department of the government.

On the whole, the *Federalist's* discussion of the legislative and executive powers indicates a decided change in political theory since the days when the legislature had been implicitly trusted and the executive degraded and despised. There is now manifested a decided suspicion of the legislature, and great anxiety as to the possible extent of its encroachments. On the other hand, there is a strong disposition to revive the executive department and intrust it with substantial powers.

As to the judicial department, the general philosophy of the *Federalist* was as follows. The judiciary was regarded as always the least dangerous to the liberties of the people.[2] This department has neither force nor will, as have the other two organs, but possesses the power of judgment only. Hence the maintenance of good gov-

[1] No. 70.   [2] No. 77 ff.

ernment has never been much imperilled by the courts, unless in combination with one of the other two departments. There is, however, great need that the judiciary be kept as far as possible independent in its position. This is particularly important in a country which is governed under a limited Constitution. Here the function of the court is to act as final interpreter of the Constitution, and to decide upon the conformity of all laws with that instrument. This does not mean, explains the *Federalist*, that the judicial is superior to the legislative power, but that the authority of the people is superior to both. For this reason, then, and in order to protect the rights of individuals against governmental oppression, the tenure of the judges should be permanent, in order that they may possess the proper independence. As in a despotic country this kind of a tenure serves as a barrier against the prince, so in a republic it is a useful protection against the encroachments of a despotic legislative body.

The *Federalist* recognizes, as every observer of political phenomena must, the great difficulty in securing an energetic, stable government, and at the same time preserving the liberties of the people.[1] The problem of the correct relation of liberty and authority is perennial. If governmental power is not granted in large measure, the safety of the state is endangered. If such authority is granted,

[1] No. 36.

there is likelihood of its abuse. The great argument against the Constitution was, that it would endanger the liberties of the people.

Admitting, however, that governmental power is liable to such abuse, the defence was made that inasmuch as confidence must be placed somewhere, it was better to risk its abuse by regularly constituted authorities than to embarrass the government and endanger the public safety by the imposition of unwise restraints upon all authorities. The American people, said the *Federalist*, cannot be "argued into anarchy" by objections raised against all energetic government. Although the necessity of popular vigilance over rights and liberties is recognized, it must be remembered that, however useful jealousy may be in a republic, "yet when, like bile in the natural, it abounds too much in the body politic, the eyes of both become very liable to be deceived by the delusive appearances which that malady casts on surrounding objects." [1] Love of liberty, then, does not always require a bilious jealousy of all government.

The *Federalist* was not an advocate of bills of rights such as were found in the Revolutionary state declarations. The preamble to the Constitution, it was said, is "a better recognition of popular rights, than volumes of those aphorisms, which make the principal figure in several of our state bills of rights, and which would sound much better

[1] No. 63.

in a treatise of ethics, than in a constitution of government." [1]   No statement better expresses the marked change of attitude since the days of the Revolution.   In 1776, to have referred to the declarations of rights as "aphorisms" which properly belong only to the domain of ethics, would have been almost equivalent to high treason, but in a few years the inalienable rights of man are thus lightly passed over.

Furthermore, it was argued that bills of rights are in general inapplicable to constitutional governments. They originated as agreements between ruler and subjects — abridgments of royal prerogative. In a popular government, however, "the people surrender nothing; and as they retain everything, they have no need of particular reservations." [2]   Such specific restrictions have no application to governments which are founded directly on the act of the people and "executed by their immediate servants and representatives." This is true of all types of popular government, but is more than ever applicable to a confederate government, where the central authority has no power except that conferred upon it by the Constitution.   In such a case the Constitution is itself the "bill of rights of the Union," and a separate declaration would be not only unnecessary but dangerous.   "Why declare things should not be done, which there is no power to do?" [3]

[1] No. 84.   [2] *Ibid.*   [3] *Ibid.*

But the *Federalist* goes beyond this, maintaining that the whole scheme of securing liberty by mere constitutional restraints is a mistaken one. All such precautions as these are mere paper barriers vainly raised up against the spirit of encroachment.[1] The true guaranty of liberty in a republican government lies in the fact that the political power belongs to the representatives chosen by the people themselves.[2] The government is in the hands of agents who derive their power from and are responsible to the people. If these chosen delegates betray their trust, there is then no resource left but the exertion of that " original right of self-defence, which is paramount to all positive forms of government." The guaranty that free institutions will be maintained, rests in the last analysis on the " general genius of the government." This alone can be relied upon for enduring results : "particular provisions, though not altogether useless, have far less virtue and efficacy than are commonly ascribed to them."[3] It is the spirit and temper of the people in which confidence must be placed, rather than the written word embodied in an instrument of government.

In judging the political theory of the *Federalist*, it cannot escape notice that the " natural-right" philosophy lies at the basis of its system. But no more can it pass unnoticed, that the doctrines of natural rights and the social compact, while

[1] No. 47.　　[2] No. 28.　　[3] No. 83.

formally accepted, are but infrequently employed in the course of argument. The truth is that popular interest in these doctrines, so widely proclaimed during the period of Revolution, had suffered a pronounced decline. The enthusiasm of the first resistance, the spirit of which was so eloquently expressed in the Declaration of Independence, had died down. The country had passed through the trying years of the war and the critical period, had come close up to the edge of anarchy, and was now ready for the establishment of government and law at any cost.

Nowhere is the change in the dominant sentiment of the people more deeply marked, nowhere more clearly expressed, than in the *Federalist*, which may fairly be taken as representative of the class or classes of people whose support secured the adoption of the Constitution. Comparison of the writings of 1763–1776, and their bold and sweeping generalizations about the rights of man, with the conservative utterances of the *Federalist*, reveals an unmistakable change of feeling and opinion. The contrast is strongly marked. The Revolutionary period emphasized the rights of man, the *Federalist* the necessity of government; the Revolutionary period demanded government of a more democratic character, the *Federalist* asked for a government of a less democratic nature. Annual elections, the feeble executive, the omnipotent legislature, the absolute division of governmental powers, with other planks in the ultra-democratic platform, were discredited by the leaders of the new school. In fact, the democratic philosophy of the eighteenth century was a perfect expression for the men and times of 1776; for it was essentially a philosophy of revolution. With the needs of 1787–1789, however, it did not harmonize and could not easily be made to agree. The Declaration of Independence represented the political theory of the American people when it had "become necessary to dissolve the political bands which had connected them with another." The *Federalist* represented the time when it had become necessary "to form a more perfect union." Its authors did not reject, but largely ignored, the rights of man. There was full recognition of the sovereignty of the people, but an impressive warning, reënforced by cogent examples from recent American history, was sounded against excessive democracy.

In addition to this there were substantial contributions made toward the solution of new problems in political science. The federal state was discussed with remarkable acumen, the theory of the separation of governmental powers was restated, the possibility of extending republican government over a large area asserted and argued, the doctrine of government under a constitution developed and applied. In all this the authors of the *Federalist* were not in advance of the political facts of the time. The old theory was outgrown; they were formulating political theories adapted to the new state of things.

The *Federalist*, however, was not the only expression of the reactionary tendency in the theory of this time. Much more suggestive in this respect was the doctrine advanced by the great leader of the Federalist party — John Adams.[1] During the earlier part of his life, Adams had been one of the most outspoken and enthusiastic advocates of the radical movement. In these days he thought that government is "a plain, simple, intelligible thing, founded in nature and reason, quite comprehensible by common sense." He indorsed the maxim that "where annual elections end, there slavery begins"; favored stripping the governor of the "badges of slavery called prerogatives"; and was vigorous in his declaration of the rights of man.[2]

In little more than a decade, however, there was evident a pronounced change in the general character of Adams's theory.[3] Influenced by the turn that events were taking in America and by the

[1] See his life by C. F. Adams ; also the essay by Mellen Chamberlain. See also "The Politics of John Adams," by Anson D. Morse, in the *American Historical Review*, January, 1899, and the *Works* of Adams in ten volumes, edited by C. F. Adams.

[2] "Thoughts on Government," 1776, *Works*, Vol. IV.

[3] Some symptoms of a reaction appeared as early as 1776. See Adams's *Works*, IX, 410, 435, 451.

fear that certain principles of the French philosophy might obtain the ascendency here, Adams was led to formulate a system of political theory widely different from that which he held in earlier days. In the first period Adams was the bold champion of the Revolution, in the second period he was equally fearless in his advocacy of strong government and of aristocratic principles.

The theory of Adams during this second period is contained in the two once famous, but now almost forgotten works, *A Defence of the Constitutions of Government of the United States of America* (1787–1788) and the *Discourses on Davila* (1790). The *Defence* was written in view of recent occurrences in Massachusetts, and also as a reply to an attack on the American system made by Turgot in a letter to the famous English theorist, Dr. Price (1778).[1] One of the principal points to which Turgot took exception was the policy in the state constitutions of dividing the powers of government and instituting a system of checks and balances, instead of concentrating all governmental powers in a single sovereign body. Adams's reply was a defence of the American system of balanced government against the French theory of centralized and un-

[1] Printed with Dr. Price's *Observations on the Importance of the American Revolution, and the Means of making it a Benefit to the World.* An extract from Turgot's letter is given in Adams's *Works*, IV, 278–281. Considerable attention was also given in the *Defence* to refutation of a radical English work by Marchamont Nedham, *The Excellency of a Free State* (1656), reprinted 1767.

divided power. The first part of this book was
published in time to find its way into the hands of
the members of the Constitutional Convention, and
doubtless exerted an influence there. The work,
although hastily put together, was effective, and
was widely read. That the author of so conservative a treatise could be elected Vice-President
of the United States shortly after, shows that its
principles were not unfavorably received.

The *Discourses on Davila* [1] was written in reply
to the *Four Letters of a Citizen of New Haven*
by Condorcet.[2] These two works, the *Defence* and
the *Discourses*, though now generally neglected,
contain the substance of Adams's ideas, and are
invaluable for an understanding of the aristocratic
theory of his time.

Adams's treatment of political theory evidences a
wide acquaintance with political history and with
the results reached by the greatest political thinkers.
He discusses, in the course of his work, the his-
tory of democratic governments in Greece, Sparta,
Carthage, Rome, Italy, Switzerland, and the United
Provinces. In the field of political theory he was
familiar with the writings of Plato, Machiavelli,
Harrington, Montesquieu, Sidney, Milton, and
Hume. His conclusions were based upon an ex-

---

[1] Davila, *Dell' Istoria delle Guerre civile di Francia*.

[2] Quatre Lettres d'un bourgeois de New Haven à un citoyen
de Virginie, sur l'inutilité de partager le pouvoir législatif entre
plusieurs corps, 1788.

tensive study (more extensive than intensive) of the world's classics in political theory and practice.[1] This transition from a philosophy based on the "rights of man" to one emphasizing the historical method within little more than one decade is certainly impressive; yet it was paralleled by the change of attitude seen in Edmund Burke during the same time. Adams's change of opinion was by no means so radical, however, as that of Burke, although it followed the same direction.

The chief points of interest in Adams's theory may be included under three heads; first, his distrust of unlimited democracy; second, his defence of aristocracy; third, his system of checks and balances. An analysis of these three leading doctrines will be presented here.

The great wave of democratic sentiment which had swept over the country during the latter part of the eighteenth century, the triumph of this movement in the Revolution, Adams's own participation in the struggle, had been by no means sufficient to keep awake in him the sentiments of an enthusiastic democrat. Such feelings had been excited, but they soon gave way to other and more characteristic tendencies of the man. Adams was not wholly anti-democratic, but he certainly did not share in that unqualified approval of democratic government which was so common, in theory at least, among his con-

[1] See *Defence*, Chaps. I–IX.

temporaries. His comparative study of republican states had inspired in him a profound distrust for an unqualified democracy, which manifested itself throughout his later life. Some of his criticisms on the general theory of democratic government may be considered here. In the first place, Adams strongly objected to the common assertion that the people are incapable of tyrannical and oppressive conduct. "We may appeal," said he, "to every page of history we have hitherto turned over, for proofs irrefragable, that the people, when they have been unchecked, have been as unjust, tyrannical, brutal, barbarous and cruel as any king or senate possessed of uncontrollable power. The majority has eternally and without one exception usurped over the rights of the minority." [1]

The people, moreover, are not only prone to tyranny ; they are jealous, exacting, and suspicious to the last degree. They not only demand outward submission to their commands, but cannot endure even a mental dissent from their will. They "will not bear a contemptuous look or disrespectful word ; nay, if the style of your homage, flattery, and adoration is not as hyperbolical as the popular enthusiasm dictates, it is construed into disaffection"; and as a result the popular suspicion is aroused and their fury breaks out "into every kind of insult, obloquy, and outrage." [2] Again, the people are no less given to luxury than

[1] *Defence*, VI, 10.   [2] *Ibid*. VI, 89.

are kings and nobles, although the latter are usually charged with the greatest extravagances. A free people, says Adams, is most addicted of all to the vices of luxury.[1] The simple democracy is, of all governments, most exposed to tumults and disorder, and such disturbances are most likely to be fatal in this kind of a state.[2] [In short, it seems that no stable government can be built upon the foundation of an unlimited democracy.] " All projects of government, formed upon a supposition of continual vigilance, sagacity, virtue, and firmness of the people, when possessed of the exercise of supreme power, are cheats and delusions." [3]

There is, says Adams, no such thing as an abstract love of equality. There can be no love of democracy as an abstract conception, but only in so far as it stands for a certain advancement of individual interest and advantage. Democracy is not desired for itself, but for what it brings with it, or for what it makes possible in the form of personal welfare. Or as Adams elsewhere says, " Mankind in general had rather be rich under a simple monarchy than poor under a democracy." [4] In brief, Adams maintains that there never was and never can be a pure democracy. In reality, " democracy signifies nothing more nor less than a nation of people, without any government at all and before any constitution is instituted." [5]

[1] *Defence*, VI, 95.   [2] *Ibid.* 151.   [3] *Ibid.* 166.
[4] *Ibid.* 97.   [5] *Ibid.* 211.

It is, nevertheless, unfair to reckon Adams among the opponents of free government. The attacks which he made were directed chiefly against immediate or unlimited democracy, and he was far from being hostile to popular government, properly checked and restrained. The common charges against him to this effect were founded upon a misapprehension of his true position. Although his assaults on democracy pure and simple were vigorously sustained, no language could be clearer than that in which he asserts the doctrine of popular sovereignty. "The suprema potestas," he declares, "the supreme, sovereign, absolute, and uncontrollable power is placed by God and nature in the people, and they can never divest themselves of it."[1] All government depends upon and represents the people. No government can exist longer than the people will to support it; they are the fountain of political power, and may vest authority wherever they choose. Adams held to the theory of popular sovereignty as the basis of government; upon this point he was never uncertain, but he did not favor democratic government of the type which the French thinkers desired. All free government, he thought, ought to contain certain limitations upon the direct action of the people, in

---

[1] *Works*, 469. Cf. VI, 113, to the effect that there can be no constitutional liberty, "where the people have not an independent equal share with the other two orders of the state, and an absolute control over all laws and grants of money."

order to render excesses on their part difficult, if not impossible.⌋

The charge that Adams was opposed to democratic institutions received support from the bitterness of his invective against unlimited democracy, and his not unfriendly attitude toward monarchy. For example, he said on one occasion that "a hereditary first magistrate at once would perhaps be preferable to elections by legislative representatives."[1] Yet this was not the final opinion of Adams, for he said later of kings that he would "shut them up like the man in the mask, feed them well, and give them as much finery as they please, until they could be converted to right reason and common sense."[2] But because of his criticism of certain phases of popular government, Adams was made the object of the bitterest denunciation, particularly by Jefferson and his associates. The object of his criticism, however, was not popular government as such, but certain evils arising from the direct and unrestrained rule of the people. It is quite likely that if obliged to choose between this type of popular government, and monarchy, he would have accepted the latter without much hesitation. This was particularly true in the days when the Constitution was being formed. After the Constitution was adopted and the government established, he accepted the government

[1] *Ibid.* 122.
[2] X, 409 (1825). Letter to Jefferson.

K

fully and without reserve. It was not a government of just the kind that he or Hamilton would have established, but it was far enough removed from extreme democracy to justify a fair trial.

The political creed with which Adams is most closely associated is that of aristocracy, and to this phase of his theory we now turn attention. No one better expressed than he the theory of the "well-born," and its wide divergence from the canons of political philosophy laid down in the Revolution. It has already been pointed out that the contemporary interpretation and application of the principles of the Declaration offered many evidences of departure from its philosophical spirit. Adams goes farther than this, however, and attacks certain parts of the theory itself. He takes exception to the doctrine that all men are created equal. This, Adams declares, is not in accord with the facts, since "nature . . . has ordained that no two objects shall be perfectly alike and no two objects perfectly equal. . . . No two men are perfectly equal in person, property, or understanding, activity, and virtue." [1] This is a clear contradiction of the Declaration, and even of his own earlier statements It is to be observed, however, that Adams does not deny that all men are born with equal rights; "every being," said he, "has a right to his own, as clear, as moral, as sacred as any other being has." [2]

[1] *Works*, VI, 285–286.
[2] *Ibid.* 453.   Letter to John Taylor (1814).

This he does not wish to dispute, confining his protest to the teaching that all men are created with equal powers or faculties. Such a doctrine seems to him "as gross a fraud . . . as ever was practised by Druids, by Brahmins, by priests of the immortal Lama, or by the self-styled philosophers of the French Revolution."[1]

Adams held firmly to the idea that men are essentially unequal. If we take a hundred men at random, he says, we shall find among them, on the average, six wealthy, six eloquent, six learned, six having the gifts of eloquence, learning, and fortune, and six having art, cunning, and intrigue.[2] Thus we have an aristocracy of thirty among the hundred, — thirty men gifted with certain extraordinary qualities which enable them to rise above their fellow-men. The following quotation gives a good picture of Adams's aristocrat: "Whenever I use the word aristocrat," said he, "I mean a citizen who can command or govern two votes or more in society, whether by his virtues, his talents, his learning, his loquacity, his taciturnity, his frankness, his reserve, his face, figure, eloquence, grace, air, attitude, movements, wealth, birth, art, address, intrigue, good-fellowship, drunkenness, debauchery, fraud, perjury, violence, treachery, pyrrhonism, deism, or atheism."[3]

The inequalities upon which Adams lays greatest stress in his theory are those of wealth, birth,

---

[1] *Ibid.* [2] *Ibid.* 456. [3] *Ibid.* 457.

and education. These are the criteria by which
the natural aristocracy may be most readily determined. The people in general may be divided into
two groups, the gentlemen and the simplemen.[1]
Gentlemen are those who " have received a liberal
education, an ordinary degree of erudition in liberal arts and sciences," and it will usually be
found that those so endowed are also "well-born
and wealthy." The simplemen, on the other hand,
or the common people, are " laborers, husbandmen,
mechanics, and merchants in general, who pursue
their occupations and industry without any knowledge in liberal arts or sciences, or in anything but
their own trades or pursuits." Some of these may
be true aristocrats, as some of the first class may
be in fact common people, but in general the two
classes may be divided by the line drawn.

These two groups are to be found in every society, and inasmuch as they exist should be recognized in the government of the state. "There is,"
says Adams, " a voice within us, which seems to intimate that real merit should govern the world, and
that men ought to be respected only in proportion
to their talents, virtues, and services." [2] The incor-
poration of this aristocracy into the government, he
regards as one of the greatest problems of political
organization. The policy of Europe, he suggests,
has been to connect "lands, offices, and families"
and to have them all descend together, and along

[1] *Ibid.* 185.   [2] *Ibid.* 249.

with them, "honor, public attention, consideration, and congratulation." [1] To this policy Europe owes its superiority over Asia and Africa. Adams asserts that no well-ordered commonwealth has ever existed without hereditary nobility, and it is an easy inference that he considered such an institution advisable for this country as well, or at least looked with suspicion on the experiment of proceeding without an order of nobility.

Adams would seem, then, to favor some system of hereditary nobility as the surest way of obtaining recognition for the virtue and talent of the community. This disposition leads him naturally to condemn the policy of rotation in office. It appears to him that such a requirement is really "a violation of the rights of mankind." [2] It is a violation at once of the rights of the candidate and of the voter; for one has a right to be chosen again, if efficient, and the elector to choose the officer for further service, if deemed advisable. No policy is so disastrous to the public interest as that of discharging, at fixed and arbitrary intervals, tried and experienced servants. Hereditary tenure is in general not inadvisable, and a life term of office is certainly commendable. The maxim "non diurnare imperia" does not, in Adams's opinion, apply to a free government. Where there are republican institutions, authority may be safely given for a long term of years or even for life, without danger to

---

[1] *Ibid.* 251.   [2] *Ibid.* 52.

the liberties of the people.   On the contrary, such
a policy of intrusting power in the hands of officers
for long terms would really be one of the guaranties of continued free government.

For the United States, Adams seemed to be
not averse to a life tenure for the chief executive,
or even an hereditary tenure.   He indicated that
terms of office may be extended until they reach
the life limit, and if this is not found sufficient,
they should be made hereditary.   " The delicacy
or the dread of unpopularity," said he, " that should
induce any man to conceal this important truth
from the full view and contemplation of the people
would be a weakness if not a vice." [1]   The elective
method, wherever tried, has been found to be a
failure; the system of hereditary tenure has the
sanction of history — the prestige that comes
from years of successful operation.   The inference
is that Adams looked to see the old system restored
in this country. [2]

From these passages, then, it is clear that Adams
had no sympathy with the radical ideas of human
equality, rotation in office, and unlimited democratic government.   He was essentially aristocratic
in his ideas.   Birth, wealth, education — these
were the points on which his eye was fixed, these
were the elements for which he desired recognition

[1] *Ibid.* 67.

[2] Cf. Hamilton's proposition in the constitutional convention.
See his *Works*, II, 393 ff.

and to which he would accord supremacy in the administration of political affairs. He believed in popular sovereignty as the basis of political institutions, and the popular welfare as their goal; but he had very little confidence in the ability of the mass of the people to administer the government successfully, or even to choose their rulers properly. The common people are the basis of the state, but the guiding hand in the affairs of government must be that of the gentlemen, the " well-born."

The relation of John Adams to the radical theory of his day is well illustrated by a correspondence upon this very question, between him and Samuel Adams (1790).[1] This interchange of views was occasioned by recent events in France, and it brings out clearly the markedly aristocratic tendencies of the one, and the equally pronounced democratic opinions of the other. John Adams, in his letters, defends the institution of nobility, upholds the superiority of the well-born, hints at hereditary rather than elective tenure of office, and betrays throughout a profound distrust of the self-governing capacity of the people.

Samuel Adams, replying, upholds the doctrine of popular rule, and criticises John Adams's statement that the people should have merely a share in the government. He asserts that the selection of rulers by frequent elections is superior to the system of hereditary tenure; for, conceding that people

[1] Wells, *Samuel Adams*, III, 297 ff.

may be occasionally deceived, the evil is not incurable and certainly will not long endure. The requisite remedy will be near at hand, whereas under an aristocratic system there is no easy way out of the difficulty.

John Adams suggests doubts as to the practicability of democratic government, because of the high degree of popular intelligence and virtue required for the successful operation of such a system. The rejoinder is that the American people do possess this extraordinary capacity for government; and furthermore, that these qualities may be strengthened by means of general education. The theory of the "well-born," Samuel Adams dissents from emphatically. The natural aristocracy, he maintains, is likely to be found among men of all ranks and conditions, regardless of birth. The cottager may beget a wise man ; the noble a fool ; hence the boundary lines of natural aristocracy are exceedingly difficult to draw, and cannot on the whole be safely marked out.

Probably the most conspicuous idea in John Adams's theory is that of an elaborate system of checks and balances in the organization and operation of the governmental system. The *Defence* was written, as already pointed out, in reply to Turgot's attack on the American plan and apology for the French idea of the centralization of powers, afterward illustrated in the French Revolution. To refute this argument, Adams collected evidence from the days of the Grecian and Roman republics down to modern times, and from the opinions of eminent philosophers beginning with Plato. He endeavored to show that unlimited and unchecked government had been everywhere attended by disaster, particularly when such government rested upon a popular basis. The earnestness of his belief in the necessity of a system of balances is indeed accountable for what is taken as dislike of democracy. In reality, his point of attack was not popular government in general; but that particular type of democracy lacking the necessary restraints.

The subject next claiming consideration is, then, Adams's system of checks and balances. Here his arguments meet the French theory advanced by Turgot, that an equilibrium of governmental powers is necessary only under a monarchical government and not required where republican institutions exist. In every state there must be, said Adams, a first magistracy, a senate or little council, and a larger assembly.[1] These three classes represent respectively the monarchical element in the government, the aristocratic element, and the democratic element. No constitution lacking these three elements can remain secure. Their existence and balance is essential to the maintenance of peace and liberty.[2] They have, he declares, "an unalterable foundation in nature."

[1] *Works*, IV, 379. Cf. Harrington, *Oceana* (1656), (Morley's edition), 29 *et seq.*   [2] *Ibid.* 579.

The best expression of this idea is found in the British Constitution, which he looked upon as "the most stupendous fabric of human invention." [1]

The people alone, as Adams reasons, are unworthy of trust, unless restrained by the balances which are advocated, and aristocracy and the monarchy alone are also prone to abuse the power intrusted to them. Adams takes particular pains to combat any objection to placing power in the hands of the monarch. An alliance between monarchy and democracy, he points out, has been necessary in order to make headway against the encroaching tendencies of the aristocracy; and it is in reality the people themselves who have supported the absolute king against the petty lords. Monarchy and aristocracy he considers as natural foes. It is, therefore, Adams suggests, the best policy on the part of the common people to intrust the whole executive power to one man, so that he may stand out as a distinct order in the state. There will then inevitably arise a jealousy between him and the aristocracy, and this very jealousy will force the monarch to ally himself closely with the common people, to become their guardian and their protector, and to keep in check all who might otherwise endanger the safety of the state. Adams saw what few Americans of his day perceived, namely, that absolute monarchy had rested upon a

[1] *Works*, IV, 358.

popular basis and had really constituted an alliance between crown and people against the aristocracy.

Adams's plan is, then, to provide for the representation of the aristocracy in one branch of the legislature; in another for the representation of the people; and finally to place as an umpire and arbiter between them a strong executive power. This arrangement of governmental authorities will secure the equilibrium of forces necessary to the welfare of the state. It will obviate the grave difficulties presented by a simple and wholly unified plan of government, by preventing the extravagances to which any one of these powers alone and unchecked is prone.

This, however, was not the only balance of powers which Adams discussed. In later years he called attention to the organization of government under the Constitution of the United States, which presents a system of checks and balances even more intricate and complex than the tripartite plan just examined. In the federal government Adams discovers no less than eight different kinds of balances. These are as follows: 1st, the states and territories against the federal government; 2d, the House against the Senate; 3d, the Executive against the Legislature; 4th, the Judiciary against the House, the Senate, the Executive and the state governments; 5th, the Senate against the President in respect to appointments and treaties; 6th, the people against their representatives; 7th, the state legislatures against the Senate; 8th, the electors against the people. Here are certainly ample guaranties against hasty action on the part of any organ of the federal government, and it is apparent that Adams so considered them.[1]

When Adams entered into active political life under the new federal Constitution, he no longer gave expression to sentiments which could so easily be interpreted as unrepublican in character. It is likely that he considered the new government as embodying in many of its features the principles he had laid down. The new Constitution was certainly more in harmony with Adams's ideas than with those of the French theorists whom he combated. In his inaugural address of 1797 Adams declared that no change in the existing government was intended. He commented on the essentially popular basis of the government with evident satisfaction and pride. He declared his preference for free republican government, and his firm attachment to the United States Constitution. In terms that suggest the inaugural of four years later, he discoursed fluently on his regard for virtuous men of all parties, and his love for equal laws, for justice, and for humanity.[2] It would, therefore, be unfair to maintain that after the Constitution was once put in force, Adams demanded a monarchy and hereditary aristocracy.

[1] *Works*, VI, 467 (1814).   [2] IX, 105 ff.

He even denied that any such idea could, by fair construction, be deduced from his writings, and asserted that "they were all written to support and strengthen the Constitution of the United States."[1] He continued to defend with unabated vigor, however, the doctrine of the inequality of men, and the necessity of elaborate checks and balances. To Jefferson he wrote (1815): "The fundamental principle of my political creed is, that despotism, or unlimited sovereignty, or absolute power, is the same in a majority of a popular assembly, an aristocratical council, an oligarchical junto, and a single emperor."[2] This was, in fact, the fundamental proposition in Adams's political philosophy, and explains his frequently undemocratic phrases. He feared the unlimited power of the people as well as the unlimited power of either nobility or king; and was steadfastly opposed to any system, popular or otherwise, which was not so constructed as to limit and restrain the governing powers. In America he considered that the despotism imminent was that of the people, hence his criticisms were directed mainly against them.

Such was the character of the reactionary theory prevalent during the early years of the republic. With some modifications this doctrine continued to manifest its existence during the first quarter

[1] X, 54. Cf. VI, 463, stating that they were written in defence of the Massachusetts constitution.   [2] X, 174.

of a century of the newly established Union. It found expression in the demand for a strong central government, in a pronounced dislike for the French Revolution, particularly in its later phases, in a certain liking for form and ceremony. It would be wide of the mark to say that the Federalists accepted all of the theory of Adams as stated in the works just analyzed. This he did not do himself in his later years. But the spirit of this work — the distrust of democracy and the tenderness for the " well-born " — was characteristic of them.[1]

[1] Cf. Publicola, a series of letters by John Quincy Adams in reply to Paine's *Rights of Man*, 1791.

A careful exposition of early American principles is preserved in the lectures given by James Wilson before the Law School in Philadelphia, 1790–92. See Wilson, *Works*, edited by J. D. Andrews, 2 vols., 1896.

Wilson laid great stress on the theory that law and political obligation do not come from a superior, but are created by the voluntary agreement of individuals, — " the consent of those whose obedience the law requires " (I, 88). He regarded even a private contract as really constituting a law. " Why not," said he, " if it had all its essential properties ? " He denied that there was any contract between king and people or between governor and governed, maintaining that the agreement is one between the individual and the whole society.

CHAPTER IV

THE JEFFERSONIAN DEMOCRACY

No sooner was the new Constitution put into actual operation than there began a decided movement away from strong government and toward individual and states rights. It seemed almost as if the people were alarmed at what they had done, and were anxious to neutralize its effect. In addition to this perhaps natural reaction after the violent agitation in favor of a strong government, there was the powerful stimulus given to democracy by the French Revolution, especially in its earlier years. This great event aroused the democratic spirit throughout Europe, and was not without its effect on America.[1] Nor should it be forgotten that just at this time Jefferson returned to his native land, ready to organize and give form to the scattered democratic tendencies. Under these auspices the new movement rapidly gained strength, and in little more than a decade was able to triumph over the Adams-Hamilton party.

The most marked characteristic of this movement was the antipathy shown toward everything

[1] On this subject see the interesting study by Charles D. Hazen, *Contemporary American Opinion of the French Revolution* (1897).

suggestive of monarchy, hereditary aristocracy, or strongly centralized government. Objection was made, for example, to any exceptional formality in addressing the President, to stamping his likeness on the coinage, to any elaborate ceremony at the seat of government. Opposition was made to the size of the standing army, to the establishment of the United States Bank, to the assumption of the state debts. Particularly was there denunciation of the administration because of its refusal to take up the defence of republican France against monarchic England. To favor Britain or even to remain neutral in the contest, it was said, was really equivalent to upholding the British form of government against the free institutions of the Revolution.

The theory of this movement is represented in such works as Thomas Paine's *Rights of Man*, which was used as an answer to the writings of Adams; in Tucker's *Commentaries on Blackstone*[1] (1803); in Taylor's *Inquiry*[2] (1814); and the various writings of Joel Barlow.[3] But by far the most

[1] H. St. George Tucker, *Commentaries on Blackstone*.

[2] John Taylor, *An Inquiry into the Principles and Policy of the Government of the United States*. A considerable part of this discursive work is taken up by a criticism of Adams's theory of aristocracy. By the same author, *Construction Construed and the Constitution Vindicated* (1820); *Tyranny Unmasked* (1822); *New Views of the Constitution* (1823).

[3] *Advice to the Privileged Orders in the Several States of Europe* (1792); *Joel Barlow to his Fellow Citizens in the United States of America* (1801); and various other letters. See *Life and Letters of Joel Barlow*, by Charles Burr Todd.

influential of the leaders in this group was Thomas Jefferson, and to a consideration of his doctrines we now turn.

No name is more often or more intimately associated with American democracy than that of Thomas Jefferson. During his lifetime he was the American democrat *par excellence;* on his death he was politically canonized, and his words are still quoted with confidence and received with respect in the consideration of almost all political questions. Brought into prominence as the author of the Declaration of Independence, identified with the growth and triumph of the Republican party, inaugurated as its first President, framing its policies and providing its philosophy, Jefferson was undoubtedly the central figure in the early development of American democracy.[1]

Though regarded as the great advocate of democracy, Jefferson bequeathed to posterity no systematic treatise on the principles of politics.[2] His *Summary View* (1774) and *Notes on Virginia* (1782) are the nearest approach to this,[3] and they can scarcely be considered an approximation. Moreover, he was not a great orator, and there is no

[1] For the life of Jefferson, see H. S. Randall's work in three volumes; also Morse's volume in the American Statesmen Series.

[2] A useful classification of Jefferson's ideas on a great variety of subjects is made by J. P. Foley, in *The Jeffersonian Cyclopædia*.

[3] See also his *Autobiography* (to 1790) and *The Anas* (1791–1806).

L

collection of addresses in which his ideas are embodied. He was, however, a great correspondent, and we have a large collection of his letters, written to such persons as Madison, John Adams, Lafayette, Dupont de Nemours, Taylor, Kercheval, Johnston, and others. From this extensive correspondence, in which topics of political theory frequently appear, together with some of his official papers, it is possible to reconstruct the theory of Jefferson, if not in minute detail, at least in general outline.[1]

The first important statement of Jefferson's political theory is contained in the Declaration of Independence. Here are eloquently expressed the now familiar doctrines of human equality, of the natural and inalienable rights of man, of the guaranty of these rights as the first cause of government, and of the right and duty of revolution when they are subverted. These doctrines, it is perhaps needless to say, were not original with the writer of the Declaration. They were the common property of his time, were on the lips of every patriot orator, and found copious expression in resolutions throughout the colonies. It was later charged that the substance of the Declaration had been "hack-

[1] References are to Ford's edition of Jefferson's writings (ten volumes), unless otherwise specified. The Washington edition contains some material not found in Ford, and *vice versa*. See also "The Jefferson Papers," in *Collections of Massachusetts Historical Society*, Seventh Series, Vol. I, edited by J. Franklin Jameson.

neyed in Congress for two years before." [1] Jefferson himself was fully conscious that the originality of the statements lay in their form, rather than in their content, and his own explanation of his work is excellent : " Neither aiming at originality of principle or sentiment, nor yet copied from any particular or previous writings, it was intended to be an expression of the American mind, and to give to that expression the proper tone and spirit called for by the occasion." [2] Jefferson crystallized the common sentiment into a very effective form, but he could not and did not claim for himself the merit of presenting to the world a series of new or hitherto undiscovered truths. This is not to say, however, that the authorship of the Declaration was not a signal distinction ; it merely changes the category in which the distinction lay.

Inquiring more closely into Jefferson's theory of inalienable rights, we find him protesting against the idea that we surrender any of our natural rights on entering into society. Jefferson argues that these rights are not given up, but, on the contrary, are rendered more secure. [3] He holds that the

[1] *Works*, X, 267. This was alleged by Pickering and Adams, who also charged that "its essence was contained in Otis's pamphlet." R. H. Lee maintained that it was copied from Locke.

[2] *Ibid.* X, 343. Cf. X, 268 : " I did not consider it as any part of my charge to invent new ideas altogether and to offer no sentiment which had ever been expressed before." — *Letter to Madison.*

[3] *Ibid.* X (1816), 32 ff. Cf. Locke, *Two Treatises of Government.*

state should declare and enforce our rights, but should take none of them from us. Reasoning in this way, it is possible, he thinks, to mark out the proper sphere of state activity. Thus, as no man has a natural right to interfere with the rights of others, it is the duty of the law to restrain every one from such interference. Every man should contribute to the necessities of society ; therefore the law should see that he does so. No man has a natural right to judge in his own cause; therefore the law must judge. Thus it appears that one does not lose his natural rights under government, but obtains a better guaranty of them.

Government is established, however, by the " consent of the governed," or at least a just government is so supported. What, then, is the nature of this consent, and how is it to be made effective amid constantly changing conditions ? Jefferson was not satisfied with a contract made once and for all, like that of Hobbes, or with a merely hypothetical contract or even with a presumption of tacit consent from the fact of residence. He looked upon the contract as a necessary foundation for legitimate government, and he considered that the agreement should have historical as well as logical validity. The principle of the social contract must be sacredly preserved in the life of the people, and Jefferson proposed two ways of insuring this end : first, by revolution ; second, by periodical renewal of the agreement.

Revolution, Jefferson did not regard with great horror, if principle were involved in the process. He did not believe in government as something so sacred in nature as to be above human criticism. He did not " look at constitutions with sanctimonious reverence and deem them like the ark of the covenant, too sacred to be touched." [1] Government appeared to him as an institution existing for the governed ; and if it failed to serve this purpose, then it might be overthrown and another erected on its ruins. So far did he go in this direction that the beneficent elements in government were at times almost lost to view. He declared his dislike of energetic government because it is always oppressive.[2] He was on one occasion doubtful whether the first state of man, without government, as he says, would not be the most desirable, if the society were not too large.[3] He thought that republics should not be too severe in their treatment of rebellions, lest the free spirit of the people be suppressed.

Rebellion, he argued, is a medicine necessary to the health of government, and its use must not be denied. It is wholesome, though bitter ; or, using another figure, it clears the air like a thunderstorm.[4] Shays's Rebellion in Massachusetts Jefferson regarded with great composure, even with complaisance. The motives of the rebels were good, he thought, though doubtless they were ill

[1] *Works*, X, 42.   [2] *Ibid*. IV, 479.
[3] *Ibid*. IV, 362.   [4] *Ibid*. IV, 362.

informed on the situation.   Better, however, that
they should take up arms than tamely submit to
what they deemed oppressive ; for, after all, it is
not rebellion that destroys a republic, but the dull
lethargy that creeps upon and paralyzes the public
spirit — "God forbid, that we should ever be twenty
years without such a rebellion."   There have been,
he continues, thirteen states independent for eleven
years, and during this time only one rebellion.
This amounts to one in one hundred and forty-three
years for each state — by no means an excessive
number.   How is it possible for a country to preserve its liberties if the rulers are not occasionally
warned of the existence of a spirit of resistance
among their subjects ?   "What signify," he asks,
"a few lives lost in a century or two ?   The tree
of liberty must be refreshed from time to time with
the blood of patriots and tyrants." [1]

The idea of adherence to the principle of the
social contract finds a less violent expression in
Jefferson's argument for periodical renewals of the
agreement.   Rebellion or revolution serves to keep
alive the public spirit ; but it acts through irregu-
lar and illegal channels, and hence is best adapted
to countries where the government is tyrannically
inclined.   For a free state, however, there are
other plans that may be followed, without passing
outside the boundaries of the law.   A convention,
reconsidering the organic law of the land and sub-

[1] *Works*, IV (1789), 467.

mitting the result of its deliberations to the people, really constitutes, he maintains, a renewal of the fundamental agreement. In this way the "consent of the governed" may be again invoked and the government reëstablished on a just foundation. Each generation, such is the argument, has a right to establish its own law. "The earth belongs in usufruct to the living; the dead have neither powers nor rights over it."[1] It follows, then, that no generation of men can pass any law binding for a period longer than the lifetime of that generation, because their law-making power ceases with their existence. If one generation could bind another, the dead and not the living would rule. Since conditions change and men change, there must be opportunity for corresponding change in political institutions, and also for a renewal of the principle of government by consent of the governed.[2]

Having established this proposition, Jefferson proceeded to determine the exact period for which a law or a constitution might be considered as an expression of the will of the community. By the use of certain tables of M. de Buffon, he found that in any given society one-half of all those over twenty-one years of age will have passed away in eighteen years and eight months.[3] Therefore, he

[1] *Ibid.* V, 116.

[2] Cf. the theory of Thomas Paine as discussed in *Political Science Quarterly*, XIV, 389 (September, 1899).

[3] *Works*, V, 118–119.

reasoned, no society can make any constitution,
law, or contract of binding force for any period
longer than nineteen years. Hence, if the society
is to adhere to the principles upon which just government is founded, there should be a revision
of the fundamental law, or at least an opportunity
for revision, every nineteen years. This plan was
defended by Jefferson as a reasonable and practicable method of maintaining a free government in
its integrity. "At first blush," said he, "it may
be rallied as a theoretical speculation, but examination will prove it to be solid and salutary." [1] He
urged that the first revenue law enacted by Congress should contain in its preamble a statement
of this theory, and that the period for the granting
of patents be limited to nineteen years; and he
manifested much concern at Virginia's failure to
adhere to the policy of periodical constitutional
revision.

Such, then, were the two methods by which the
consent of the governed might be made the constant basis of government — by periodical renewal
of the contract, or, if this were impossible, by
rebellion or revolution. Neither of these methods,
however, was novel in political speculation when
Jefferson propounded them. The idea of a "fre-

---

[1] *Works*, V, 123. See VI (Washington edition), 136, 197;
VII, 15, 359. Madison, in reply to Jefferson (in Madison's Writings,
I, 503–506), urges the debt owed by the living to the dead and
advocates the doctrine of "tacit consent."

quent recurrence to fundamental principles" was common to the time and was often expressed in the Revolutionary state constitutions;[1] while the plan for a revision of the Constitution was not so radical as the provision actually made in Vermont and Pennsylvania for a council of censors and a septennial constitutional revision.[2]

Having considered Jefferson's theory as to the basis of the government, it is now in order to examine his position as to the various classes of government.[3] What, then, was his opinion of monarchy? The government of a king Jefferson regarded, at least in the earlier part of his life, with utter abhorrence. Though not the equal of Paine in the vigor of his invective against kings, he was but little inferior. He declared that "no race of kings has ever presented above one man of common sense in twenty generations."[4] Again: "There is not a crowned head in Europe whose talents or merit would entitle him to be elected a vestryman by the people of any parish in America."[5] Writing in 1810, he stated that, to his personal knowledge,

---

[1] Massachusetts (1780), Art. 18; Pennsylvania (1776), Art. 14; New Hampshire, Art. 38; North Carolina, Art. 21; Vermont, Art. 16.

[2] See Jameson, *Constitutional Conventions* (4th ed.), sec. 544.

[3] *Works*, IV, 362. Jefferson classified societies into three groups: (1) those destitute of government; (2) those in whose government the will of every one has a just influence; (3) those whose governments rest on force.   Letter to Madison (1787).

[4] *Ibid.* IV, 426.   [5] *Ibid.* V, 8.

Louis XVI was a fool; and in the same category were included the kings of Spain, Naples, Sardinia, and Denmark, and the queen of Portugal; while the successor to Frederick the Great he characterized as a mere hog.[1] Moreover, he thought that if there were any efficient hereditary monarchies, their power would decay in the course of a few generations. Jefferson's favorite and perhaps most effective form of attack upon his opponents was to arouse the suspicion that they were at heart monarchists, longing for the restoration of royalty.[2] In later years, however, after the failure of the European revolutions to establish democracy, he was inclined to concede that under certain conditions a monarchy might really be the most desirable form of government.[3]

The next point of inquiry is Jefferson's opinion of aristocracy. Judging from his famous utterance, "All men are created equal," he is generally regarded as the great champion of human equality. Against this is sometimes urged the fact that the ownership of slaves is hardly in keeping with ideas of universal equality. It should not be forgotten, however, that Jefferson was really opposed to the institution of negro slavery and more than once

[1] *Works*, V (Washington), 515.

[2] In 1824 he said that he had charged the Federalists with adherence to the *forms*, that is, the ceremonies, of the British government, not with a desire to introduce the British *form*, *i.e.* the monarchy. *Works*, X, 309–310.

[3] See letter to Lafayette (1823) in *Works*, X, 279 ff.

went on record against it, as in his proposition for a Virginia constitution[1] (1776) and in the report on the "Government for the Western Territory" (1784).[2] Later in life he was forced to abandon his early hope that slavery would soon cease to flourish in America, yet he still believed in the ultimate extinction of slavery and declared (1814) that "the love of justice and the love of country plead equally for the cause of these people."[3] He said that the hour of emancipation was advancing with the march of time and urged continual effort, "softly but steadily."

Aside from this point, however, it is easy to show that Jefferson was not at all a believer in the absolute equality of men.[4] In this connection it is interesting to examine his correspondence with John Adams upon this very question of aristocracy. Adams denounces in set terms the theory of the equality of all men, declares that society is divided into two classes, "gentlemen" and "simplemen," and demands the legal recognition of this difference in ability.[5] Jefferson does not deny the

---

[1] *Works*, II, 26.

[2] *Ibid.* III, 429. In this report occurs the provision : "After the year 1800 of the Christian æra, there shall be neither slavery nor involuntary servitude in any of the said states otherwise than in punishment of crimes whereof the party shall have been convicted to have been personally guilty."   [3] *Ibid.* IX, 477 ff.

[4] With the Declaration of Independence should be read Jefferson's proposed constitution for Virginia (1776), II, 7 ff. See also the propositions of 1783, 1794, and 1816.   [5] See *ante.*

existence of an aristocracy among men, but distinguishes between the *natural* aristocracy and the
artificial aristocracy. One is based upon virtue
and talent, the other upon wealth and birth. The
"natural aristocracy" appears to him as the "most
precious gift of nature," and highly useful for the
purpose of instructing and governing society. He
even goes so far as to say, "That form of government is the best which provides the most effectively for a pure selection of these natural *aristoi*
into the offices of government."[1] The "artificial
aristocracy," based on wealth and birth, is mischievous, even dangerous, and should not receive legal
recognition. In reply to Adams's proposition that
the aristocracy should be represented in one legislative chamber and the people in the other,[2] he
urges that the separation of the pseudo-aristocracy
from the genuine should be left to the people themselves. Some mistakes will doubtless be made,
but the really good and wise will generally be
selected.[3] Jefferson, it may be said, believed in
an aristocracy, but only in the sense that the best
fitted for governing should rule, and that the selection of the *aristoi* should be made by popular election rather than on a basis of birth or wealth. He
wanted aristocratic rulers democratically chosen.

[1] *Works*, IX, 425.

[2] *Works* of John Adams, IV, 379.

[3] *Works*, IX, 426. See Jefferson's explanation of the difference
in opinion between Adams and himself.

But in this connection it must be remembered that the democracy of his day was not the democracy of ours. As late as 1824, Jefferson estimated that a majority of the freemen in Virginia were excluded from the franchise, and there were many inhabitants who were not even freemen.[1]

Having reviewed his ideas on monarchy and aristocracy, it remains to consider Jefferson's doctrine of democracy. What was the theory of " Jeffersonian democracy " ? The doctrines of natural rights and the " consent of the governed " have already been examined; but, more specifically, what was his idea as to the characteristic features of a democratic government ? This is not easy to determine ; for, in the first place, his notions were never systematically and not always clearly expressed; and, in the second place, there are contradictions between his political theory and his practical politics. The theory of Jefferson, the political scientist, and the practice of Jefferson, the man of affairs, are not always free from inconsistency. An effort will be made here, however, to show as clearly as possible from the scattered sources at command what Jefferson's theory of democracy really was.

Jefferson defines a republic as "a government by the [its] citizens in mass, acting directly and personally, according to rules established by the

[1] On Aristocracy, see Taylor, *Inquiry*, *passim* ; Tucker's *Blackstone*, Appendix to Vol. I, 37 ff.

majority." [1]   Governments are republican in proportion to the degree of direct action on the part
of the citizens,[2] and there are of course many vary-
ing degrees.   This is, however, only a very general
statement and lacks definiteness of outline.   One of
the best supplementary explanations is that found
in Jefferson's first inaugural address.[3]   Here are
laid down the main principles which should obtain
within a democracy.   They include, among others,
the following propositions: equal and exact justice; jealous care of the right of election by the
people; the rule of the majority; [4] the preservation of the guaranties of civil liberty, such as freedom of religion, freedom of the press, the habeas
corpus and jury trial; the subordination of the
military to the civil authority; and economical
administration.   In these phrases are summed up
his democratic program, and under his type of
government they would all be found in operation.

Further evidence as to Jefferson's notion of

[1] Letter to Taylor, in *Works*, X, 28.   See also letters to Dupont
de Nemours X, 22 ff.; to Judge Johnson, X, 226; and to Gerry,
VII, 327.

[2] "Action by the citizens in person, in affairs within their reach
and competence; in all others by representatives chosen immediately and removable by themselves, constitutes the essence of a
republic." — *Letter to Dupont de Nemours*, X, 24.

[3] *Works*, VIII, 1 ff.

[4] *Ibid.* VIII, 4.   "Absolute acquiescence in the rule of the
majority, the vital principle of republics from which there is no
appeal but to force."

democracy is given by examination of what he once termed the "two hooks" upon which republican government depends.[1] These were an educational system and a scheme of local government. Keenly appreciating the necessity of popular intelligence as a basis for successful popular government, Jefferson was a constant advocate of all measures for the diffusion of knowledge among the masses. If government rests upon public opinion, he said, then our first and foremost care is to see that this opinion is kept right.[2] Opinion that is unenlightened and unsound would be the death of free government. He once said that, if forced to choose between a government without newspapers and newspapers without a government, he would not hesitate to choose the latter alternative, assuming that every man received the papers and were capable of understanding them. Jefferson exerted himself in behalf of educational institutions in his own state, and to his earnest efforts was largely due the establishment of the University of Virginia.[3]

The second "hook" was local government. Referring to his experience at the time of the Embargo Act, Jefferson said: "I felt the foundations of the government shaken under my feet by the New England townships."[4] He recommended

[1] *Ibid.* IX, 453.   *Ibid.* IV, 360.
[3] See Randall's *Jefferson*, III, 461.
[4] *Works*, VI (Washington edition), 544.

for Virginia a system of local government modelled quite closely after the New England type, to take the place of the "large and lubberly divisions into counties." "Wards" were to take charge of the elementary schools, to care for the poor and the roads, and to have a system of justices, constables, and police.[1] But the "ward" was merely one step in the scheme of governmental gradation which Jefferson had in mind. He conceived that liberty should be secured, not only by a tripartite division of governmental powers, but also by a further distribution among a series of organizations extending from ward to nation. First should come the elementary republics or wards, then the county republics, then the states, and finally the nation. Governmental powers should be delegated "by a synthetical process to higher and higher orders of functionaries, so as to trust fewer and fewer powers in proportion as the trustees become more and more oligarchical."[2] Local government would thus be made a part of the complicated "check and balance" system in the intricacies of which despotism would be entangled and rendered powerless.

Another feature in the Jeffersonian program should perhaps receive mention at this point; namely, the plea for the subordination of the military to the civil authority. He argued against a large standing army as a likely instrument of

[1] *Works*, VII (Washington edition), 357; also V, 524.
[2] *Ibid.* VI (Washington edition), 543.

oppression. Absolute governments must depend upon force, but a free state, he held, should place its confidence in the good-will of its citizens. So far as military power is necessary for purposes of defence, the need should be supplied by a well-disciplined militia. A standing army was associated with monarchical power, and it was, therefore, a part of the republican policy to reduce the army and the navy to as low a footing as possible. Under Jefferson this was the line of conduct followed by the administration. In this way an alleged monarchical tendency was checked and at the same time the expenses of government were reduced, although the Embargo Act involved an exercise of power like that of a " consolidated government." The suppression of the military power was undoubtedly one of the features in the Republican plan for governmental regeneration — indeed, it has been urged that this was the real significance of the transition in 1801 ;[1] but Jefferson did not present any very elaborate arguments upon the question, and it did not occupy a very prominent place in his political theory.

Thus far this inquiry has extended into Jefferson's definition of a republic and an examination of various features included in the program of such a government. Yet all these considerations fail to show what was the real essence of Jeffersonian democracy. They reveal in part his policy, but his policy was never complete either in theory

[1] Ford, *The Rise and Growth of American Politics*, 131.

M

or in actual practice. That which gave life and color to all these measures for democratic reform was the article in the Jeffersonian political creed which must now be considered. The distinctive and characteristic feature of his doctrine is most clearly expressed in his correspondence with John Adams; here may be seen the real difference that divided these two great leaders, one the advocate of the "well-born," the other the apostle of democracy — their opinions characteristic of two great parties and of two great schools of political thought. This difference has already been indicated, but may here be better explained and more appropriately emphasized.

It has been shown that Adams was anxious for a balanced government of the most complex nature, including, as one of its elements, a legal recognition of the aristocracy, and that he appeared to doubt and distrust the capacity of the people for any high degree of self-government.

Against such a theory, Jefferson maintained that men are naturally divided into two classes: (1) those who fear and distrust the people; (2) those who identify themselves with the people, have confidence in them, consider them as the most honest and safe, although not always the most wise, depositories of public interests.[1]

---

[1] *Works*, VII (Washington edition), 376. Cf. Madison, *Dialogue between a Republican and an anti-Republican* (1792), in *Works*, IV, 483.

In the opinion of the first class, the masses must be held in check by physical and moral force, and can be restrained in no other way; men are essentially incapable of ruling themselves, and must be governed by authorities independent of their will and not subject to their judgment. But the second class, on the other hand, argues Jefferson, place their trust in popular capacity for self-government, maintaining that man is a rational animal, possessing a natural and innate sense of justice, and that for the preservation of peace and order he does not require restraint from above or outside, but is competent to choose his own rulers and hold them dependent on his will. The same idea as to the two classes of opinions is expressed in a letter to Dupont de Nemours, in which Jefferson says: "We both love the people, but you love them as infants whom you are afraid to trust without nurses, and I as adults whom I freely leave to self-government." [1]

The essence, then, of Jefferson's democracy was confidence in the self-governing capacity of the great mass of the people — a belief in the ability of the average man or of average men to select rulers who will conduct the administration in general accord with the interests of the society. The divergence of opinion just here made Adams an aristocrat and Jefferson a democrat — not that

[1] *Works*, X, 23; one of the best of the statements of democratic principles.

Adams had no confidence, or that Jefferson had all confidence, in the people, but the degrees of confidence differed widely. We might say that one looked with suspicion on the people first of all, the other distrusted first the government and after that the people. Both favored a balanced government; but Adams desired primarily to prevent violent action on the part of the people, whereas Jefferson's first aim was to prevent oppression by the government; one reasoned that the people should be watched, the other that the government should be kept in constant view.[1] Confidence in the people was, therefore, the distinguishing characteristic in the *theory* of Jeffersonian democracy. In practice, however, the early "democracy" was aristocratic in the nature of its rule and continued to be so until the time of Jackson, when the democratic theory found a more complete expression in political institutions.

It must further be noted that Jefferson's theory of democracy was by no means so doctrinaire as is often supposed. He did not argue that democracy was equally adapted to all times, places, conditions, and peoples, as some have assumed. Confident of the ultimate triumph of democratic principles, he was not eager for their immediate

---

[1] Letter to Dupont de Nemours, in *Works*, X, 22. Cf. also VIII, 127: "What is practicable must often control pure theory, and the habits of the governed determine in great degree what is practicable."

and universal application. Nothing could be clearer than his statement that "the excellence of every government is its adaptation to the state of those who are governed by it." The Sage of Monticello was not so blind a devotee of democracy as to believe that civil and political liberty need no firmer basis than a paper constitution. To Lafayette he said that liberty becomes, "with an unprepared people, a tyranny still of the many, the few, or the one." [1] Again, he expressed doubt " whether the state of society in Europe can bear a republican form of government," and therefore advised " a hereditary chief strictly limited." [2] The cause for the failure of the continental revolutions is discovered in the fact that " the mob of the cities, the instrument used for their accomplishment, debased by ignorance, poverty, and vice, could not be restrained to rational action." [3] Discussing American conditions, he comes to the conclusion that the Spanish-American states are not ready for republican institutions, since their experience " has disqualified them for the maintenance or even knowledge of their rights." [4] Louisiana

---

[1] *Works*, IX (1815), 505.

[2] *Ibid.* X (1823), 280, "A hereditary chief strictly limited, the right of war vested in the legislative body, a rigid economy of the public contributions and absolute interdiction of all useless expenses, will go far toward keeping the government honest and inoppressive."

[3] *Ibid.* VI (Washington edition), 227.

[4] *Ibid.* IX (1811), 322; also IX, 430, 435.

is not ready (1803) for the exercise of complete political liberty and should obtain it only " in proportion as we find the people there riper for receiving the first principles of freedom." [1]   Jefferson points out that in America economic conditions favor democracy.[2]   Here every one owns property or is at least so well situated as to be interested in the maintenance of law and order.   It seems, then, that "such men may safely and advantageously reserve to themselves a wholesome control over their public affairs and a degree of freedom, which, in the hands of the canaille of the cities of Europe, would be instantly perverted to the demolition and destruction of everything public and private."   Elsewhere he remarks that the Americans will continue to be virtuous and retain their democratic form of government as long as they remain an *agricultural* people ; but " when they get piled upon one another in large cities, as in Europe, they will become corrupt as in Europe." [3]   In one instance he even goes so far as to say that the people here "would go on as well under an absolute monarch while our present character remains of order, industry, and love of peace." [4]

Jefferson believed fully in democracy and was confident of the ultimate triumph of the system, but he was too keen and careful an observer to

[1] *Works*, VIII, 275.   Cf. Paine, to the same effect.
[2] *Ibid.* IX, 428;   IV, 479.
[3] *Ibid.* IV, 479.   [4] *Ibid.* X, 31.

think that all people were capable of adopting the American system in his day. This may not have been in harmony with his ideas on natural rights; but as he himself said, theory and practice are not always in accord, and "the habits of the governed determine in great degree what is practicable."

Some interesting light is thrown on Jefferson's philosophy by noticing upon what systematic political theorists he was most dependent, and which of them, in his opinion, best expressed the true principles of political science. From the classical writings, Jefferson apparently derived little inspiration. Aristotle he knew,[1] but thought of little value; and Plato's writings he considered as so much worthless "jargon."[2] The chief source from which Jefferson drew his inspiration is commonly supposed to have been the philosophers of the eighteenth-century democracy in France. It is often said that his head was turned by French ideas, that he was a "Rousseauist," and that the speculative Jefferson was really a Frenchman. The extent of the French influence upon Jefferson was, however, far less than is generally supposed. Montesquieu and Rousseau, who might be presumed to have had a large share in determining his views, seem to have affected him very little. Montesquieu he held in no high esteem. "I am glad," he says, "to hear of anything which

---

[1] *Ibid.* VII (Washington edition), 31.
[2] *Ibid.* IX, 462.

reduces that author to his just level, as his predilection for monarchy, and the English monarchy in particular, has done mischief everywhere, and here also to a certain degree."[1] Rousseau is not discussed or recommended for reading by Jefferson; nor do the latter's theories show as much resemblance to Rousseau as to other French writers. Jefferson recommended Condorcet's *Esquisse d'un Tableau Historique des Progrès de l'Esprit Humain*, and probably obtained from this source his ideas on human "improvability." The only French work cited with enthusiasm is that by Destutt de Tracy, *Commentaire sur l'Esprit des Lois*, of which Jefferson had a translation made into English (1811), so that it might circulate freely in this country. He referred to Tracy's work as the "most precious gift the present age has received,"[2] "giving the most correct analysis of the principles of government which has yet been offered;" although he did not agree with all the theories contained in it, notably the doctrine of a plural executive.[3] But this work did not appear until long after the early and more radical period in Jefferson's life was over. The Declaration of Independence antedated it by thirty-five years, and Tracy himself had been influenced in no small degree by American publicists, as appears from

[1] *Works*, V (Washington edition), 535. Cf. VIII, 24.
[2] *Ibid.* IX, 305, 500.
[3] Letter to Tracy, *ibid.* IX, 305.

his eulogy of our federal system of government. It is hence impossible to impute the paternity of Jefferson's ideas to this work.[1]

Indeed, it is unnecessary to go outside of the English theory of politics to find ample precedent upon which Jefferson might draw. In the English writers, particularly of the seventeenth century, are found revolutionary and democratic principles of the most decided character,[2] anticipating not only Jefferson, but in large measure Rousseau himself. As I have indicated above, when Jefferson's rivals wished to detract from his fame as author of the Declaration, they could point to the substance of this instrument in the words of Locke: the ideas were the common property of the time — not borrowed from Rousseau or Montesquieu. Jefferson's theory followed a line of thought already marked out during the English revolution by Milton, Sydney, and Locke, and taken up by colonial thinkers before Rousseau had begun to write.[3]

When called upon for advice as to the best political literature, Jefferson recommended Locke and Sydney of the earlier writers, and of the later: Priestley's *Essay on the First Principles of Government;* Burgh's *Political Disquisitions;* Chipman's *Sketches of the Principles of Government; The Fed-*

---

[1] The commentary appeared first in America, and eleven years afterward in France (1822).

[2] See G. P. Gooch, *English Democratic Ideas in the Seventeenth Century.*   [3] See *ante*, Chap. I.

eralist, which he once commended as "the best commentary on the principles of government which was ever written," and Tracy's *Commentaries*. Jefferson was also an intimate friend of Thomas Paine, and there are many common points in their theories. In a letter to Paine he assured him that the Americans are "firm and unanimous in their principles of republicanism, and there is no better proof of it than that they love what you write, and read it with delight. The printers season every newspaper with extracts from your last, just as they did before from your first part of the *Rights of Man*." [1]

On the whole, it appears that, so far as the revolutionary character of his theory was concerned, Jefferson was little in advance, logically, of his predecessors. The difference between Jefferson and Locke, for example, was not so much in fundamental principles as in the development of and deductions from these principles. Jefferson and Locke were both democratic and revolutionary in theory, but Jefferson went farther than Locke in his advocacy of democratization of the government. Between the *Fundamental Constitutions* of Locke and the Jeffersonian program there was a wide difference. Locke's attitude toward the organization of the government was wholly aristocratic, while that of Jefferson was essentially democratic. They agreed in their destructive, but not in their

[1] *Works*, VI, 87.

constructive, program. Both were opposed to absolutism; but Locke feared, while Jefferson favored, the erection of a "numerous democracy."[1]

In conclusion, what should be said of Jefferson's rank as a political theorist? The important service rendered by the Sage of Monticello was not the scientific elucidation of theory. The doctrines he advocated had all been discussed and developed long before his time, and he did not improve much on the classic analysis of Aristotle, the reasoning of Locke, or the brilliant logic of Rousseau. He cannot be classed as one of the great political thinkers. He did not inquire deeply into the nature of the state, its forms of organization, or any of the numerous problems arising out of the complex relations of political association. He did not write systematically at all, and what he did write was notable rather because of its rhetoric than because of its scientific depth or clearness. Tested by the canons of the schools, Jefferson falls far short of the stature of a great political philosopher.

What, then, shall be said of this personality so preëminent in the annals of American democracy? What was the source of his power, and what the significance of his career? One great cause of his power was the unusual sagacity and astuteness that made him a great party leader. With a

[1] See, on the source of the ideas of colonial theorists, Lewis Rosenthal, "Rousseau in Philadelphia," *Magazine of American History*, XII, 46.

"machine" that was ill organized, if organized at all, and with little patronage, Jefferson's political genius guided the Republicans on to the destruction of their rivals. Another cause was his singular gift for vivid statement of popular ideas. He crystallized the common democratic sentiment, giving it form and power. He was great in his ability to interpret and express popular feeling. And finally, he had great confidence in the people. He believed in their capacity for self-government, had confidence in the soundness of their judgment, and was hopeful of the future of democratic institutions. In spite of the many inconsistencies in his conduct, Jefferson stands out as the great apostle of the democratic faith in his day. He appeared as the advocate of the "people" against the claims of "monarchists" and "aristocrats." He not only defended the people on theoretical grounds, but he was identified with a fairly definite program of democratic reform, a part of which he was successful in carrying out, and much of which was realized later under the Jacksonian democracy. He stood for the extension of the suffrage, periodical revision of the Constitution, religious liberty, subordination of military to civil authority, the maintenance of local governments as a barrier against excessive centralization, and for a certain democratic simplicity in place of the elaborate ceremony of kings and courts. This was the framework of his political system, while the life and spirit of it was faith in the self-governing capacity of the people.

What is said of Jefferson may be taken as typical of the school with which his name is connected. He organized the party, furnished its policies and its principles, and for eight years offered a practical illustration of the type of thought for which he stood. When the political theory of Jefferson is stated, that of the Jeffersonian democracy has been outlined.

In conclusion on the theory of this epoch, it may be said to have begun with a reaction against democracy and to have closed with the triumph of the popular doctrines. The great work of the reactionary party was the adoption of the Constitution and the establishment of the federal government on a firm basis. Their chief concern was with the maintenance of law and order, and they were interested only secondarily in the guaranty of human rights. This was the secret of their success and the cause of their failure as well. In the accomplishment of their task they necessarily antagonized some of the democratic doctrines of their time; and certain of the leaders, such as Adams and Hamilton, developed and expressed decidedly aristocratic ideas. Notwithstanding the explanations made at a later date, it is evident that Adams and his school leaned away from the people; or perhaps it would be more accurate and just to say that they favored strong and efficient government, whether popular or not. If they must choose between strong government and popular government, they would stand for an adequate and effective political system. When once the central government was fairly established, the opposition, aided by the movement in France, rapidly gained strength, and soon was able to obtain control of the administration. Their return marked the re-action from government to liberty again. Although guilty of much misrepresentation of their oppo-nents' position, and of many inconsistencies in their conduct, the Jeffersonian Democrats had greater confidence in the masses, and were ready to do more for popular government than was the conser-vative school.[1] They looked forward to a contin-ued process of democratic development; the other school looked backward toward the long-tried ré-gime of England, half expecting a return to an order like that of earlier days, when the demo-cratic impulse had spent its force.

Notwithstanding the democratic character of the Jeffersonian theory, the program involved in this was by no means carried out. Even un-

---

[1] It should not be forgotten that in 1787 Jefferson himself enthu-siastically endorsed Adams's *Defence*. " I have read your book with infinite satisfaction and improvement," he said. " It will do great good in America. Its learning and its good sense will, I hope, make it an institute for our politicians, old as well as young." — Letter to Adams, 1787. *Works* (Washington edition), II, 128.

der the democratic régime, there still remained a
strictly limited electorate, property qualifications,
long terms of office, and little participation of the
people in the election of their officers. The government was still in the hands of the freeholders
and the gentry. The theory of the Jeffersonians
was in many respects an advance upon that of
the government party, but its practice was still in
many ways aristocratic. The development of democracy was begun by the Jeffersonian democracy,
but its full realization was left for another time
and another party.

CHAPTER V

THE JACKSONIAN DEMOCRACY

THE radical movement which was destined to break down the power of the landed aristocracy, level the old barriers of exclusiveness, and open the way for government of a more popular character, took the form of Jacksonian Democracy. Its leaders made few contributions to democratic political theory, but they broadened the application of principles already familiar. By expanding the electorate, a revolution was made in the basis of the democracy, and radical changes in the superstructure were equally conspicuous. To the more important features in this movement, attention will now be directed.[1]

Two great forces were back of the Jacksonian democracy. These were, in the first place, the frontier conditions and ideas in the West and South; and, in the second place, the growth of

[1] On this period, see J. B. McMaster, *United States*, IV, V; S. N. Thorpe, *Constitutional History of the American People;* H. J. Ford, *Rise and Growth of American Politics;* F. A. Cleveland, *The Growth of Democracy in the United States;* James Schouler, *Constitutional Studies.*

cities and an industrial class. By 1830 nine new states had been added to the original thirteen, and by 1850 there had been sixteen admitted, of which only two, Maine and Vermont, were not on the Western frontier. In these new states the conditions, economic and social, were highly favorable to the development of the democratic spirit. Frontier life tended to produce self-reliance, independence, and individuality. It developed a sense of equality on the part of the members of the community. There was no great wealth, no highly polished society, no leisure class, and no historic tradition; the conditions were accordingly unfavorable to aristocratic theory or practice. To the hardy pioneers, the idea of a *jure divino* king, an hereditary nobility, or a specially privileged class was ridiculous in the extreme; while religious or property qualifications, permanent or long tenure of office, and similar restrictions were altogether unacceptable. They firmly believed in the sovereignty of the people, and, furthermore, in the necessity of giving to the mass of the population, as far as possible, the direction of public affairs. Anything in the shape of special privilege or class exclusiveness became at once an object of suspicion and distrust; but confidence in the people was always met with hearty applause, and was the surest way to popular approval.

A second cause was the increase of the city population, and the development of other than

N

agricultural pursuits. By reason of this development there came into existence a population and
a set of interests different from those of the freeholders' aristocracy. They demanded the right to
share in the active exercise of political power,
exerted pressure in this direction, and helped to
bring about the same state of affairs in the East
that was being realized in the Western and Southern states.[1]

This democratic tendency found expression in
national politics through the election to the Presidency of Andrew Jackson. In his personality the
new leader embodied the characteristics of the new
democracy. His defeat of John Quincy Adams, the
skilled and accomplished statesman, marked the advent of another type of chief executive and the
end of a long line of the old school Presidents.
To many grave thinkers, the election of Jackson
seemed the triumph of " King Mob," and portended
the ascendency of the worst elements of the people, the rule of an ignorant and incapable democracy. They thought that republican institutions
were threatened with the very gravest danger, and
would not have been surprised to see them wholly
subverted.

The importance of the new departure was soon
felt in the national government. The President
regarded himself as the representative of the peo-

[1] See on this point the debates in the Massachusetts Convention
of 1820, and the New York Convention of 1821.

ple, and asserted the rights of the executive against
the legislature and the judiciary as they had never
been asserted before. In the days when state constitutions had first been formed, overwhelming predominance had been given to the legislative department;
and in the national government also, Congress had
occupied the most conspicuous place up to this time.
Congressmen had nominated candidates for the
Presidency; had already directly chosen two Presidents; their law-making power had seldom met with
executive check; they had occupied the foremost
place in the direction of the affairs of the nation.
In the days of Jackson, the rule of "King Caucus"
was overthrown in favor of the less aristocratic
nominating convention. The long dormant veto
power was brought out and used in a way that had
never been thought of in the old régime. The
constitutional strength of the executive was for
the first time revealed, and the legislature met its
first decisive check.

Fear of the executive was soon aroused, and the
most painful anticipations of presidential tyranny
were expressed. The Whig party was organized in opposition to what its leaders considered
the abuse of the executive prerogative. Clay,
Calhoun, and Webster, the ablest intellects of the
time, struggled hard in defence of Congress, denouncing the action of the President in the most
unsparing terms. Webster said: "The contest
for ages has been to rescue liberty from the grasp

of executive power. . . . To this end, all that
could be gained from the imprudence, snatched
from the weakness, or wrung from the necessities
of crowned heads, has been carefully gathered up,
secured and hoarded, as the rich treasures, the
very jewels of liberty." [1] The executive, he urged,
has always been regarded "as a lion which must
be caged." The executive power is not the defender of liberty; but "our very security depends
upon our watchfulness of it." The President,
he denounced as "a Briareus (who) sits in the
centre of our system, and with his hundred
hands touches everything, moves everything, con-
trols everything." Clay was equally vigorous in
his attacks on the executive. The power of the
President, he said, "is felt from one extremity
to the other of this vast republic. By means of
principles which he has introduced and innova-
tions which he has made in our institutions, alas!
but too much countenanced by Congress and a
confiding people, he exercises uncontrolled the
power of the State. In one hand he holds the
purse, and in the other brandishes the sword of
the country. Myriads of dependants and partisans, scattered over the land, are ever ready to
sing hosannas to him, and to laud to the skies
whatever he does. He has swept over the government during the last eight years like a tropical
tornado. Every department exhibits traces of the

[1] *Congressional Debates*, Vol. X, Pt. II, p. 1681 (1834).

ravages of the storm."[1] To the leaders of the Whigs, indeed, it seemed that, as in the seventeenth century in England, the people were threatened by the power of the executive, and should find their natural ally in the legislature. This was clearly expressed by Calhoun when he said, that he considered Congress "the great central point where all power must receive its sanction and direction;" and that the large amount of discretionary authority which must under every government be lodged somewhere, should be placed in the hands of the legislature. Still more radically this theory was stated at times. For example, it was said on the floor of the Senate: "The executive power which represents the common force of society is, in every just theory, and in the nature of things, inferior to the legislative power, which is the representative of the common intelligence and the common will, and that, too, precisely in the degree to which brute force is inferior to reason."[2] The essence of the Whig doctrine was that the legislature is naturally the closest representative of the people, and that the executive should be an object of constant suspicion and distrust.[3]

[1] *Ibid.* XIII, Pt. I, p. 438 (1837). Cf. X, Pt. I, p. 1314, on the Whigs as opponents of executive prerogative.

[2] *Ibid.* Vol. XIII, Pt. I, 469.

[3] A very rhetorical statement of the anti-prerogative men was that made by Mr. Sprague in the Senate, January 29, 1834. "I may be deemed an alarmist. There is cause for alarm. When one

The legislature, however, had reached the climax of its power in the days of the Revolution, and there was now a pronounced reaction against that department. This was one of the most significant points in Andrew Jackson's administration. He announced himself as the representative of the people in as true a sense as the Congress, and declared his independence of, or better, his right to an equal rank with, the other two departments. The executive, since the time of the Revolution shorn of power, again found strength to assert himself in the affairs of state. It may fairly be said that one of the first fruits of the new democratic régime was a decisive victory for the executive, representing the people, over the congressional aristocracy inherited from the Revolution. It was the old story over again, of a strong executive supported by the masses of the people against a well-intrenched aristocracy; and the victory rested with the executive. Jackson undoubtedly believed that he was the representative of the people against the legislative aristocracy; the people apparently

man, encroaching upon Congress, the Senate, and the judiciary, arrests and rolls back the course of legislation; interprets laws, treaties, and constitutions; assumes the sole power of appointment, — holding at the same time absolute control over the army, the navy, the post-office, an affiliated press, and the whole swarm of executive officers, — and now superadded to all this, tremendous money power, the fiscal agency ingrafted upon banking capital, — can liberty be safe? Safe — when a boa-constrictor is closing around her his crawling and crushing folds?"

regarded him as their champion in the conflict, and
were willing to trust him with great powers in
order to insure the victory.

A similar expansion of the executive power is
noticeable in the individual states. In fact, the
movement began there, and not in the national
government. The selection of the governor was
taken away from the legislature and submitted to
the direct vote of the people ; [1] the term of office
was materially lengthened ; [2] the great weapon for
the defence of the executive prerogative, the veto,
was in general vested in the governor, [3] and also a
larger share of the appointing power. At the
same time, the former high property qualifications
were removed, and the position was made accessi-
ble to all citizens so far as wealth was concerned.
In short, there arose a new idea in regard to the
executive and his place in the scheme of government. This was well expressed by one of the delegates to the New York Convention of 1821. "An
erroneous idea," said he, "seems to have prevailed
in relation to the powers and origin of the governor. Who is he ? and by whom is he appointed ?
Does he derive his authority from the king of Great
Britain ? Is he an usurper ? If so, let us unite to

[1] Penn., 1790; Del., 1792; Ga., 1824; N.C., 1835; Md., 1837;
N.J. 1844; Va., 1850.

[2] Penn., 1790; Ga., 1789; Va., 1830; Del., 1831; N.C., 1835;
Md., 1837; N.J., 1844.

[3] Ga., 1789; Penn., 1790; N.H., 1792; Conn., 1818; N.J., 1844.

depose him.   But, sir, he is the man of the people
— elected by their suffrages and identified with
their interests.   He is a watchful sentinel to guard
us from evil and a zealous friend to admonish us
of error."

It is evident, then, that one pronounced feature
of the democratic movement in the first half of the
century was the elevation of the executive and the
degradation of the legislative power.   The early
distrust of the executive, which once took the form
of a fear that monarchy might return, had disappeared, and also the early confidence in the legislature.   Popular suspicion seemed to be directed,
not so much against a tyrannical monarchy, as
against "encroaching aristocracy."   The public
was willing to intrust large powers to one man,
but was jealous of the authority of a legislative
coterie, or a "banking aristocracy," or aristocracy
in any shape or form.   As has often been the case,
the instrument by which the aristocracy was overthrown, in this instance also, was a powerful executive.   In the national field this change centres
around the career of Andrew Jackson; in the
states the same tendency was at work, readjust-
ing the balance between the legislative and the
executive power.

Another point in national administration was carried for the radical democracy, when the principle
of rotation in office and the "spoils system" obtained recognition.   This was primarily a victory

for party organization, but the idea of rotation in office was a democratic one. This result had already been partly achieved by the provisions in state constitutions for short terms of office, and in many instances by limitations upon reëligibility. But now the general principle was accepted that all offices should be held for short terms only, in order that all citizens might have better opportunity to secure a position. The idea rested on the assumption that one man is about as well fitted for any office as any other man, and may, therefore, be safely intrusted with official responsibility. It was diametrically opposed to the doctrine that office should be held on the ground of special fitness, and that long tenure of office gives one, in a sense, a vested right to the position.

By no one was the popular notion more clearly stated than by Jackson himself in his first annual message to Congress. Here are found the two ideas on which the new system rested; namely, that experience is not very important for a public servant, and secondly, that a long tenure of office is actually detrimental to good public service. "There are, perhaps, few men," said Jackson, "who can for any great length of time enjoy office and power without being more or less under the influence of feelings unfavorable to the discharge of their public duties." And again he argued that "the duties of all public officers are, or at least admit of being made, so plain and simple that men of intelligence may readily qualify themselves for their performance; and I cannot but believe that more is lost by long continuance of men in office than is generally to be gained by their experience." He further urged that the proposed measure "would destroy the idea of property in office now so generally connected with official station; and although individual distress may be sometimes produced, it would, by promoting that rotation which constitutes a leading principle in the republican creed, give healthful action to the system." Such was the doctrine of rotation in office as announced by President Jackson.

This view seems to be that experience had before entering office is unnecessary, and experience gained after entering office is apt to make the officer less fit to serve the public. John Taylor, in his *Inquiry*, asserted that more talent is lost by long continuance in office than by the system of rotation. Talents are called out by the prospect of employment, and "smothered by the monopoly of experience." On the floor of the United States Senate it was predicted that in time opportunities will be enlarged, "till it shall become a matter of course that each individual shall strive to qualify himself to discharge the duties of any office to which he may be called."[1] It was, in fact, generally believed that no great skill is necessary for the work of governmental administration; and, on

[1] *Congressional Globe* (1835), 23d Congress, 1st Session, I, 273.

the other hand, that an officer long in the public service would lose sympathy with the people,
and become a devotee of officialism and bureau-
cracy. Life estate or even long estate in office
was attacked by the democracy of this time in the
same way that monarchy and aristocratic privilege
had been at an earlier time. This attack was one
part of the great movement which swept away
what was left of privilege, and opened the way for
the democratization of political institutions. That
some of the ideas accompanying this advance
should be crude, radical, or extreme, was in the
nature of things to be expected.

One of the most important measures of this
period was the general extension of the suffrage
from the "property" basis to a "manhood" basis.
This change went down to the very roots of the
political society, and for that reason deserves the
most careful attention. At the time when the republic was founded there were very strict limitations on the electorate. Political power was kept
tightly in the hands of the freeholders, who were
to all intents and purposes "the people." These
qualifications began to disappear, however, soon
after the establishment of the federal government.[1]
Few of the new states entering the Union adopted
the property requirement, and the old states slowly

[1] On this point see the authorities already cited, Poore, *Charters and Constitutions;* and the debates in the constitutional
conventions of the various states.

abandoned the restrictions found in their constitutions. Stubborn resistance to the tendency was often encountered, notably in the case of Virginia, New York, Massachusetts, and Rhode Island; yet the advance was sure, no backward step was taken, and by the middle of the century property qualifications for suffrage had been practically abolished in all the states. A few restrictions were still in existence, but these were not oppressive in character, and excluded no large section of the community. In the majority of the states, however, even these restrictions were omitted, and the broad principle of manhood suffrage (white) received full recognition. The old property qualifications were outgrown and a new democracy sprang up, based, not on the freeholders, but on the whole body of adult male citizens. The electorate was enormously expanded, and there came into existence a type of democracy which made that of Revolutionary days seem like a limited aristocracy.

Recognition was won for this new idea only after a bitter and protracted struggle. The doctrine that suffrage should depend upon property was tenacious of life, and clung desperately to its hold on the state constitutions. The property requirement was supported by some of the ablest men in the nation, and it is from one point of view surprising that the opposite principle was able to make headway against such talented advocates. John

Adams, Daniel Webster, and Joseph Story defended the property qualification in Massachusetts. In New York Chancellor Kent bitterly opposed the adoption of universal suffrage; in Virginia there were arrayed against the extension of the franchise, Madison, Monroe, Marshall, Randolph, and Upshur. The opposition to the freehold principle could boast of no such formidable champions.

The earnestness displayed in the defence of property, and the ability with which the cause was conducted, are such as might have been expected from a class long accustomed to the possession of the right to govern. To this dominant class, the plan of extending the suffrage to practically all male adults appeared to be fraught with the very gravest danger. The project seemed to them to be without foundation either in reason or in justice, and they did not see how it could result in anything but the subversion of democratic institutions. The results of the adoption of the principle of universal suffrage as predicted by the famous jurist, Kent, were the abuse of liberty, the oppression of minorities, the disturbance of chartered privileges, the degradation of justice, unequal taxation, crude and unstable legislation. " I hope, sir," said the venerable judge, "we shall not carry desolation through all the departments of the fabric erected by our fathers. I hope we shall not put forward to the world a constitution such as will merit the

scorn of the wise and the tears of the patriot." [1]
On every hand, it was urged that the freeholders
are the safest and most conservative depository of
political power.   They were considered as the
only class capable of actively entering into political affairs.   Frequent and always unfavorable con-
trasts were drawn between the solid class of landed
gentry, and the commercial and laboring classes
found in the cities, with the uniform conclusion
that political power might be most safely intrusted
to those who held the land.   This idea was of
course connected with the theory, sanctioned by
Jefferson himself, that a democracy thrives best
where it has an agricultural population as its basis.
Profound distrust of the capacity of the urban population for the exercise of political power helped materially to stiffen the resistance made by the ruling
class to sharing its authority with others. [2]   From

[1] *Debates in the New York Convention of 1821*, 219 ff. In the
Virginia Convention of 1829–1830, there was an animated and extended debate in which almost every phase of political opinion was
represented.

[2] Kent, *op. cit.*, 222. In the New York Convention, one speaker
referred to " the ring-streaked and speckled population of our large
towns and cities, comprising people of every kindred and tongue."
p. 253. Referring to the commercial classes, Root had said a little
before this : " Will not these classes feel as strong an interest in sus-
taining them (the judges) as the farmer back in the woods ? . . .
Have they not more frequent occasion to resort to them for the
protection of their rights ? " p. 223. In the Virginia Convention one
enthusiastic orator expressed the belief that " if there are any
chosen people of God, they are the cultivators of the soil." p. 366.

the strength displayed by the old aristocracy at this
time, one may judge of the importance and the
significance of the new democratic movement.[1]

In behalf of an increase in the electorate, the
argument was less brilliantly conducted, but was
none the less convincing and effective. Sometimes
the plea was made in the interest of the commercial
class, or the laboring men, or of those who had
done military duty for the state, but were nevertheless excluded from participation in the suffrage.
Sometimes it was asserted that the franchise is a
natural right, and that therefore men cannot be
justly deprived of it; but this was not always contended. The greatest difficulty seemed to be that
of uprooting the idea that only the holders of
property have an interest in government strong
enough to justify giving them a voice in its direction. The proposition that men who own no land
in the community should have a share in the political power was contrary to long-established English
custom, and to the practice in America since the
early days of settlement here. The introduction
of any other idea was necessarily difficult.

The case of the liberals was most clearly stated
in the argument that "our community is an association of persons — of human beings — not a
partnership founded on property." Thus the result was made to turn on the question whether

[1] See Debates in Massachusetts Convention of 1820; New York
Convention of 1821; Virginia Convention of 1829-1830.

property or human personality is the more fundamental element in civil society, or what their relative importance is.   One party denounced the rule
of mere numbers as illogical and absurd, and
showed that it is wholly impossible to carry out
the principle fully.[1]   The other party, with equal
logic, showed that if property were the only consideration, voting power ought, then, to be proportioned
according to wealth.   The suffrage extensionists, in
reply to the property argument, laid great stress
on the elements of virtue and intelligence in society, and declared these were as worthy of consideration as the mere ownership of a tract of land.
As one disputant said, there is nothing in property
that "by enchantment or magic converts frail, err-
ing man into an infallible and impeccable being."
It was shown that the non-freeholders are not
eager for an opportunity to plunder the rich, but
that they are responsible and reliable citizens who
may safely be intrusted with the exercise of political power.   This assertion was pointed by the fact
that many citizens who owned no real estate were
so prosperous and wealthy that they could not
well be looked upon as untrustworthy individuals
who would use the ballot to the perversion of the
state.

Slowly the old idea that the holders of real

[1] Randolph referred to the rule of "King Numbers."   The reply
was made that "there is no other monarch save King Cypher,
King Blood, King Sword, or King Purse."   *Virginia Debates*, 389.

estate are the political people was discredited and abandoned, and the way opened to practically all citizens of mature years. The land-holding class abdicated, and the mass of the people was intrusted with the power of political control. This was by far the most important change made during the Jacksonian epoch, for it radically altered the foundation of the republic.

At the same time, the property qualifications for office-holding became unpopular and were cast aside. When the new states came in, these requirements generally found no place, and the old states, one by one, abolished the severe requirements of colonial and Revolutionary days.[1] A few states, notably Delaware and Massachusetts, clung persistently to these early provisions or remnants of them almost down to the end of the nineteenth century, but they were exceptions. Generally speaking, by the middle of the century property qualifications for office in the United States were a thing of the past. Office was no longer the monopoly of the few, but was thrown open to all so far as wealth was concerned.

With these restrictions on suffrage and office went those of a religious character. A majority of the original thirteen states disqualified Roman Catholics, and all but New York and Rhode Island

[1] Md., 1810; Penn., 1838; Mass. (except for governor), 1840; N.J., 1844; Conn. 1845; N.Y., 1845; Ga., 1847; Va., 1850; N.H., 1852.

o

imposed a religious test of some kind. These restrictions endured for only a short time, however, and very early began to drop out of the state constitutions. The Protestant clause was first abandoned, and finally the religious tests were omitted altogether; Protestant, Roman Catholic, Jew, Unitarian, and those of no religious profession were placed on the same footing in the political world. The tendency of the time was wholly opposed to conditioning political rights on religious considerations, and although the case was ably argued by those who defended such restrictions, they were unable to make effectual resistance to the demand that religious belief and political capacity should not be connected by the law of the land.[1]

With the abolition of these tests disappeared the provisions for public taxation in support of churches in the states which had inherited religious establishments from the Revolution. The establishment of religion had been forbidden the national government in the Constitution, and the same provision was adopted by the states a little later.[2] By 1833 the provisions for taxation in support of ecclesiastical organizations had been abolished, except

[1] See the argument in the Massachusetts Convention of 1820–1821 *passim;* also the North Carolina Debates (1835), especially the speech of Judge Gaston in favor of religious toleration, 264–305. Consult in this connection Phillip Schaff, *Church and State in the United States,* and Sanford H. Cobb, *The Rise of Religious Liberty in America.*

[2] Va., 1785; S.C., 1790; Md., 1810; Conn., 1818; Mass., 1833.

in New Hampshire, where the Revolutionary clause is still found in the constitution.

Thus was completed that separation of church and state, which has since been a characteristic feature of American institutions. The idea was early stated by Jefferson, but was not at that time able to win a place for itself. The line of reasoning, however, was substantially that which was later followed. He urged that rights of conscience were not surrendered in the original contract, but were retained by the individual, and that government has, therefore, no jurisdiction over that field. Government, said he, can interfere only in respect to such acts as are injurious to others; but "it does me no injury for my neighbors to say there are twenty gods or no god. It neither picks my pocket, nor breaks my leg." He denied that uniformity of belief was desirable, pointing out the advantages arising from variety. But even if desirable, such uniformity was not attainable by the use of coercion. The only effect of the use of force, he maintained, was "to make one half of the world fools, and the other half hypocrites." [1]

The same principle was strongly stated by Madison. He argued that state support of religion is unjustifiable because, in the first place, the right to religion is inalienable. It is a duty to the Creator, and is a reserved right in the social contract. Interference in this matter violates the principle of

[1] *Notes on Virginia* (1784), III, 261–266.

equality by allowing some men the free exercise of
religion, and forbidding it to others. It gives the
legislature unwarranted jurisdiction, and confers
power on civil magistrates to act as judges of religious truth — a capacity in which they are not
fitted to serve. Such measures, he urges, are not
needed for the advancement of the Christian religion, nor do they tend to strengthen the civil
government. The effect of an attempt to enforce
such laws is simply "to enervate the laws in
general and to slacken the bands of society." [1]

The abolition of religious tests and church establishment during this period was a recognition of
these ideas. In general the line of reasoning followed was about that indicated by Jefferson and
Madison. The underlying cause seems to have
been the multiplicity of sects, which was highly
favorable to mutual toleration, rather than antipathy to religion as such.

Another feature of the democratic movement
during the first half of the nineteenth century was
the increasing participation of the people in the
election of their officers. In the earlier period
this power had been largely in the hands of the
legislature, and hence the choice of officers was,
to that extent, indirect. With the increasing emphasis on the people, however, and the reaction
from the early confidence in the legislatures, there

[1] " Remonstrance to the General Assembly of Virginia on the support of religious teachers" (1785). *Works*, I, 162–169.

came a decided change. Elections were taken out of the hands of the legislative bodies, and officers were chosen directly by the popular vote. In the national government, popular voting under the district system took the place of election by the legislature in the choice of representatives in the House, and the choice of presidential electors was also taken away from the legislature. In the states a tendency in the same direction was clearly evident. The choice of governor was taken away from the legislature and conferred upon the people, thus rendering him less dependent upon the legislative branch of government. Other officers, such as the treasurer and the auditor, were given over to popular election in place of choice through the legislature. Many minor officers were also made directly elective, such as clerks of court, sheriffs, and justices of the peace. The theory upon which this action rested was that the legislature is a more or less aristocratic body, and that the people should participate directly in the choice of their officers.

In this same connection should be noticed the popular opposition to certain elements in the judicial system, which were considered as aristocratic. The courts, state as well as national, were objects of suspicion and often of open hostility.[1] The

---

[1] See McMaster, Vol. III, 153 ff., for account of "judge-breaking" in Pennsylvania, Maryland, and New Hampshire; Burgess, *Middle Period*, 195 ff.

Federal Supreme Court was feared because of its alleged encroachment upon the rights of the individual states, but the commonwealth courts also met with opposition from the newly awakened democratic sentiment. This desire to put a check on the judiciary was expressed in two ways; namely, by an abbreviation of the judicial term of office, and by constitutional provision for the election of the judges by the people. In the early days of the Republic, the tenure of the judges had generally been during good behavior. Life tenure, however, was obnoxious to the new democracy, and was repudiated as occasion offered, particularly in the South and West, and also in some of the Eastern states.[1] The tenure for life was replaced by a shorter term of from five to fifteen years, six, seven, and eight years being the most common periods allotted. Popular election of the judges was less easily carried through than the shortening of the term. At first, provision was made for the election of justices of the peace and minor officers, but toward the middle of the century popular election of the higher courts began to find general favor. This movement was looked upon with alarm by the conservative class, but the idea made rapid progress as constitutions were constructed and reconstructed, and soon won a general victory. In the period from 1846 to 1853, no fewer than

[1] Of the old states, Penn., 1838; N.J., 1844; N.Y., 1846; Va., 1850; Md., 1851.

thirteen states recognized the elective principle in the choice of judicial officers of the highest grades.[1] Thus, with the abandonment of life tenure of office and the adoption of a popular system of judicial election, the democracy triumphed in the third great branch of government — the judiciary.

Another evidence of the democratic tendencies of this period is the method in which changes in the fundamental law were made. Of the Revolutionary constitutions, only two were submitted to the people, the others being adopted by convention alone. By 1830 the practice of submitting constitutions to a popular vote for ratification had become frequent; and in the period from 1830 to 1850 only two constitutions went into operation without having received popular sanction at the polls.[2]

Summing up the democratic movement of this period, we have the following results. The electorate was largely increased by the abolition of property qualifications. Religious and property requirements for office-holding were abandoned, terms of office were shortened, the principle of "rotation in office" was accepted, provision was

[1] Cal., Ia., Ky., La., Md., Mich., Mo., N.Y., Ohio, Penn., Tenn., Va., Wis.

[2] Del., 1831; Ark., 1836. Cf. Cleveland, *op. cit.*, 113; Jameson, *Constitutional Conventions.*

made for popular election of officers, the legislative department of government became an object of suspicion, and the executive was correspondingly advanced in popular favor. These numerous and important changes marked the rise of a new democracy, widely different from that of Revolutionary times, or the early days of the Republic. The new type of government was as much an advance on that of the Revolutionary period, as that of those days was upon the contemporary government in England. The only exception to the democratic movement was the position in regard to slavery. In the Southern states, accompanying the democratic changes in government, there were laws of increasing severity in respect to those held in bondage. With this exception, the new democracy had taken the country by storm.

In spite of these marked democratic changes, there was little advance in the fundamental principles of political theory. The Jacksonian democracy carried out in large measure the ideas which the Jeffersonian democracy either had not thought of carrying out, or was unable to carry out. The theory was not new, but such a wide application of these ideas was a decided innovation. In fact, there was on some points a perceptible reaction from the principles of 1776. This was notable in the case of the contract theory, which was subjected to important modifications. Story, for example, held that the doctrine of the contract " requires many limitations and qualifications when applied to the actual condition of nations, even of those which are most free in their organization. Every state, however organized, embraces many persons in it who have never assented to its form of government, and many who are deemed incapable of such assent, and yet who are held bound by its fundamental institutions and laws."[1] On the other hand, Calhoun and his associates, who upheld the cause of slavery, repudiated altogether the "natural right" theory of politics and came out boldly with another doctrine. With these two tendencies coincided that of the German refugee, Lieber. Thus the Revolutionary theory, although still widely accepted and defended by many writers and thinkers,[2] was already seriously undermined. Although the organization of the government and the spirit of social institutions was more democratic than before, there were strong evidences of a change in the character of the political theory. This movement was in the direction of a new basis for democracy — a new theory of republican institutions, fundamentally different from that of the founders of the Republic. The nature of this

---

[1] *Commentaries*, sec. 327.

[2] See *Considerations upon the Nature and Tendency of Free Institutions* (1848), by Frederick Grimke — a diffuse work covering the entire field of politics; Nathaniel Chipman, *Principles of Politics* (1833), 1st edition, 1793.

new philosophy will be considered in a subsequent chapter on modern tendencies.[1]

[1] Attention may be called at this point to a change in the prevalent theory as to the form of the contract upon which society rests. In Revolutionary times it was a common opinion that the parties to the agreement were the king, or government, and the people. The later thinkers distinctly repudiated any contract between governor and governed, and held that the agreement was one between individuals. The governors, it was held, were not parties to a contract, but the mere agents or servants of the people. Cf. Madison, *Works*, IV, 63; John Taylor, *Inquiry*, 424; James Wilson, *Works*, I, 272.

CHAPTER VI

THE POLITICAL THEORY OF THE SLAVERY
CONTROVERSY

ONE of the most interesting developments of
political theory in the United States is that which
arose out of the controversy over slavery in the
years between 1830 and 1860. During the period
of the Revolution and the early days of the Republic the general sentiment was unfriendly to slavery.[1] The existence of the custom was lamented
by such men as Washington, Jefferson, Monroe,
and Adams. There was general regret that the
institution had ever been planted in America, and
it was hoped that it would in time be abandoned.
In the Northwest Ordinance of 1787 the anti-
slavery principle was recognized, and later in the
abolition of the slave trade. Slavery was gradually
abolished in the Northern states, and the Colonization Society represented the desire to put an end
to it in the South. No effort was made to defend
the institution or to present it as an ideal basis for

[1] William Poole, *Anti-Slavery Opinions before 1800;* S. B.
Weeks, "Anti-Slavery Sentiment in the South," in *Publications of
the Southern History Association* (1898).

the political and economic structure of a society. At best, slavery was regarded as a necessary evil.

Certain influences were at work, however, that tended to bring the question of slavery into greater and greater prominence. On the economic side, there was the invention of the cotton gin and other contrivances which made possible the rapid expansion of the cotton industry, and thus offered new fields for the employment of slave labor. On the political side, the territorial expansion of the United States precipitated a bitter struggle as to the status of the new acquisitions, and gave rise to problems of the gravest character. And, finally, like oil on the flames, came the agitation of the Abolitionists. The beginning of the period of controversy may be placed at 1830. In that year occurred the July Revolution in France; in 1831 the Southampton massacre in Virginia; and in the same year the foundation of the *Boston Liberator.* During the thirty years following this time, while the conflict between slavery and anti-slavery was at its height, the doctrines of both sides were fully stated, and the philosophy of slavery discussed in all its aspects.

In the course of this discussion many different sides of the question were considered. From the economic point of view inquiry was made as to whether slavery was or was not a profitable institution, and how it compared with the system of free labor.[1]   From the constitutional point of view, questions of profound importance were discussed, involving the power of Congress in the territories, the admission of new states, the concept of United States citizenship.   From the ethical side, inquiry was made to determine whether the relations of slave and master rested on a proper moral basis. There was also discussion from the standpoint of religion as to whether slavery was contrary to the principles of Christianity, and particularly as to whether slavery was sustained by the Scriptures. And finally, there was an animated controversy as to whether the status of slavery is consistent with the principles of political science.   This is the inquiry which forms the subject of this chapter. Upon what theory was the practice of slavery defended, upon what principles was the attack upon it conducted?   What was the political theory of the anti-slavery forces?   What was the political theory of the pro-slavery party?   How were they related to each other?

The bitterest attacks on slavery were made by the Abolitionists, but they were not the only or perhaps the typical opponents of the system.   The forms which the anti-slavery theory took were many and various, ranging from the statesmanlike views of such men as Lincoln to the radical utter-

---

[1] On this point see H. R. Helper's work, *The Impending Crisis of the South* (1859).   With this compare *Southern Institutes*, by G. S. Sawyer, a member of the Louisiana Bar (1859).

ances of the extreme Abolitionists of the Garrisonian type.[1]

In this discussion an analysis will be made of
three forms of the anti-slavery theory : first, the
theory of the radical Abolitionists; second, the
philosophic argument; and third, the doctrine of
the statesmen. These theories are not very much
different in final analysis, but in form they show
divergences which should be noted. This method
of classification is, no doubt, open to certain objections, but is perhaps useful in distinguishing the
various shades of political thought.

The impulse to the anti-slavery crusade was
given by the radical Abolitionists, and their doctrines and tendencies may therefore be first considered. This group of agitators differed from the
conservative class in that they demanded the im-

[1] On this period, see James Schouler, *History of the United
States;* Hermann von Holst, *The Constitutional History of the
United States;* J. W. Burgess, *The Middle Period;* Henry Wilson,
History of the Rise and Fall of the Slave Power; J. F. Rhodes,
History of the United States; J. C. Hurd, *The Law of Freedom and
Bondage.* For statements of the anti-slavery theory, see William
Jay, *Miscellaneous Writings on Slavery* (1853); William Goodell,
Slavery and Anti-Slavery (1852); Richard Hildreth, *Despotism in
America* (1854); Wendell Phillips, *Works;* Daniel R. Goodwin,
Southern Slavery in its Present Aspects (1864); Albert Barnes, *The
Church and Slavery* (1857), *Scriptural Views of Slavery* (1856);
T. S. Goodwin, *The Natural History of Secession* (1865); Debates
in Congress, especially Sumner on the crime against Kansas, 1856,
1st Session, 34th Congress, Appendix. An excellent summary of the
situation is given by J. E. Cairnes in *The Slave Power* (1862).

mediate and unconditional abolition of slavery without concession or compromise. They differed
from the philosophic group in that they reasoned
in general less strictly and carefully, being given
to action rather than to reflection. The fundamental premise of the Abolitionists was about the
same as that expressed in the Declaration of Independence; namely, that all men are created equal
and are endowed with a number of inalienable
rights, which are independent of all government,
and cannot justly be taken away by any government. They regarded liberty as a birthright of
man, and not as a privilege to be enjoyed under certain conditions. Consequently, they looked upon
slavery as a piece of monstrous injustice to those
deprived of their natural liberty.

In the platform of the National Anti-Slavery
Society (1833) the following declaration was made :
"The right to enjoy liberty is inalienable. To
invade it, is to usurp the prerogative of Jehovah.
Every man has a right to his own body, to the
products of his own labor, to the protection of
the law, and to the common advantages of society."
With this general statement of principle perhaps
all the opponents of slavery could agree ; but with
the violent conclusion drawn, not all were in harmony. This conclusion was that "all those laws
which are now in force, admitting the right of
slavery, are, therefore, before God, utterly null and
void." It was characteristic of the Abolitionists,

however, to be intolerant of delay, and to demand immediate emancipation. They did not believe in postponing the day of liberation, because they could not see the necessity for any long period of preparation. They considered that liberty is an innate faculty of man, and that he requires no special training for its effective exercise. "Liberty," said one, "being the birthright of every man, the natural and normal condition of his existence, all the preparation he needs for its enjoyment is born with him. He gets his fitness for liberty as he gets his hands and feet — not by education, but by inheritance." It was expressly denied that a good government is fit only for the best of people, that is, "the most wise, virtuous, and intelligent." If this were true, it was said, then one might, with equal logic, maintain that "bad children should have bad parents, or that sick people should have worse treatment than those in health." [1]

To those holding such views, the argument for the postponement of emancipation because of the unfitness of the negro was looked upon as fallacious and dangerous. "Gradualism," as it was termed, was repudiated at every point. "Has not the experience of centuries shown," said Garrison, "that gradualism in theory is perpetuity in practice?" Acting on this principle, they attacked and over-

[1] William Hosmer, *The Higher Law* (1852); see especially Chap. XIII, on the Capacity of Slaves for Civil Government.

threw the Colonization Society, denounced slavery as a " combination of death and hell," branded the Constitution of the United States as a " covenant with death and an agreement with hell," and declared for a dissolution of the Union. Inability to see any possible justification for the institution of slavery led them to say of slaveholders: " They ought not to be allowed seats in Congress. No political, no religious copartnership should be had with them, for they are the meanest of thieves and the worst of robbers. We should as soon think of entering into a compact with the convicts at Botany Bay and New Zealand. . . . We do not acknowledge them to be within the pale of Christianity, of republicanism, of humanity." [1]

The ultra-radical wing of the Abolitionists did not stop at denunciation of slavery and of the United States government for failing to put an end to it. They went on to denounce all systems of government as such. This doctrine took the form of the " non-resistance " or " no-government theory," of which Garrison and Noyes were the great champions, and of which the New England Non-Resistance Society was an organized expression. This body declared in 1838 that its members could

[1] *Boston Liberator* (1841). Garrison said on one occasion, that his manner of expressing himself was unpleasant because of its plainness and directness. He could, he said, " be as smooth and politic as any one, but I do not so choose, and much prefer nature to art." *Life of Garrison,* by W. P. and F. J. Garrison.

P

not "acknowledge allegiance to any human government," nor would they oppose any such government by resort to physical force. In accordance with this principle they disclaimed any particular love for the United States. "We love the land of our nativity, it was said, only as we love all other lands. The interests, rights, liberties of American citizens are no more dear to us than those of the whole human race." They recommended that no physical force be employed either for or against their fellow-men; that all should refuse to hold office or to vote, and none should invoke the aid of the courts.[1]

The principle on which this action or inaction was based was that of opposition to coercion as a means of securing obedience. The use of violence they looked upon as a wholly irrational and un-Christian way of maintaining order. Since all governments are based on this principle, it follows that they are, "in their essential elements and as at present administered, all anti-Christ; that they can never by human wisdom be brought into conformity with the will of God."[2] If this is true, then all Christians are obligated "to come out now and be separated from the kingdoms of this world." All

[1] This idea had also a religious basis in the "holiness" or perfectionist movement. The non-resistance idea was also adopted by various socialistic organizations. See J. H. Noyes, *History of American Socialism.*

[2] Garrison's *Life*, II, 202.

governments, whether despotic, monarchical, or republican, are to be supplanted by the " King of Kings and Lord of Lords, who is to rule in righteousness." [1] The laws of this kingdom are written upon the hearts of men, not upon parchment; they depend not on human, but on divine wisdom; the weapons of this kingdom are not carnal, but spiritual. It was, therefore, urged upon all Christians to withdraw their allegiance from any human government, and regard themselves as subjects of the kingdom of God only.

The following statement gives an adequate summary of the views of this party : " As every human government is upheld by physical strength, and its laws are virtually enforced at the point of the bayonet, we cannot hold any office which imposes upon its incumbents the obligation to compel men to do right on pain of imprisonment or death. We therefore voluntarily exclude ourselves from every legislative and judicial body and repudiate all human politics, worldly honors, and stations of authority. . . . If *we* cannot occupy a seat in the legislature or on the bench, neither can we elect *others* to act as our substitutes in any such capacity. It follows that we cannot sue any man at law to compel him by force to restore anything which he may have wrongfully taken from us or others; but if he has

---

[1] See the letter of Noyes to Garrison (March, 1837), *Life*, II, 145–148. In 1837 Noyes nominated Jesus Christ for President of the United States.

seized our coat, we shall surrender up our cloak rather than subject him to punishment." [1]

The capture and return of fugitive slaves in the midst of free communities occasioned frequent expressions of the right of resistance to government, and in some cases of even more radical sentiments. In his famous 11th of March speech, Seward declared that "there is a higher law than the Constitution," and maintained that slavery was contrary to the laws of God. [2] In the famous Van Zandt case, Chase argued that the fugitive slave law was unconstitutional, because the Constitution is a "free constitution." [3] It was designed, he said, "to establish as written law certain great principles of natural right and justice, which exist independently of all such sanction." Slavery, he declared, was contrary to natural right, and " no legislature can make right wrong, or wrong right." Even if there are no express restrictions in the Constitution, "there are certain vital principles in our national government which will ascertain and overrule an apparent and flagrant abuse

---

[1] Declaration of sentiments adopted at the Peace Convention held in Boston, September 18–19, 1838.

[2] *Congressional Globe*, 31st Congress, 1st Session, Appendix. Cf. Frederick Bancroft, *The Life of Seward*, I, 242 ff. Seward refused to explain what he meant by "higher law," or what its practical application would be.

[3] An argument for the defendant, submitted to the Supreme Court of the United States at the December term, 1846, in the case of Wharton Jones *v.* John Van Zandt, 93.

of legislative power." He further declared that no court was bound to regard an unjust law, but on the contrary was obligated to refrain from enforcing the provisions of any such act.

In a time when statesmen like Seward and Chase could speak like this, it was to be expected that more radical men would go much farther in this direction.[1] A striking example of this was the treatise on *Civil Disobedience* by the famous author, Thoreau (1849). Evidently exasperated beyond all bounds by the attitude of the government, state as well as national, Thoreau expressed his opinion of government in general, in terms by no means flattering. He declared that the best government is no government at all, and that when men are fully developed, they will have none. The value of government, he did not estimate very highly. It is at best an expedient, said he, but "most governments are usually, and all governments are sometimes, inexpedient."[2] Even in America government accomplishes but little, for what has been done here is due largely to the character inherent in the American people, and this would have accomplished even more, " if

[1] Cf. *The Higher Law in its Relation to Civil Government with Particular Reference to the Fugitive Slave Law*, by William Hosmer, 1852; C. K. Whipple, *The Non-Resistance Principle, with Particular Application to the Help of Slaves by Abolitionists* (1860).

[2] Cf. *Slavery in Massachusetts* (1854). With Thoreau compare Emerson's individualistic theories, contained in the essays on *Self-Reliance* and *Politics*.

the government had not sometimes got in its way." Government is, indeed, very often a hindrance to human activity. "Trade and commerce," said Thoreau, "if they were not made of india-rubber, would never manage to bounce over the obstacles which legislators are continually placing in their way." Whenever government comes into conflict with conscience, the former must yield. One must be, said he, in his expressive phrase, a man first and a subject afterward. In view of the attitude of our government toward slavery, he maintained that no one could conscientiously associate himself with the American political system, but must withdraw the support given to it, whether in the shape of personal service or of a contribution of property as taxes. If a few men would adopt this policy and adhere to it for a time, he felt confident that both war and slavery would soon be given up. Doubtless this might involve the imprisonment of the person offending; but in this case the prison is the "only home in a slave state in which a free man can abide with honor." [1] It is true that one who resists the government may find it difficult to live in as great comfort as he might otherwise enjoy.

---

[1] Thoreau himself acted on this principle and spent one night in jail as a consequence — a punishment he was disposed to ridicule, however. "I saw," said he, "that the state was half witted, that it was as timid as a lone woman with her silver spoons, and that it did not know its friends from its foes, and I lost all my remaining respect for it and pitied it."

"You must hire or squat somewhere, and raise but a small crop and eat that soon," but this may well be done for the sake of a clear conscience. It was ingeniously suggested, however, that one is not obligated to forego any advantage offered him by the state, since he is really at war with the commonwealth, and on this basis is entitled to take from the enemy whatever he can get.

No government, said Thoreau (and this is the beginning and the end of his theory), can have any "pure right over my person and property but what I concede to it." We have progressed from absolute to limited monarchy, thence to democracy; but it is possible to take one step more in organizing the rights of man. The ideal state must regard the individual as "a higher and independent power," from which its own authority is derived, and must treat him accordingly.

Such was the theory of the radical Abolitionists, and this is the direction in which it led. It has already been stated that the fundamental premise in the political philosophy of this school was the original and inalienable liberty of all men. Starting from this highly individualistic premise, it is easy to see how the most radical conclusions were reached, even the abolition of government, or refusal to take any part in it, and in other cases refusal to affiliate with any of the churches.[1] To such

[1] For an exposition of the tendencies of ultra-radical Abolitionism, see the *Life of William Lloyd Garrison*, by W. P. and F. J. Garrison.

men as Garrison, the emancipation of the slaves was only a small part of the program. They believed in the broader idea of "universal emancipation," by which they understood "the emancipation of our whole race from the dominion of man, from the thraldom of self, from the government of brute force, from the bondage of sin. This was emancipation evolved into a mystical and transcendental sort of "Perfectionism," marked by a coming-out from the church and the state.[1] It would of course be unfair to suggest that all Abolitionists indorsed such doctrines as these, but to the radical wing they were acceptable, and the tendency of Abolitionism was necessarily radical.

Radical Abolitionism was in fact only a part of a larger movement which swept over the North. Transcendentalism, idealism, humanitarianism, were dominant in the philosophy of the time during which the anti-slavery crusade was at its height. Religious and social reforms of every description, genuine and sham, were eagerly taken up and were propagated with the greatest enthusiasm. In the religious world these tendencies found expression in a decided liberal movement which sometimes took the form of a demand for no religion at all. New sects arose with strange doctrines; the Mormons, for example, made many converts at this

[1] The "come-outers" believed in coming out of the churches on account of their failure to take a proper stand on the slavery question.

time, while the Millerites proclaimed and awaited confidently the advent of the millennium. Social-istic ideas flourished, and experiments such as those of Brook Farm and Icaria were undertaken. A vigorous assault was made upon Masonry and a powerful political party formed on the basis of this idea alone. The temperance movement was actively carried on and won notable victories. The agitation for women's rights was begun, and able champions of the cause appeared. The environment was favorable to the rapid and rank growth of reforms and crusades, many of them utterly impracticable, but all of them pushed on with the greatest devotion and en-thusiasm. Abolitionism was only one part of a great current of liberal and humanitarian senti-ment that was sweeping over the country. The frequent blending of the anti-slavery movement with these other tendencies made it still more difficult for the South to understand or to value properly the real significance of the anti-slavery agitation.

A more philosophic presentation of the anti-slavery theory was that made by a certain group of thinkers of which William E. Channing[1] and Francis Wayland[2] were the ablest representatives.

[1] *Essays on Slavery* (1835).

[2] *The Elements of Moral Science*, by Francis Wayland, president of Brown University (1835), one of the strongest works on the anti-slavery side.

The method of these men presents a decided contrast to the simple style and language of Lincoln, on the one hand, and to the fiery utterances of the Garrisonian Abolitionists on the other. The starting-point in this theory was the proposition that every man is a rational and moral being. As such, he must be recognized by all as a person, and cannot be regarded as a thing merely. He is an end and purpose in himself and cannot be a mere instrument to accomplish the ends or purposes of others. He is a person, and cannot, philosophically, ethically, or politically, be justly deprived of all the prerogatives of personality. All men, it was asserted, are equal in the essential and fundamental elements of their humanity. All men are endowed with a rational nature as distinguished from the animals; all men are gifted with the faculty termed conscience; all men have the capacity for development. These attributes are common to humanity, the universal characteristics of rational beings; in these respects all men are equal.

Endowed with these high characteristics, all moral beings possess certain rights, which may be summed up as the right to exercise one's powers and to promote the happiness and virtue of one's self and others, as one sees fit, and so far as one does not interfere with the equal rights of others. A more specific enumeration is found to include the following. All men as rational and moral beings have a right to exercise and develop their intellect ; they have a right to inquire into their duty ; to be respected by others in accordance with their moral worth ; to receive a fair equivalent for their labor ; to sustain domestic relations; and other such fundamental rights arising from the fact that man is a moral personality. These rights are the prerogatives of every individual. He cannot give them up if he would ; they are inherent and inalienable, an essential part of his nature, indispensable to the proper performance of his function in the world. These rights must not only be regarded by other individuals, but they must be respected and maintained by the government. " Right," says Channing, "is older than human law. Law ought to be its voice." Considerations of expediency should not be allowed to weigh against these rights, for the good of the individual is really of more importance than the welfare of the state. It is a more sacred, exalted, enduring interest than any accessions of wealth or power to the body politic.[1] It was conceded, however, that there are extreme cases in which these rights may be suspended for their ultimate and permanent security, and in the interest of the community at large.

The conclusion was, then, that slavery, which is subversive of all these rights, must be regarded as fundamentally unjust — a usurpation of the sacred prerogatives of humanity. Slavery makes of man

[1] Channing, *op. cit.*, 47.

a thing, a piece of property, whereas he is essentially and primarily a person. It constitutes a system that cannot possibly be justified on any rational basis.

Furthermore, it was pointed out that the influence of slavery was unfavorable to the growth of democracy. The spirit of liberty, it was said, cannot live and flourish in an atmosphere of human slavery. Free institutions rest upon the basis of a love of liberty, but this is destroyed or impaired by the practice of slavery. The contempt for human rights as manifested in the treatment of the slave leads to a universal contempt for all the rights of men, and must bring on a general decline of the spirit of liberty. Democracy,[1] it was said, implies that one has learned to obey as well as to command. In a slaveholding community the habit of command is acquired, but that of obedience is little cultivated, except by the slaves. Hence the tendency is to make men arrogant and imperious, and consequently ill-adapted for democracy. The claim was made, therefore, that the influence of slavery is ultimately fatal to the liberty-loving spirit upon which free government rests. Democracy cannot exist with slavery as its basis. If, as some say, democracy is dependent upon a slave system, then such a government is scarcely worthy of perpetuation. "Those who tell us," said Channing, "that slavery is a necessary condition of a republic, do

[1] Channing, 100.

not justify the former, but pronounce a sentence of reprobation on the latter." [1]

In brief, then, what we have called the philosophical argument against slavery was, that every rational moral being has the right to develop his own powers, is an end or purpose in himself, and cannot justly be held as property by any other man. Slavery was therefore regarded as a status contrary to the rights of every or any human being. It was conceded that the community is justified in imposing a certain degree of restraint upon its members, but emphatically denied that slavery is a proper means for this, since it amounts to the permanent subversion of all rights. The tendency with this school was altogether toward the consideration of the rights of the individual in contrast to those of the community. What they were endeavoring to do, was to show that in every political system a large field of autonomy should be left to the individual, and that only under exceptional circumstances should he be reduced to a condition where he would enjoy no rights at all.

One of the ablest and certainly the most representative statement of the anti-slavery theory was that made by the great leader of the conservative emancipation party — Abraham Lincoln. His reasoning was not that of an agitator or of a philosopher; yet it was profound, it was stimulating, and it

[1] *Ibid.*, 103. Cf. Richard Hildreth, *Theory of Politics* (1853), also *Despotism in America* (1854).

was politically masterful.   Since it represented the opinion of a large group of men who were neither radical Abolitionists nor acute philosophers, the theory he advanced is worthy of careful examination.

As Lincoln viewed the situation, there should be no repudiation of the teaching of the Declaration that all men are created equal.   He firmly believed that that doctrine, properly understood and applied, should still be regarded as a foundation principle of free government.   He would not admit that the Declaration was intended to apply only to the British colonists, or to the whites alone, or to any class or caste of men ; but he did not interpret this statement to mean that all men are equal in all respects.   The Fathers "did not mean to say all were equal in color, size, intelligence, moral development or social capacity."[1]   What they did mean was that "all men are equal in the possession of certain inalienable rights among which are life, liberty, and the pursuit of happiness."   It was not understood that all men are exactly equal in all respects, nor was it intended to confer political equality upon all men alike and immediately.   This was not the purpose of the founders of the republic. They meant merely "to declare the right so that enforcement of it might follow as soon as circumstances should permit."   The Declaration was intended to be, and in fact is, a fundamental principle to serve as an ideal for free society, "constantly

[1] *Works*, I, 232.

looked to, constantly labored for, and even though never perfectly attained, constantly approximated, and thereby constantly spreading and deepening its influence, and augmenting the happiness and value of life to all people of all colors everywhere." [1] Not only is it to serve as an ideal toward which men should struggle, but it is also to prevent a return to the past — an impressive warning "to all those who in after times might seek to turn a free people back into the hateful paths of despotism."

To the institution of slavery, therefore, Lincoln was wholly opposed. He did not demand for the negro equal social and political privilege with the white, but on the contrary expressly disclaimed any such desire. He did claim for the black man " the right to put into his mouth the bread that his own hands have earned," and asserted that in this respect he is the equal of every other man. The fact that others are more highly endowed cannot be used to justify them in depriving their inferior of the little that he does have. The alleged right of the superior to enslave the inferior man, he regarded as contrary to justice and the principles of all free government. " No man," said Lincoln, "is good enough to govern another man without that other's consent." [2] "When the white man governs himself, that is self-government; but when he governs himself and also governs another man, that is more than self-government — that is despot-

---

[1] *Ibid.*   [2] *Ibid.* I, 195.

ism." The whole argument from the right of the superior to enslave and oppress the inferior, he denounced as identical in object and effect with the old plea for "classification, caste, and legitimacy." Whatever form this reasoning may assume, it is in reality "the same old serpent"; it is a principle essentially hostile to free and popular government.

Such doctrines, he argued, are "the vanguard, the miners and sappers, of returning despotism." These ideas must be driven out not only for the sake of the black man, but in the interest of the white as well, for they are a menace to his own equality and freedom. It must not be supposed that freedom and slavery can permanently endure side by side. One must overthrow the other, and one principle be everywhere recognized. "This is a world of compensation," said Lincoln, "and he who would be no slave, must consent to have no slave. They who deny freedom to others, deserve it not for themselves, and under a just God cannot long retain it." Thus Lincoln not only maintained that this nation could not permanently endure half slave and half free, but also formulated the universal law that freedom and slavery cannot permanently exist side by side.

Lincoln believed that there are two great theories of society. [1]   According to the "mud-sill"

[1] Annual address before the Wisconsin Agricultural Society at Milwaukee (1859). *Works*, I, 580 ff. See also II, 105. Annual Message to Congress (1861).

theory, capital always takes precedence of labor, and must be honored and rewarded accordingly. Capital employs either hired laborers or slaves, both of which classes tend to remain in their dependent position. Education and labor are regarded as incompatible, while the educated and the laboring classes are separated by a sharp dividing line. "A Yankee who could invent a strong-handed man without a head would," said Lincoln, "receive the everlasting gratitude of the 'mud-sill' advocates."

According to the other theory, labor is prior to and independent of capital. The laborer is not limited to the so-called laboring class; for there is a large group of those who "mingle their own labor with capital." All men are or should be educated, so that the sharp distinction between the educated and the laboring classes tends to disappear. This system, which Lincoln champions, opens the way to all, inspires all with hope, and tends to develop energy and to improve the condition of all.

It is evident, then, that Lincoln looked upon the conflict between slavery and its adversaries as one part of the great struggle between liberty and despotism, and believed that American slavery could not long be tolerated without endangering the foundations of American liberty. In his opinion slavery and despotism were inextricably interwoven. He did not, however, demand the immediate emancipation of the slaves, nor did he ask

Q

or expect that they be placed on terms of entire equality with the whites. Admitting the inequality of the races, he did not think it logical or expedient to conclude that the inferior race should be wholly deprived of political rights. Such a course he considered as selfish and unjust, and sure to bring retribution upon those who attempted it.

This is, in general outline, the anti-slavery theory. In spite of the widely different forms in which the idea was stated by agitators, philosophers, and statesmen, there was a fundamental agreement underneath all this diversity. The point of union was the belief that all men are created equal, and are endowed with certain natural rights which must everywhere be respected. In every form of theory the very term " slavery " was assumed to be synonymous with injustice, and scarcely any argument was needed to show its enormity. In the Revolutionary days the climax in the denunciation of Great Britain had been the charge that the colonists, taxed but not represented, were being reduced to the level of slaves, and no one had thought of saying that slavery might be a benefit to both ruler and ruled. Slavery had been considered then, as it was later regarded by the anti-slavery party, the very name for tyranny and oppression of the most execrable kind. To justify slavery would be to subvert the foundations of free government — a crime against civilization and humanity.

In respect to the practical program most suitable to the conditions, there was a wide difference between such men as Lincoln and those of the Garrisonian type. One party demanded the immediate and unconditional emancipation of the slaves as an act of simple justice to those in bondage, trusting to the ability of the newly made freemen to take and use their liberty without danger to themselves or to the nation. The other party, although denouncing slavery as an evil, and demanding its ultimate abolition, clearly perceived the great difficulties involved in the transition from bondage to freedom, for the negro and for the community in general. They therefore counselled a policy of moderation and conservatism.

The pro-slavery theory was almost wholly the product of the three decades preceding the outbreak of the Civil War. Before this time no organized or well-sustained effort was made to defend slavery, but it was generally treated in an apologetic way. As late as the controversy over the admission of Missouri, it was said that the entrance of slavery into new territory was not expected to strengthen the institution, but to weaken it by scattering the evil. In 1832, in the Virginia legislature, the whole question of slavery was discussed, and emancipation was openly and strongly urged by many. The increasing bitterness of the attacks on slavery, however, touched the pride of the South, and aroused its leaders to find a justification for the institution. In the face of the furious arraignment made by the Abolitionists, it seemed necessary to assume some other attitude than that of indifference toward the question. As Calhoun said, the discussion " has compelled us of the South to look into the nature and character of this great institution, and to correct any false impressions that *even we* had entertained in relation to it." [1]   As a result of this reinvestigation of the question, the opinion of the Southern leaders was radically changed. They no longer apologized for slavery, they defended it; they not only defended it as a necessary evil, but upheld it as a positive good.

The formulation of the pro-slavery theory may be attributed in large measure to John C. Calhoun, assisted by such able associates as Stephens and Davis, together with a clever group of thinkers, including Bledsoe,[2] Simms,[3] Sawyer,[4] Dew,[5] and others.[6]

[1] *Works*, II, 180 (1838).

[2] A. T. Bledsoe, Professor of Mathematics in the University of Virginia, *An Essay on Liberty and Slavery* (1856).

[3] Dr. W. G. Simms of South Carolina, *The Morals of Slavery* (1837). This was an answer to the writings of Miss Martineau and other persons.

[4] George S. Sawyer, *Institutes of Slavery* (1859).

[5] F. R. Dew (professor in William and Mary's College), *Review of the Debates in the Virginia Legislature* (1833).

[6] See *The Pro-Slavery Argument*, containing "Memoir on Negro Slavery," by Chancellor Harper; "Letters on Slavery"

In order to make an adequate defence of slavery, it was found necessary to abandon certain ideas that had been conspicuous during the Revolutionary period. The Declaration of Independence, with its assertion that all men are created equal and are endowed with certain inalienable rights, was not in harmony with the practice of slavery, and must be repudiated or explained away. This, however, proved no barrier to the new movement, for the defenders of slavery rejected the principles of the natural-right school of political theory, and constructed their political system on another basis.

In the first place, the proposition that all men are created equal was subjected to the most severe criticism on the part of the pro-slavery school. It was maintained that unless taken in some very qualified sense, such an assertion was incapable of proof. Calhoun declared that: "Taking the proposition literally, there is not a word of truth in it. It begins with, 'all men are born,' which is utterly

(Letter to Thomas Clarkson), by Governor J. H. Hammond of South Carolina (1845); also Simms, *op. cit.* and Dew, *op cit.; Lectures on the Philosophy and Practice of Slavery*, by William A. Smith (Randolph-Macon College, 1857); *Studies on Slavery*, by John Fletcher (Louisiana, 1852); *Slavery in the United States*, by J. K. Paulding (1836); *Slavery ordained of God*, by F. A. Ross (1859); *American Slavery*, by Rev. Samuel Seabury (1861). Many interesting contributions to this subject are contained in *The Industrial Resources of the South*, by J. D. B. de Bow (1853), a collection of articles published in *De Bow's Magazine*. See also *The Southern Literary Messenger*.

untrue. Men are not born. Infants are born. They grow to be men." [1] He found it difficult to see how so unreasonable an idea could ever have become current among reasonable men. Governor Hammond alluded contemptuously to the " much-lauded but nowhere accredited dogma of Mr. Jefferson that all men are born equal." [2] Simms said that this phrase was " a finely sounding one, significant of that sentimental French philosophy then so current." [3] When the Fathers spoke of equality, what they really had reference to, was the equality of the American states among other states of the world, or at the most the equality prevailing among white men.

Not only are men created unequal, such was the line of reasoning, but this very inequality must be regarded as one of the essential conditions of human progress. Calhoun did not hesitate to assert that the advance of human civilization depends upon the inequality that exists among men. There have always been and there must always be, he argued, a front and a rear rank in the onward march of humanity ; to reverse or confound this order, would check the advance of the race. This fundamental fact that individuals or races are unequal, is not an argument against, but rather in favor of, social and political advancement. [4] Others maintained that inequality is the necessary

---

[1] *Works*, IV, 507–512.   [3] *Ibid.* 251.   Cf. Fletcher, *op. cit.* 399.
[2] *Pro-Slavery Argument*, 110.   [4] *Works*, I, 57.

principle upon which all government rests; that inequality is the source of all harmony in the universe; even that the souls of men in the future state must be unequal.[1] In short, the doctrine that all men are created equal was wholly repudiated as a basis for political theory. Emphatic denial was entered on grounds of both fact and philosophy. From either point of view, it was regarded as untenable and absurd.

Again, the doctrine of natural rights—that every individual possesses certain rights which are not derived from government, and of which he cannot justly be deprived by government—was either abandoned entirely or interpreted in such a way as to lose all application to the institution of slavery. The repudiation of this theory of natural rights was most emphatically made by the famous Dr. Cooper of South Carolina.[2] He attempted to show that even on the hypothesis of an original state of nature it could not be assumed that all men are endowed with the same rights. Force, either of body or of mind is, said he, the basis of all rights. "The universal law of nature is force. By this law the lower animals are subdued to man, and the same law governs the relations between men."[3] In fact, there is no law of nature of the character

[1] Fletcher, *op. cit.* 407.
[2] *Lectures on the Elements of Political Economy* (1826). With this compare his *Essay on the Foundation of Civil Government,* (1787); reprinted 1826. [3] *Ibid.* 56.

conceived by such thinkers as Grotius, Pufendorf, and Vattel. The so-called law of nature, and with it the natural rights claimed under such a law, consist merely of "systems fabricated by theoretical writers on a contemplation of what might usefully be acknowledged among men as binding on each other."[1] What is right, in the proper sense of the term, is only that which is granted and protected by society. That which society refuses to acknowledge is not a right and has no character of a right. In other words, there is no body of natural rights obtained independently of all government, but only those rights which the society considers it expedient to grant.

Calhoun, also, scouted the idea of a state of nature, natural rights, and a social contract. He believed that the "state of nature" is purely hypothetical and fictitious, and he placed no confidence in the conclusions drawn from such an hypothesis.[2] In his opinion, government is not to be regarded as a mere matter of choice, but must be considered, on the contrary, as a fundamental necessity, organized and maintained in obedience to a purely natural instinct of man. There is consequently no need to presume a state of nature, and reason from this to the formation of political institutions. The whole structure erected on the foundation of the natural-right theory seemed to him to be worth-

[1] *Lectures on the Elements of Political Economy*, 54.
[2] See on this point Chap. VI.

less speculation, unnecessary to consider when once the weakness and imperfection of the corner-stone is discovered. For his part, he was determined to disregard the individualistic political theory of the seventeenth and eighteenth centuries, and to construct his political science upon another foundation. There was no hesitation or uncertainty in his attitude: he did not attempt to reconcile divergent views; he simply rejected outright the fundamental tenets of the old school.

Not all of the defenders of slavery, however, were willing to part with "the rights of man." There were many and ingenious interpretations of the law of nature, intended to bring it into accord with the practice of slavery. Thus it was admitted in one instance that there are natural rights with which every human being is endowed; but a closer examination of these rights shows that they contain nothing to interfere with the status of slavery. Among these natural rights it is found that one has in early life "the right of such absolute control by others as that his will may retain its self-acting power unimpaired." It also appears that an adult is entitled to have such a political organization as will afford "that system of appliances which develops and matures the self-acting power of his will." Now, the negro in slavery is under an institution which will allow the fullest development of the "self-acting power of his will," and thus may be said to have the full possession of his natural rights.[1] Another writer declared that there are certain inherent and inalienable rights, but at the same time denied that liberty and property are among these. These rights are subject, he reasoned, to the general good, and occasion may demand their sacrifice on the part of some members of society.[2]

It is evident from these authorities that the doctrine of natural rights was either wholly repudiated, or so interpreted as to obviate any objection to slaveholding. This did not necessarily mean that the principles of democracy were entirely given up, but rather that the principles on which the Fathers had thought democracy must be based, were fallacious and inadequate. It was believed that such doctrines were not essential to the existence of republican government, and that they might better be made less prominent in the new political science.

Having rejected the idea that all men are created equal, and possess from the hour of their birth certain inalienable rights, it was asserted that the status of the individual should be determined by his ability or capacity. John C. Calhoun maintained that the theory of the equal right of all men to the same degree of freedom is contradicted by the most evident and unmistakable facts. Liberty, he reasoned, is not inborn in men; it is not a natural inheritance, given to every man, but a condition dependent upon a high degree of human develop-

---

[1] Wm. A. Smith, *Philosophy and Practice of Slavery* (1857).
[2] A. T. Bledsoe, *An Essay on Liberty and Slavery* (1856).

ment.   Liberty is the "highest reward bestowed
on mental and moral development, combined with
favorable circumstances." [1]   It is not a status into
which men are born, but one for which they must
struggle, and which can be reached only by those
who are most highly endowed.   Liberty is not
given to man at the beginning of his career, but is
the distant goal which he reaches at the end.   The
same idea was clearly stated by Bledsoe in his *Essay on Liberty and Slavery*, where he urged that
there is no natural and inherent right to political
power or privilege, except that arising from
superior fitness or capacity.   He denounced the
"French idea" that liberty may be obtained through
formal equality, and held that, on the contrary,
liberty depends on equality of intelligence and
virtue.   "The most illiterate peasant," said he, "may
at a glance grasp the idea of equality; the most
profound statesman may not, without much care
and thought, comprehend the nature of liberty." [2]

Particular emphasis must be placed on this doctrine, for it was just at this point that the pro-
slavery and the anti-slavery party sharply diverged.
It was a part of the Abolitionist argument that
freedom is inborn in all men, is an essential
part of their nature, something of which they cannot justly be deprived.   Calhoun and his followers
maintained, on the contrary, that liberty is not born
with man, not a natural and inherent right, but

[1] *Works*, 511.   [2] *Op. cit.* 129.

a privilege, a reward of which all are not equally worthy, for which individuals or races must demonstrate their fitness. This fundamental difference between the doctrine of the pro-slavery party and that of the Revolutionary Fathers and the Abolitionists, is deserving of careful attention, for it is the clew to the philosophic controversy between the opposing schools. It marks the scientific parting of the ways.

Assuming, then, that liberty is not a gift impartially bestowed by nature on all men, but only upon the few, the pro-slavery party declared that the negro race is unworthy of liberty and incapable of self-government. The contrast between the white man and the black man, in all those points that are characteristic of civilization, was a staple item of argument. It was asserted that the negro "stands at the lowest point in the scale of human beings."[1] If human beings at all, they are of the most degraded species.[2] The negro is not merely "a lamp-blacked white man debased by slavery," but a being essentially and fundamentally inferior in mind and body. Contemporary authorities in the scientific world were invoked to show that the racial characteristics of the negro stamped him as an inferior order of man.[3] It

[1] "Nature and Destiny of the Negro," by J. C. Nott (1850), in De Bow, *Industrial Resources*, II, 308.

[2] *Ibid.* II, 203.

[3] *Ibid.* II, 308.

was even urged that the negro could not be a descendant of Adam, but must be derived from some other distinct and inferior species.[1] More common was the assertion that the negro is descended from Ham, upon whose race both God and nature have set a curse, as shown by the concurring authority of the Scriptures and natural science.[2]

Not only was it asserted that the negroes were manifestly inferior, but the ground was also taken that they were incapable of ever becoming, even approximately, the equal of the white race. It was said of the negro races that "no moral or physical agencies can redeem them from their degradation;" to attempt to relieve them from their natural inferiority is idle in itself, and may be mischievous in its results. The negro must, therefore, be regarded as an essentially inferior race, and, moreover, as incapable of rising very far or very soon from this natural and divinely appointed status of degradation.[3]

It follows, then, that the black man cannot be considered as a fit subject for the exercise of civil

[1] *Ibid.* 203, and III, 315–329. Article on Negroes, by Dr. Cartwright. Cf. *Negro-mania*, by John Campbell (1851). There was at this time considerable discussion as to the multiple origin of the human race.

[2] Sawyer, *Institutes of Slavery*, 116.

[3] "The negro cannot be schooled, nor argued, nor driven into a love of freedom. His intellect cannot be schooled, nor argued, nor driven into a love of freedom." De Bow, *op. cit.* II, 204.

or political rights. Governor McDuffie said that the negroes are "utterly unqualified, not only for rational freedom, but for self-government of any kind," and this fairly expressed the sentiment of the slavery party. If the negro is unfit to govern himself, there can be no injustice in governing him without his consent. To do for him what he could not do for himself, and what must be done by some one, is not to commit an injustice, but to confer a benefit. Hence, the slave is not to be regarded as a hapless victim of oppression; he is under no despotic power; there are laws which protect him, in his place, as inflexible as those which his proprietor is required to obey in his place. "Providence," said Hammond, "has placed him in our hands for his good, and has paid us from his labor for our guardianship." [1]

In brief, the contention was that if there are two races existing side by side, and the inferior race is incapable of self-guidance and self-government, this race must be taken in hand and governed by the superior. It had also to be shown that the institution of slavery did no more than what was necessary for the regulation of the lower race; in other words, that the relation between the races was that of guardian and ward, and not that of exploiter and victim.

[1] Hammond, *op. cit.* 274. Cf. Bledsoe, *op. cit.* 115; Samuel Seabury, *op. cit.* 91. Others held slavery to be the result of sin; cf. Fletcher, *op. cit.*

Such reasoning, however, was only a defence of slavery, and the advocates of the cause were unwilling to rest their case at this point. They attempted to show, not only that slavery was not an evil, but that it was a positive good; that it was not only tolerable under certain unfortunate conditions, but essential to the highest type of society. Inspired by this motive, Calhoun declared in Congress that "there has never yet existed a wealthy and civilized society in which one portion of the community did not, in point of fact, live on the labor of the other." [1] He maintained that the performance of menial duties is wholly inconsistent with the life of a freeman. "No Southern man," said he, "not even the poorest or the lowest, will, under any circumstances, submit to perform (either of) them. He has too much pride for that, and I rejoice that he has." [2] Fortified by this belief, Calhoun was ready to say that the institution of slavery "forms the most solid and durable foundation on which to rear free institutions"; [3] and Governor McDuffie could declare that "domestic slavery, instead of being a political evil, is the corner-stone of our republican edifice." With the same idea in mind, Alexander H. Stephens, on the verge of the Civil War, proclaimed that slavery, rejected by the Revolutionary Fathers,

[1] *Works*, II, 631 (1837).
[2] *Ibid.* IV, 505.
[3] II, 632.

"is become the chief stone of the corner in our new edifice."[1]

The pro-slavery party reasoned that in a society where all are equally free, and share alike in political privileges, some of the citizens must of necessity be occupied with the performance of menial duties. But one who engages in such labor has not the leisure necessary for political observation and reflection, and hence is unqualified for the performance of the duties that devolve upon him. Consequently, the average of the political society is greatly lowered by the presence of this body of citizens, who are of necessity unworthy and unfit. Whenever any considerable proportion of this element is present, the otherwise pure republicanism is defiled and its possibilities of development are seriously limited. On the other hand, in a community where the drudgery of society is performed by a particular class devoted to that purpose, and excluded from participation in political rights, the remaining part of the community may be formed into a democracy of the very highest type. There will be fewer members of the democracy, but they will be of a superior grade; they will enjoy the necessary leisure for the cultivation of political affairs, and so will be able to maintain a much more perfect and efficient kind of a democracy than would otherwise be possible. The members of such a democracy will

[1] Speech at Savannah, Georgia (March 21, 1861), in Moore's *Rebellion Record*, I, D, 44–48.

be men of great capacity for self-government, and among them the principles of free government can be carried out to an extent impossible among a mixed population containing a large element of inferior stock. For example, where a slave class is found, there is no necessity for the existence of an order of nobility or an hereditary monarchy, since the lower class is wholly under the control of the higher, and in the higher class itself such distinctions of rank are not necessary. In a mixed political society some such device as this is required in order to impress the masses with the dignity and majesty of the government. But where all the undesirable and unfit elements have been eliminated from the political society, these artificial devices are unnecessary and may be abolished. The ruling class exists by virtue of natural capacity alone, and within that class there may safely be established the most liberal type of a democracy. Here may be seen "the perfect spirit of equality so prevalent among the whites of all the slaveholding states."[1]

This argument as to the function of a slave class in a democracy is, it will be observed, almost identical with that made by Aristotle in his *Politics;* and it was to his political theory that the slavery apologists returned.[2] In proof of the theoretical justice

---

[1] Dew, *The Pro-Slavery Argument,* 461.

[2] Calhoun recommended Aristotle as among the best writers on government. Letter to A. D. Wallace (1840), in the *Correspondence,* p. 469.

R

of slavery, his reasoning was repeated, and the example of the Greek democracies was cited to show the desirability of such a social and political institution.

In fact, the whole question of the relative advantages of slave and free society was discussed in all its different phases. The conditions in the cities of the North and in England were contrasted with the state of affairs in the South, and conclusions drawn to the decided advantage of the latter. The rule of the capitalist and his indifference to the poverty of the masses was compared with the benevolent paternalism exercised over the negro by his master; and the free laborer was said to be in a much more miserable state than the slave. This kind of argument was reënforced by illustrations drawn from material afforded by the state of the laboring classes in England and by the frequent denunciations of contemporary society by the socialists. It was often asserted that, on the whole, the condition of free labor was inferior to that of slave labor, and that if anything needed reform, it was the condition of the white slaves, "tantalized with the name of freedom, to which their condition gives the lie." The assertion was made that in every way — economically, socially, morally, and politically — a slave society is superior to a society built on a foundation of free labor. Apologies were no longer made for slavery, but it was pointed to with feelings of pride, and was really considered among intelligent leaders of opinion as the "corner-stone of our republican edifice," the very best foundation possible for a civilized society. Within four years of the Thirteenth Amendment, Alexander H. Stephens rejoiced in the discovery of a new type of organization — slavery — and declared the new government the first in the world based upon "this great physical, philosophical, and moral truth." Other societies had been built on the slavery of the same or similar races; but now, for the first time, a foundation was laid, perfectly in accord with the laws of nature, since nature, in this instance, has fitted the enslaved race for that particular condition. And he further asked, "May we not, therefore, look with confidence to the ultimate universal acknowledgment of the truths upon which our system rests?"[1]

The climax or rather the anti-climax of this style of reasoning is found in the writings of the radical, George Fitz-Hugh.[2] His work on *Sociology for the South, or the Failure of Free Society*, 1854, is considered here, not because typical of the thought of the pro-slavery school, but as an illustration of the extremes to which their argument might be and in this case actually was forced.

Fitz-Hugh favored the abandonment of any sort of philosophy as applied to government. "Philosophy," he said, "will blow up any government that is

---

[1] *Op. cit.*

[2] By the same author, *Cannibals All, or Slaves without Masters* (1857). For a sketch of his life, see Appleton, *Encyclopædia.*

founded on it. . . . If we would have our people normal and our institutions permanent, we should repudiate our political abstractions and adopt religious truths in their stead." [1] Notwithstanding this denunciation of philosophy, he proceeded to develop a system of his own. A fundamental part of his creed was the doctrine that liberty is not, as generally supposed, a good. Liberty, said he, is an evil which government is intended to correct. This is the object of political society, and all government is really slavery. " Sin," he said, " began with the desire for liberty and the attempt to attain it in the person of Satan and his fellow-angels." [2] He declared that as civilization advances, liberty recedes, since " what is needed is good government and a plenty of it — not liberty." The idea that liberty is good for men, he ridiculed as the " most false and foolish that ever entered the human mind. The only free people in the world are the Digger Indians of the valley of the Great Salt Lake and the Australians of New Holland. They know nothing of government, of society, of castes, classes, or of subordination of rank ; each man digs for worms and climbs for birds' eggs on his own hook : they are perfectly free, famished and degraded." [3]

Slavery he considered as the best possible basis for any society. Moreover, Fitz-Hugh discovered a resemblance between the philosophic bases of slav-

[1] *Sociology*, 114–115.   [2] *Ibid.* 170.   [3] *Ibid.*

ery and socialism, which the advocates of neither
of these systems would be willing to admit. In
common with the socialists he attacked the principle
of free contract, considering its results as cruel as
the war of the sword, or theft, robbery, and murder.
A Southern plantation was an ideal type, he thought,
of a socialistic society. The feelings and interests
of the masters prevent undue pressure on the
laborers; they are protected from the evils of
competition and are assured employment and
support. His only objection to socialism was,
"that it will not honestly admit that it owes its
recent revival to the failure of universal liberty and
is seeking to bring about slavery again in some
form." [1] No effective combination of labor can be
made, said Fitz-Hugh, until men are willing to
surrender their liberty and subject themselves to a
despotic head or ruler — "this is slavery, and
toward this socialism is moving." This theory of
Fitz-Hugh was not, it may be said, the philosophy
of the great body of the pro-slavery school and
cannot be taken as representative of them. His
extremely radical ideas illustrate, nevertheless, one

[1] *Ibid.* Fitz-Hugh favored providing for a system of entailment
of property. "We need not fear the mad-dog cry of aristocracy. . . . We have the things, exclusive hereditary property and
aristocracy, in their utmost intensity; let us not be frightened at the
names." Fitz-Hugh was not alone in his radical theory. Governor
Hammond, in a letter to Calhoun (1850), expressed the belief that
"free government and all that sort of thing has been a fatal delu-
sion and humbug from the time of Moses." *Correspondence*, p. 1212.

phase of the intellectual movement and as such are worthy of examination in the same spirit in which the theory of the radical Abolitionists is studied.

Such, then, was the character of the theory by which slavery was defended. The individualistic philosophy of the eighteenth century and of the Revolutionary period was rejected. The doctrine that all men are created equal was denied, and the possession of inherent and inalienable "natural rights" was disputed or the force of the doctrine weakened by interpretation. It was shown that political rights and civil liberty cannot justly be demanded by all, but belong only to those who possess intellect, morality, and political capacity. If this is true, then an inferior race or class unfitted for political life may properly and justly be held in a state of servitude by a class or race that is politically capable; and this servitude may properly extend to the entire abolition of civil and political rights, even of any legal status whatever. Such a system is not undemocratic, but on the contrary tends to foster the spirit of liberty and to develop free institutions to the highest degree of perfection, since the lower classes are eliminated from politics and the political people are composed of those of the highest grade and most capable of administering democratic government. The complete servitude of a lower class to a highly democratic ruling class is not only possible, as the ancient Hellenic democracies conclusively show, but this is on the whole the most advantageous kind of a governmental-social structure that can be devised, especially when the slaves are taken from an inferior race, naturally unfitted for participation in political life.

As the Abolitionist crusade was a part of a world-wide humanitarian and philanthropic movement, so the pro-slavery theory had certain features in common with an intellectual movement of the time. The characteristics of the slavery apologists were those of the natural scientists rather than those of the philanthropists.[1] The leaders in the defence of the slave system regarded human life as essentially a struggle in which the fittest survive, and thought that in spite of certain elements of cruelty in this process the system was on the whole beneficent in its results. They believed that they were among the fittest, holding their position by the authority of the inexorable fiat of nature, and they were not primarily interested in the elevation of the lower classes, or in the amelioration of their condition. Abolitionism, they regarded as sentimental, idealistic, and impracticable, classing it with socialism, spiritualism, free-thought, anti-masonry, "teetotalism," and other "isms" of the day. They justified themselves as practical men, viewing with impartial eye the actual

[1] The method of argument employed by the slavery apologists was not, however, the same as that of the natural scientists. The pro-slavery reasoning was, to a great extent, *à priori* and deductive.

and inevitable conditions of social life and progress, perceiving the difficulty of reversing the operation of the laws of nature, and little disposed to tamper with movements in that direction. They regarded slavery as a social necessity decreed by the laws of nature, and they looked upon any attempts to alter this state as wholly idealistic and impractical.

In conclusion, a few words may be said by way of summarizing the discussion. It is clear that at the bottom of the controversy between the radical Abolitionists and the pro-slavery party, there was a fundamental difference of opinion as to the nature of human liberty. The abolitionists thought that liberty is the birthright of all men; the defenders of slavery thought it the possession of those only who are fit. The Abolitionists thought that as far as rights are concerned, all men are created and should continue to be equal; and consequently they were bitter in their denunciation of the denial of these rights; the opposite party thought that rights do not belong to men simply as men, but because of the superior qualities, physical, intellectual, moral or political, which are characteristic of certain individuals or races. The Abolitionists argued, in accordance with their belief, that the negro ought to be put in possession of the original and natural rights which are justly his, and of which he is wrongfully deprived. The slaveholders contended that

the negro, being an inferior order of man, should
be kept in a state of complete subjection for his own
and for the general good. Thus in both theory
and practice, there was an almost irreconcilable
difference between the two parties.

Between the conservative anti-slavery element
and the slave party there was a less marked
contrast. Although these opponents of slavery
declared that all men are born with certain rights,
they did not demand complete equality for the
races. It was therefore recognized that there must
be a certain restraint of certain classes under certain conditions, and no demand was made for equal
liberty or for immediate liberty for all members
of the community. Between this group and the
slavery party, the question was really one as to how
far individual conduct may be regulated and for
how long. The defenders of slavery insisted that
the negro is entitled to no rights at all, politically
speaking, and moreover that the nature of the
black man is such as to make this status permanent.
On the contrary, the anti-slavery party declared
that a certain body of rights should be granted to
every one — not necessarily full participation in the
exercise of political functions, but at least something in advance of complete and permanent subjection to the will of a master. Upon this point
the two parties differed sharply. Had the pro-
slavery party been willing to grant the negro even
a modicum of civil rights, and to concede and

make provision for his capacity for future exercise
of further rights, the gulf between these positions
might have been spanned.

A further difference of opinion was that concerning the influence of slavery upon society in
general, and democratic institutions in particular.
The apologists for slavery believed that such a
system was economically advantageous, socially
elevating, and that politically slavery made possible the very highest type of democratic government; in brief, that a slave society was superior at
almost every point by which civilization may be
estimated.   The opponents of slavery regarded the
practice as wasteful from the economic point of
view, demoralizing socially, and with special emphasis urged that the existence of a system of slavery is incompatible with the maintenance of democratic institutions, since the characteristic qualities
which make democracy possible are diametrically
opposite to those fostered under slavery.   One side,
then, regarded democracy as properly applicable
to the whole society, the other as a relation within
a certain class not inclusive of the whole society.
This difference corresponds closely to that already
considered; namely, as to whether liberty is the
birthright of all, or the reward of the fittest.

From the standpoint of modern political science
the slaveholders were right in declaring that
liberty can be given only to those who have political capacity enough to use it, and they were also

right in maintaining that two greatly unequal races cannot exist side by side on terms of perfect equality. But the conclusion drawn from these premises was by no means a legitimate one. It did not follow that because the negro was not the equal of the white man, and could not well exercise the same political rights, that therefore he should be deprived of all rights whatever. Because he was not entitled to equal political rights, it did not follow that he should not even have a personality in the eyes of the law. This was the fatal *non sequitur* that led to the violent abolition of slavery in the throes of a terrible civil war. But, on the other hand, the Abolitionists were guilty of an equally rash generalization in assuming as they did at the close of the war, that because the negro is entitled to some rights, he should immediately and without any preparation be placed in full possession of the highest political rights. As the slavery party blundered in giving the negro no rights, the radical Abolitionists blundered in giving him, at one stroke, all rights.

CHAPTER VII

POLITICAL THEORY IN RELATION TO THE NATURE OF THE UNION

THE question of national organization is the most difficult problem that the United States has yet been called upon to solve. Possessing all the characteristics commonly attributed to nations, — common race, language, religion, geographical unity, — the full expression of this nationality met with stubborn resistance, and was realized only after the bloodiest war of the century had been fought. Even in colonial days there was evident the strongest reluctance to form any union at all binding in nature. During the enthusiasm of the Revolutionary movement a decidedly national attitude was assumed, but in the Articles of Confederation this was abandoned. In the formation and adoption of the Constitution there was a reaction in which the national spirit was conspicuous. From the very first days of the Republic, however, there was marked divergence of opinion in regard to the nature of the new Union. The Eleventh Amendment, the Kentucky and Virginia Resolutions, the Hartford Convention, Nullification, — all were evidences of the general difference of opinion as to

the character of the federal Union. With the rise
of slavery to the position of a national issue, the
defenders of this institution made states-rights a
part of their platform. Thus the unnational doctrine was associated with a particular section of
the country and with the life of a particular institution. It had a local habitation and a name. The
conflict accordingly became more and more des-
perate, until the final appeal was taken to the
arbitrament of arms.

The purpose of this chapter is to describe and
analyze the political theory underlying the various
doctrines as to the nature of the Union developed
during this period. The compromise theory prevalent at the time of the adoption of the Constitution, the states-rights theory developed by
Calhoun, and the nationalist doctrine in the legal
form given it by Webster, and in the more scientific shape later assumed, form the large groups
under which these doctrines may be classified and
discussed.

The question as to the nature of the American
Union was an important one, theoretically and
practically, in the days when the Constitution was
pending. The new government involved, it was
seen, a closer union than that under the old Confederation, and yet it was not desired to form a
centralized state, a "consolidated republic." The
Confederation was too closely allied to anarchy; a
centralized state, it was feared, would be equiva-

lent to tyranny. This difficulty was discussed by the *Federalist* and was explained with such consummate skill as to constitute a satisfactory solution for the political problem then immediate and pressing. The United States was the first type of the modern "Bundes-Staat," and the *Federalist* was breaking new ground; nevertheless, the theory then developed profoundly influenced the thought of America, and also at a later date that of Continental countries. The new Union was variously termed a "Compound Republic," a "Confederate Republic," and a "Confederacy," an assemblage of societies, or an association of two or more states into one state. "The extent, modification, and objects of the federal authority," it was explained, "are mere matters of discretion. So long as the separate organization of the members be not abolished; so long as it exists by a constitutional necessity for local purposes, though it be in perfect subordination to the general authority of the Union, it would still be in fact and in theory an association of states or a confederacy." [1]

The nature of the new Union, it was held, is neither wholly national nor wholly federal, but contains both national and federal elements in combination. Considering the foundation of the government, it is federal, since the Constitution must be ratified by the several states. In regard to the organization of the legislative power, the

[1] *Federalist*, No. 9.

new Union is partly national and partly federal, one House resting on a national and the other on a federal basis. The executive is also constituted in a mixed federal and national way, since the electoral vote is distributed partly in accordance with the principle of state equality, and partly according to population. Viewing the operation of the government, it is seen to be national and not federal, inasmuch as it acts directly on individuals and not through the states. In the extent of its powers, however, the Union is federal, because its jurisdiction is limited to specific objects, and all else is left to the states. Lastly, as respects the amending power, it is found that the government is partly federal and partly national, since neither the principle of unanimity nor that of proportionality obtains exclusively. It thus appears that the government, as organized in the Constitution, must be regarded neither as a pure confederacy nor yet as a "consolidated republic"; but should really be placed in a class by itself. It is a new type of government peculiar to American conditions — a form at once national and federal, happily combining the characteristics of both.

In harmony with this idea of the mixed character of the Union, was the theory that sovereignty is capable of division and actually is divided in the United States. This doctrine was current at the time when the Constitution was adopted, was generally accepted until the days of Calhoun, and still

remains the theory of the federal courts. In the
letter of the Constitutional Convention to Congress,
it was expressly declared that "all rights of independent sovereignty" could not be secured to the
states under a system of federal government.[1] In
the *Federalist*, also, the division of sovereign power
was frequently suggested. Thus it was said that
the old Confederation attempted to accomplish
impossibilities, "to reconcile a partial sovereignty
in the Union, with complete sovereignty in the
states ; to subvert a mathematical axiom by taking
away a part, and letting the whole remain."[2] It
was shown that in Rome "the legislative power
in the last resort resided for ages in two different
bodies, which were distinct and independent;"[3]
that is, the Patricians and the Plebeians. It was
asserted that the new Constitution does not reduce
the states to the rank of provinces, but leaves them
in possession of "certain exclusive and very important portions of sovereign power."[4] The states
will still hold "all the rights of sovereignty which
were not by that act exclusively delegated to the
United States."[5] In a consolidated system the
local authorities are wholly subject to the central
government; but in the proposed Union the "local
authorities form distinct and independent portions
of the supremacy, no more subject to the general
authority than the general authority is to them

[1] *Journal of Congress*, XII, 165.   [2] No. 4.
[3] No. 32.   [4] No. 9.   [5] No. 31.   Cf. No. 82.

within its own sphere." [1] The states may not be fully sovereign, but they have at least a residuary sovereignty. There are, in fact, many sovereignties existing side by side. The real sovereignty rests, however, not with state or federal government, but with the "people." "The ultimate authority," it is said, "wherever the derivative may be found, resides in the people alone." [2] But who the "people" were, whether of the several states or of all the states taken collectively, the *Federalist* was careful not to answer. This was a question left for coming generations.

It is a fair conclusion, then, that at the time when the Constitution was adopted, the prevalent opinion was that in some way or other sovereignty was being divided between the states and the Union. [3] It is a mistake to suppose that the states thought they were renouncing all of their sovereignty, or that they thought they were giving up none of it. There were, of course, some who believed in one or the other of these two ideas; but in gen-

[1] No. 39. [2] Nos. 33, 45, 82.

[3] See John Dickinson, "Letters of Fabius," p. 179; Noah Webster, "An Examination into the Leading Principles of the Federal Constitution," p. 46 (both the foregoing are in Ford's *Pamphlets*); Elliot, *Debates*, II, 129, 143, 356. John Adams said (1790): "Our new government is an attempt to divide a sovereignty — a fresh essay at imperium in imperio. It cannot, therefore, be expected to be very stable or very firm." *Works*, IX, 564. In this connection see a discussion on "Social Compact and Constitutional Construction," by A. C. McLaughlin, in *The American Historical Review* (April, 1900).

eral it was thought that a compromise was being made between states and Union, and that a division of sovereignty was involved in this. If the question were ever raised as to where the ultimate controlling power in the community is located, the answer was, "with the people," without particular inquiry as to just what was meant by this.[1] In the Revolutionary days "people" had stood for the opposition to the king, and this old idea was used to conceal the difficulty involved in a wholly different situation.

This idea of the divisibility of sovereignty was early enunciated by the United States courts, notably in the case of Chisholm v. Georgia (1792). The declaration was made that "the United States are sovereign as to all the powers of government actually surrendered. Each state in the Union is sovereign as to all the powers reserved."[2] Succeeding decisions gave expression to the same theory that sovereignty is capable of division and actually has been divided under the American system. The opinions of the courts were permeated with the idea of the division of sovereign powers between the states and the Union.[3]

[1] Cf. James Wilson's argument in the Pennsylvania Convention on this point, Elliot, *Debates*, II, 504.

[2] 2 Dallas, 435.

[3] Cf. Ware v. Hylton, 3 Dallas, 232 (1796): "The several states retained all *internal* sovereignty and . . . Congress properly possessed the great rights of *external* sovereignty." Cherokee Nation v. Georgia, 5 Peters, 26: "They have in Europe sovereign and

One of the staunchest champions of the theory of divided sovereignty was James Madison. He maintained that the American government was neither federal nor national; it was *sui generis*, federo-republican, unique in the nature of its construction, a "nondescript to be tested and explained by itself alone,"[1] an illustration of the adaptability of republican institutions to new and difficult conditions. To his mind nothing was clearer than the proposition that sovereignty may be divided. If it cannot, he urged, then "the political system of the United States is a chimera, mocking the vain pretensions of human wisdom."[2] Or again, "It is difficult to argue intelligibly concerning the compound system of government in the United States without admitting the divisibility of sovereignty."[3] In this case it is necessary "to abandon abstract and technical modes of expounding and designating its character," and regard the Constitution as a "system hitherto without a model."[4] He found that the sovereignty was divided between the states on the one hand and the Union on the other, so that the whole society, as he said, consists in a number of partial sovereignties.[5] Moreover, he charged that the main pillar of nullification was

demi-sovereign states, and states of doubtful sovereignty. But this state, if it be a state, must be a grade above them all." See McCulloch *v.* Maryland, 4 Wheaton, 316; Worcester *v.* Georgia, 6 Peters, 591–592.

[1] *Works*, IV, 420–421.   [2] *Ibid.* IV, 61.
[3] *Ibid.* IV, 394.   [4] *Ibid.* IV, 420–421.   [5] *Ibid.* IV, 393.

the assumption that sovereignty is a unit at once indivisible and inalienable.[1]

Up to the time when the theory of Calhoun became influential, the characteristic American doctrine was that in the United States, whatever might elsewhere obtain, the sovereignty had been divided into several portions without the destruction of its life principle. Replying to Calhoun's argument for unqualified state sovereignty, Sena-

[1] Frederick Grimke, *Nature and Tendency of Free Institutions* (1848), argued that " when we assert that the sovereignty is inalienable or indivisible, we, in effect, impose *limitations* upon the sovereignty, which is a contradiction," p. 527. He held that in the United States sovereignty is divided between the " states united " and the " states severally," pp. 519–520. Nathaniel Chipman, *Principles of Government* (1833), concluded that there is an external sovereignty vested in the United States, but no provision made in the Constitution for an internal sovereignty, 142 ff. Sovereignty is also divisible: "the opinion formerly entertained that the sovereignty of a state was a sort of indivisible essence, a power absolute, uncontrolled and uncontrollable, has been corrected in modern times. Experience has shown it capable of division." p. 273. Cf. E. D. Mansfield, *The Political Grammar of the United States* (1834), 520–521; John Taylor, *New Views of the Constitution* (1822), Sec. 13. Nathan Dane, *General Abridgment and Digest of American Law* (1823–1829), Vol. IX, Appendix, holds that sovereignty may be indivisible by " a people standing alone as in Russia or France," but in " a family political connection," like the United States, we " give and distribute almost *ad infinitum* delegated powers, or what is vaguely called sovereignty," Sec. 8. It also appears that " though the nation is sovereign, the power of the general government is limited, and so, strictly and accurately speaking, is no sovereign," Sec. 18. On the omission of the term " sovereignty " in the Constitution, see Sec. 35.

tor Rives of Virginia, himself a states-rights man of the old school, said (1833): "Sir, this is a novelty unknown to the founders of the Constitution, and has sprung up in a hotbed of local politics. At the period of the adoption of the Constitution it was distinctly made known and understood that to the extent to which sovereignty was vested in the Union, that of the states was relinquished and diminished." If the idea of a double sovereignty seemed to be without adequate historical precedent, so was the whole American system without parallel. As democracy seemed impossible until put in practice in America, so with the division of sovereignty. The fact that such a condition was not elsewhere to be found did not constitute an argument against its acceptance, but was rather a testimony to the "peculiar adaptability of republican institutions."

As has already been indicated, the progress of this idea was facilitated by the prevalence of the theory of popular as opposed to governmental sovereignty, and by the general belief that the New World had really little to do with the Old World conception of government in general or of sovereignty in particular. The wide acceptance of this idea throughout the United States made it for a long time possible to quiet the contention between the states and the Union by referring them to that authority above both; namely, the "people." When the contest between nationalism and particularism entered the acute stage, however, this doctrine became less easy to maintain. The difficulty long concealed behind the complicated governmental machinery and the ambiguous term "people" became evident, the compromise doctrine was rejected by both North and South, and the battle fought out between the sovereignty of the states and that of the Union.

It should not escape notice, however, that Joseph Story early distinguished two uses of the term "sovereignty" in such a way as to obviate the difficulties inherent in the idea of double supremacy. He observed that "by sovereignty in its largest sense is meant supreme, absolute, uncontrollable power, the *jus summi imperii*, the absolute right to govern."[1] But the term, he showed, is also used in another and more limited sense, signifying "such political powers as in the actual organization of the particular state or nation are to be exclusively exercised by certain public functionaries without the control of any superior authority." In this sense, he continues, the sovereignty "may be of a very limited nature. It may extend to a few or many objects. It may be unlimited as to some, it may be restrained as to others." In this use of the term, sovereignty is not the ultimate political power, but that which, "under the given form of organization," is exercised "without the control of superior authority." From this point of

[1] *Commentaries*, Secs. 207, 208.

view it is easy to regard sovereignty as theoretically divisible and as actually divided between the states and the Union, understanding that the "absolute right to govern" still remains in its original unity and integrity. Sovereignty in the limited sense is divided; in the broader sense it remains one.

In this connection attention should be called to an application of the social-contract theory to the nature of the Union. This doctrine of contract was capable of different application, but in the hands of Madison and others was employed to combat the theories of the extreme states-rights party. It was conceded that the Union was formed by an agreement to which states, and not individuals, were the parties, but the binding force of the contract was emphasized in the very strongest way. The fact that the Union rests on a contract, it was said, should not be made an excuse for abandoning it at will. On the contrary, the very fact that it is a contract entitles it to the highest respect. "It is," said Madison, "the nature and essence of a compact that it is equally obligatory on the parties to it, and of course that no one of them can be liberated therefrom without the consent of the others, or such a violation or abuse of it by the others as will amount to a dissolution of the compact." [1] The states, then, may in an extreme case exercise their revolutionary right, but

[1] *Works*, IV, 63.

they cannot legally dissolve the Union at pleasure. They are bound as states by virtue of the contract.[1]

Of this nature was the theory of the Union proclaimed by Jackson in his message of 1833 on the nullification question.   His position was, that, without inquiring closely into the exact form of the national contract, "it is sufficient that it must be admitted to be a compact and to possess the obligations incident to a compact."   The parties to the agreement cannot dissolve the association without "acknowledging the correlative right in the remainder to decide whether that dissolution can be permitted consistently with the general happiness." Owing to the wide prevalence of the social-contract theory in America, this appeal to the binding force of a contract was an exceedingly effective argument to use.   It was an easy step from the doctrine that governments derive their powers from the consent of the governed, to the idea that if the states had consented or contracted to form a government, they were bound by that agreement. The more strongly it was believed that the only legitimate basis of government was consent, the greater was the emphasis placed on the obligation of a contract or agreement, whether between states or individuals.   And just as it was thought that the social contract must not be interpreted by any one citizen, but by the majority, so it was reasoned that the agreement between the states should be

[1] Compare Lincoln's Inaugural Address.

interpreted by the majority, and not by any one of them at pleasure. The one-sided repudiation of a contract voluntarily entered into was, according to this theory, wholly unreasonable, and contrary to the analogy both of private law and of the social contract on which the society rests. By this line of reasoning the conclusion was reached that the Union, although created by the voluntary act of the states as states, was not an association from which a state could depart at pleasure without consulting its fellow-states.

None of these compromise ideas, however, offered a satisfactory solution of the problem. In the course of a generation after the Constitution was adopted, they were supplanted by well-defined doctrines of state sovereignty on the one hand, and national supremacy on the other. The conflict between nationalism and particularism, intensified by the agitation over the slavery question, passed out of the realm of compromise. Rigid dogmas were framed upon either side, their validity stubbornly asserted, and the conclusion found in the field of armed conflict.

Definite form was first given to the particularistic theory. The feeling of state sovereignty, strong from the first, had been aroused to vigorous protest by the summons issued against the state of Georgia from which resulted the eleventh Amendment; by the Alien and Sedition Laws; again by the war with England; by the tariff of 1832; finally by the fear that the Union and slavery were incompatible. The outgrowth of this sentiment was the doctrine of Nullification and Secession. To the political philosophy underlying these ideas attention must now be given.

In its earliest form the states-rights idea was based on the current theory of the social contract. Analogies were drawn between the social contract and the federal contract.[1] The formation of the Union by the states was compared to that of a state by the individuals; reference was made to the natural rights of states, and it was suggested that the states, like individuals, might abandon the association of which they were members, if abused or oppressed. This analogy between social and federal contract was implied in the Kentucky and Virginia Resolutions.

The doctrine was exploited by the Virginia jurist, H. St. George Tucker, in his *Commentaries on Blackstone* (1803). The states, said Tucker, are united in a confederacy, but still remain independent and sovereign. Each is still a sovereign state, still capable, should the occasion require, of resuming the exercise of its functions to the full extent. Whenever the common government becomes subversive of the rights of any state, it may secede as the states seceded from the old Confederation. This is a natural right of which

---

[1] This argument had been used by James Wilson, although not in defence of states-rights. *Works*, I, 539.

"no force or compact can deprive the people of any state, whenever they see the necessity and possess the power to do it." [1]   The state has the same right to withdraw from or overthrow the federal government as the individual has, under the Declaration of Independence, to overthrow any political system which has become oppressive.   But this, it will be observed, gave the states only a revolutionary right of resistance or secession, and it also involved the recognition of the social contract.[2] Both of these ideas were repudiated by the later defenders of the cause of the states.

The finally accepted statement of the states-rights doctrine was made by the great political philosopher of the South, John C. Calhoun.   The work in which his ideas are most systematically expressed is, *A Disquisition on Government*, accompanied by *A Discourse on the Constitution and Government of the United States*, one of the ablest treatises on political theory that appeared in the first half of the last century.[3]   This, taken in connection with the numerous public utterances of Calhoun, affords a basis for the study of his political philosophy.

[1] *Commentaries*, I, 187.

[2] Tucker speaks of the contract as partly social and partly federal; also of a division of sovereignty between states and the government; but nevertheless maintains that a state may at will withdraw from the Confederation.

[3] Published posthumously. See Calhoun's *Works*, edited by Richard K. Cralle ; *Correspondence* of John C. Calhoun, edited by J. Franklin Jameson, in Vol. II, *Annual Report of the American*

An analysis will first be made of his theory of nullification, and then of the doctrine of secession with which he is associated. The inquiry is directed in the first place, then, to the general attitude of Calhoun toward the fundamental question of the origin of the political society.

Calhoun condemned in no uncertain terms the time-honored hypothesis of a pre-civil " state of nature " and the origin of government by means of a contract.[1] This had been the theory of the revolutionists in the seventeenth and eighteenth centuries, and continued to be the prevailing American doctrine even in the nineteenth. In fact, this hypothesis of an original " state of nature " and the contractual character of government had been one of the leading principles of " the Fathers " ; the theory of contract had even been extended from individuals to the relations between the states ; it was recognized in many of the state constitutions ; adopted by men of all parties, aristocrats as well as democrats ; and was generally accepted as the correct theory of the origin of political institutions. In the politics of Calhoun, however, there was no place for the assumptions of the *Naturrecht* phi-

Historical Association for 1899. Of especial importance are Calhoun's speeches on The South Carolina Exposition (1828), Vol. III; The Force Bill (1833), Vol. II; Reply to Webster (1833), Vol. II; Reception of Abolition Petitions (1837), Vol. IV; Veto Power (1842), Vol. IV. See the *Life of Calhoun*, by H. von Holst.

[1] Cf. ' A Study of Nullification in South Carolina," by D. F. Houston, in *Harvard Historical Studies*, Vol. III (1896).

losophy, and he had no sympathy with this interpretation of the nature of government. The "state of nature" he regarded as a mere fiction, an unwarrantable hypothesis. "Instead of being the natural state of man, it is, of all conceivable states, the most opposed to his nature, most repugnant to his feelings, and most incompatible with his wants. His natural state is the social and political."

Government is not artificial and unnatural, but perfectly natural in the sense that it is necessary to the development and perfection of human powers. Government is not a matter of choice, depending for its origin and continuance on the caprice of the individual; on the contrary, it is a primary necessity of man, and, " like breathing, it is not permitted to depend on our volition." [1] There are, reasons Calhoun, two fundamental elements in the constitution of man : one the selfish, the other the social instinct or tendency. Of these two, however, the stronger is the selfish tendency, and as a consequence, there arises conflict between individuals which must be in some way controlled. The instrument by means of which this control is effected is government — a necessity arising out of the essential nature of man.[2] *Society* is necessary to man; *government* is necessary to society. But government itself contains the germ of evil,

[1] *Ibid.* 8.
[2] *Ibid.* 1-4. Calhoun avoids using the term "selfish," substituting " direct " or " individual."

and must in its turn be controlled or balanced. To this end is erected a *constitution* intended to hold in check the destructive tendencies found in government. This constitution bears the same relation to government that government bears to society; as government restrains the selfish tendencies of the individual, so the constitution checks the selfish tendencies of the government. There is this difference to be noted, however, that government is of divine origin, whereas the constitution is a human device and construction. There *must* be a government; there *may* be a constitution.[1]

The organization of the constitution Calhoun regards as one of the greatest of political problems. How can the government be given the powers necessary and yet be restrained from oppressing the members of the society? Calhoun's answer to this perennial problem is that there must be created an *organism* " by which resistance may be systematically and peaceably made on the part of the ruled to oppression and abuse of power on the part of the rulers." [2] This result may be effected by establishing the responsibility of the rulers to the ruled through the exercise of the right of suffrage — the primary principle in the establishment of constitutional government. Yet this alone is inadequate to afford the necessary protection; " it

[1] *Ibid.* 8.   [2] *Ibid.* 12.

only changes the seat of authority, without coun-
teracting, in the least, the tendency of the govern
ment to oppression and abuse of its powers." [1]
We are still confronted by the imminent danger
that the majority of the electors will prove to
be tyrannical and oppress the weaker minority
as intolerably as the most irresponsible government.

Calhoun enters, therefore, on a vigorous polemic
against the despotism of the majority. He asserts
that the tendency of the majority is to assume all
the rights belonging to the people. Although
only a fraction, they assume to be and act as
the whole people ; while on the other hand, the
minority is treated as if it were nothing at all.
Again, Calhoun points out the probability that
great political parties will arise, that their organization will become increasingly centralized, and
that continually stricter party discipline will prevail. Offices will come to be regarded as the
legitimate reward of the victorious party, while
recognition of other than partisans will be excluded. Party strife will become fiercer and fiercer
as it becomes more factional, and will finally result in an appeal to force and the establishment
of absolute government. [2]

Nor is there any way by which this inherent

[1] *Ibid.* 14.
[2] *Ibid.* 42. Calhoun had before him the spoils system inaugurated
by Jackson. See Vol. II, 435.

tendency may be effectively restrained.   It may be urged that a sufficient check is found in the power of public opinion to keep party spirit within reasonable limits.   But to this Calhoun is not ready to assent.   He concedes the great strength of public sentiment, particularly that of modern times in its highly developed form, but does not consider it even yet as an effective barrier against the tendencies of the majority.   Public opinion itself may be just as despotic as the majority party, just as radical and unreasonable, and consequently just as uncertain a defender of the rights of the minority. Nor are constitutional restrictions or the separation of powers of sufficient force against the majority.   All restrictions must be interpreted, all requirements carried out, by the prevailing party. The minority is helpless and must submit to any adjustment of constitutional balances that may commend itself to the majority.[1]

The "tyranny of the majority" is, then, one of the fundamental propositions in the theory of Calhoun. Majority rule is always liable to abuse at the hands of a party, an interest, or a section, which interprets constitutional law, determines public opinion, arrogates to itself the right and privilege properly belonging only to the whole people.   With dramatic power Calhoun pictures the inevitable advance of majority encroachment and aggres-

[1] *Disquisition*, 22 ff.   See Madison's defence of majority rule, II, 330.

sion.[1] Application of this principle is made in reference to the question of taxation. Under the operation of the numerical majority, says Calhoun, a party
or section obtaining power may easily abuse and oppress another section found in the minority. Taxes
may be levied by the majority section, which burden chiefly the minority section; not only this, but
these taxes are actually returned by the minority to the majority, virtually bounties paid by the
weaker to the stronger party. The case in point
was that of the protective tariff, which he considered was levied for the benefit of the North at
the expense of the South. It seemed to him,
therefore, an excellent illustration of the "majority tyranny" upon which so much emphasis had
been laid.

In place of the dangerous, "*numerical* majority,"
Calhoun presents his doctrine of the "*concurrent*
majority." "All constitutional governments," says
Calhoun, "take the sense of the community by its
parts, each through its appropriate organ."[2] On
the other hand, those governments in which power
is centred in an individual or a body of individuals,
even including the majority, may be regarded as
absolute governments. The principle upon which

---

[1] It is interesting to note that Calhoun objected to party caucuses
and conventions "because they are irresponsible bodies, not known
to the Constitution." The election of the President, he held, should
be left to the electoral college as the framers of the Constitution
intended. *Works*, Vol. IV, 394.

[2] *Disquisition*, 36.

T

they rest is, in last analysis, force, in contrast to
the principle of constitutional governments, which
is that of compromise.   Under the "concurrent"
or "constitutional" majority system this principle
of compromise will be made effective by giving
"each interest or portion of the community a
negative on the others." [1]   Without a "concurrent
majority" there can be no negative; without a
negative there can be no constitution.   Calhoun
declares that "it is this negative power — the
power of preventing or arresting the action of the
government — be it called by what term it may —
veto, interposition, nullification, check, or balance
of power — which, in fact, forms the Constitution." [2]
The positive power makes the *government*, but
the negative power makes the *constitution*.   The
essence of the "concurrent majority" is, then, the
veto power granted to the various separate interests.
Governmental action is conditioned, not upon the
consent of a majority of *individuals*, but upon that
of various *interests*.

The advantages of such a system are presented
with great enthusiasm.   With a "concurrent majority" there will be a greater degree of attachment
to the state than is otherwise possible.[3]   Attention
will be attracted not so much to party as to country.
The government will not discriminate against any
one interest or group, and hence there will be no violent resentments and animosities provoked as under

[1] *Disquisition*, 35.   [2] *Ibid.*   [3] *Ibid.* 47.

the rule of the absolute majority. Consequently there will result a higher development of "common devotion." Politically and morally there must follow, according to Calhoun, loftier standards of conduct under this régime of compromise than under that of force. Moreover, under this system there may be obtained a higher degree of liberty.[1] Government will be effectually restrained from arbitrary and oppressive conduct by the veto power of the various interests, and thus political freedom will be guaranteed. In any other government, indeed, liberty can be little more than a name; the "constitutional majority" alone makes it a reality. By the same logic, civilization and progress are fostered by the system of compromise, for under it are secured liberty and harmony — two great factors in civilized development.[2] On the whole, Calhoun would conclude that the "organism" known as the "concurrent" or "constitutional" majority is eminently adapted to realize the great ends of government included under the protection and perfection of society.

Two objections may be raised against the proposed system, Calhoun concedes; namely, its complexity and its ineffectiveness. To the first of these he replies that the simplest of all governments are absolute and that all free governments are of necessity complex in their structure. Hence this style of argument applies to the whole philosophy

[1] *Ibid.* 59. [2] *Ibid.* 61.

and practice of free governments, which he does
not consider it necessary to defend. Nor is the
objection to the effectiveness of the proposed
system regarded as serious. Calhoun maintains
that in times of real stress the compromise principle
is not unfavorable to the passage of necessary
measures, and that any policy agreed upon is far
more enthusiastically supported than if compelled
by force. Obedience will be rendered, not from a
selfish or sectional motive, but from a higher sense
of obligation to country. An analogy to the compromise principle is discovered in the unanimity
required of a jury before decisive action can be
taken. As circumstances lead the jurors to a
unanimous decision, so the far more imperious necessities of government will lead to a compromise
and agreement in the affairs of state. Historical
illustrations of the compromise are afforded by the
experience of Poland with the *liberum veto*, by the
Confederacy of the Six Nations, the Patricians and
Plebeians in Rome, the Lords and Commons in
England, and by the United States, if the original
intention of the Fathers were carried out.

It is now evident that Calhoun's argument all
leads up to the defence of a particular theory of
public law in the United States. "Concurrent" or
"constitutional" majority is simply the prolegomena
to nullification. The individual states of the Union
are to enjoy a veto on the proceedings of the general
government, thus establishing the principle of action

through the concurrent instead of the numerical majority. A state may reject any measure of the general government regarded as inconsistent with the terms of the Constitution; may, in other words, nullify the proposed action of the federal government. If three-fourths of the states support the action of the government, the nullifying state must either yield or withdraw from the Union.[1] Thus a constitutional means of defence is possessed by each state; there is no possibility of tyrannical conduct on the part of the " numerical majority "; and the action of the " concurrent majority " is assured. Nullification, in Calhoun's eyes, was not only a theory of the relation of the states to the Union, but it was a theory of constitutional government in general; founded not merely in the particular system of the United States, but equally essential in the frame-work of any free constitution.

In South Carolina for example, he points out, representation in the legislature is distributed on the basis of property, population, and territory. Representation in the senate is based on election districts, and thus gives to the southern part of the state the predominance in that body; the house is based on property and population, thus giving the northern part of the state the majority there. As the governor, the judges, and all important officers are elected by the legislature, there is

[1] See *Discourse,* 297 ff.

established an equilibrium between the sections. "Party organization," says Calhoun, "party discipline, party proscription, and their offspring, the spoils principle, have been unknown to the state."[1] The same principle and similar methods might well be introduced, he thinks, into other states and there be followed by like beneficent results.

As already stated, nullification as conceived by Calhoun was not simply a theory of the American Union, but a fundamental doctrine of free government. Whether the political theory of nullification was chronologically or only logically antecedent to the constitutional theory of nullification, is a matter which need not here be discussed; the important fact is that in the developed thought of Calhoun, the "concurrent majority" was declared to be a vital element in constitutional government.[2]

The next object of inquiry is Calhoun's statement of the doctrine of secession. The germ of this theory is found in Calhoun's conception of the nature of sovereignty. In the early years of the Republic it had been generally believed that in

[1] See *Discourse*, 405.

[2] Calhoun favored a plural executive for the United States. This, he urged, was the practice in Sparta, Rome, and even England, where the cabinet is the real executive. In the United States there should be one of the members constituting the executive from each of the two great sections of the country. *Discourse on Constitution and Government*, 392–395. Calhoun's opposition to Jackson's use of the executive power would also lead him to favor a plural executive.

the United States there existed a divided sovereignty. The states were sovereign in certain matters, the national government sovereign in certain others, and each was supreme in its proper sphere. If any ultimate sovereign was thought of, it was the people as contrasted with the government.

Calhoun, however, was wholly intolerant of any theory of divided sovereignty. To him this was logically impossible and contradictory. He reasoned that in its very nature sovereignty must be indivisible. " To divide is to destroy it ; " sovereignty must be one, or it is not at all. There can be no state partly sovereign and partly non-sovereign ; there can be no association composed of half-sovereign states on the one hand, and a half-sovereign government on the other. The vital principle of the state, its life and spirit, cannot be sundered ; it must remain one and indivisible. Thus in Calhoun's doctrine, all compromise was rejected, and the doctrine of the indivisibility of sovereignty presented in its clearest and most striking light.

Applying this argument to the nature of the Union, Calhoun asserted that the states were originally sovereign, and that they had never yielded up their sovereignty. They could not surrender a part and retain another part, but they must either have given up all, or have retained all ; the states must be fully sovereign or fully subject. This was the alternative which Calhoun urged with relentless logic. Given the original sovereignty of the states, and the indivisibility of sovereignty, either the states must be sovereign communities and the United States a mere agent, or the United States must be sovereign and the states wholly subordinate. In Calhoun's theory there was no opportunity given for a division of the field between the states and the Union; such a compromise was excluded.[1] It is true, he concedes, that the central government enjoys the right to exercise sovereign powers, but it does not have the true sovereignty from which these powers are only emanations. The central government acts as a sovereign, but it is not a sovereign. It wears the robes of authority only by sufferance of the legitimate owner, the states.

To the central government there are delegated by the states certain attributes of sovereignty, such as the war power, the taxing power, the power to coin money; but these powers do not constitute sovereignty. In Calhoun's theory these attributes of sovereignty may be divided, and the supreme authority itself remain unimpaired.[2] Thus the states do not surrender the sovereignty; they merely forego the exercise of certain of its attributes, and these are liable to recall at any moment

---

[1] Cf. *Works*, Vol. II, 232, 233, in reply to Clayton and Rives.

[2] *Discourse*, 146. "There is no difficulty in understanding how powers appertaining to sovereignty may be divided, and the *exercise* of one portion delegated to one set of agents and another portion to another."

by the state from which derived. In fact, neither federal nor state *government* is supreme, for there is a determining power back of both. One must distinguish, he maintains, between the constitution-making power and the law-making power; the former alone is sovereign, and to its act is due the formation and organization of the government.[1] The constituent power in any state concedes both to the state government and to the national government certain powers or attributes of sovereignty; but as it may recall the power granted to the state government, so with equal right it may recall the authority delegated to the central government. Throughout this process the sovereign power remains intact. The practical conclusion which he draws is, naturally, that the states may at any time rightfully assert their sovereign prerogative and withdraw from the Union.

It is further important to notice how, on Calhoun's basis, he differentiated the United States from a league or confederacy. What line of demarkation could he draw between the political organization under the Articles of Confederation and that effected under the Constitution? Calhoun declared that the main difference between these two types of association consisted in the fact that the Confederacy lacked one essential feature of the "Republic," namely, a fixed and stable government. The so-called "government" of a confederacy is

[1] *Discourse*, 191.

"nearly allied to an assembly of diplomats," meeting to determine certain policies, and then leaving their execution largely to the several parties to the agreement. "Our system is the first that ever substituted a *government* in lieu of such bodies. This, in fact, constitutes its peculiar characteristic. It is new, peculiar, and unprecedented." [1] Among the changes involved in the passage from Confederacy to "Republic" was, in the first place, a change in the source from which power was derived. The Confederacy obtained its authority from the state governments; the "Republic" from the sovereign communities themselves. The Confederacy was a mere league between governments; the "Republic" is a "more perfect union" between sovereign communities. Another point of difference is that in the "Republic" there is needed a much more careful specification and enumeration of powers than was required in the Confederacy, where the states themselves were immediately concerned in the administration. [2] Furthermore, under the Confederacy the state governments were superior to the central government, which was merely their agent; but in the "Republic" the federal and the state governments are equals and coördinates. [3] Both are inferior in rank to the constitutional convention of the state which gives them life. Lastly, there was a change in the method of executing the commands of the central government. The Con-

[1] *Discourse*, 163.   [2] *Ibid.* 164.   [3] *Ibid.* 167.

federacy acted through the states; the " Republic " is authorized to act directly upon individuals.[1]

The difference, then, between the " Republic," or a federal system, and a "nation" must be sought, not in the character of the powers exercised, but in the basis upon which they rest. It matters not how large the power of the federal government; if that power may be recalled by the states, the federal government is subordinate and they are sovereign. The federal government may have possession; the states have ownership: and they may at any time evict their tenant, or any one of the states may claim its share of the estate.[2]

Of the influence of Calhoun there is no question. He was easily the first in rank among the theorists of his school, and his ideas dominated the South. His political theories became the dogma of the particularistic party; they were pressed with the most rigid and unyielding logic, and led straight to the trial of arms in the Civil War. After the close of this struggle, the theory of states-rights was again stated by such authorities as Jefferson Davis,[3] Alexander H. Stephens,[4] and Bernard J.

[1] *Ibid.* 168.

[2] Calhoun's theory found expression in the constitution of the Confederate States.

[3] *The Rise and Fall of the Confederate Government* (1881).

[4] *A Constitutional View of the Late War between the States* (1868), p. 70. Cf. *A Brief Inquiry into the True Nature and Character of our Federal Government*, by A. P. Upshur (1840), a review of Story's *Commentaries.*

Sage,[1] but little was added to what had already been said by Calhoun. His doctrines still stand as the most perfect formulation of the particularistic idea which played so large a part in the first two generations of the life of the Republic.

The nationalist theory of the Union, like the particularistic doctrine, did not develop immediately on the establishment of the Constitution. The first great champion of the cause was Daniel Webster, who contributed more to the strengthening of Union sentiment than any other one man. Webster's theory, however, was constitutional in nature, rather than philosophic. He attempted to show from the language of the Constitution itself, without much discussion of philosophic or historic considerations, that the Union was formed by a contract between individuals which resulted in the establishment of a supreme law and government, and that the states as such were not concerned in this agreement. "The people of the United States" he understood to mean the people of the whole Union, and not of the several states. The Union is not merely a compact between states to form a new Confederacy, but an agreement between individuals to form a national government. "It is established," said he, "by the people of the United States. It does not say by the people of the several states. It is as all the people of the

---

[1] *The Republic of Republics, or American Federal Liberty*, by P. C. Centz (Bernard J. Sage), 1865. See especially Chap. VI.

United States that they established the Constitution." Thus the Constitution of the United States was formed just as any state constitution; namely, by means of an agreement between individuals.

But a state constitution, although created originally by an agreement between individuals, was not regarded as a contract, but as a *law*. It was created by an agreement, but when that agreement was once made, there came into being a law proper. To use an analogy from private law, the agreement has become an "executed contract." "When the people agree to erect a government," said Webster, "and actually erect it, the thing is done, and the agreement is at an end. The compact is executed, and the end designed by it is attained." [1] The same argument was made by Story, who urged that a constitution falls under the definition of law as laid down by the eminent authority, Blackstone. "It is," said he, "a rule of action prescribed by the supreme power in the state, regulating the rights and duties of the whole community. It is a rule, as distinguished from a temporary or sudden order — permanent, uniform, and universal. It is also called a rule to distinguish it from a compact or agreement, for a contract is a promise proceeding from us, law is a command directed to us." [2]

[1] *Works*, III, 468 (1833). Reply to Calhoun.
[2] *Commentaries*, Sec. 339. Cf. the *Federalist*, No. 33. Nathan Dane, *General Abridgement and Digest of American Law* (1823–1829), Appendix, Sec. 14 ff.

On this basis it was denied that the Constitution of the United States could be regarded as a contract, and the assertion made that it must be considered as a law in the strict and proper sense of the term. It is, in fact, the supreme law of the land, and carries with it the very highest degree of obligation. The Union is not a mere treaty relation which may be denounced at will, but an agreement as obligatory and indissoluble as the social contract on which the whole fabric of society rests. Hence a state has no more right to question the authority and supremacy of the Constitution than a citizen of Massachusetts has to question the constitution of that state ; not even as much right, for the Constitution of the United States is the supreme law of the whole society. The individual may exert the original right of revolution, but he has no legal right to resist the constituted authorities of the nation.

Webster's doctrine was, then, that the Union is not a treaty relation between sovereign states, as Calhoun argued, or a contract between states by which the sovereignty of the contracting parties is diminished, as Madison contended ; but it is a *law*, resting on a social contract between individuals, and in which the states as such had no part. The Constitution is a government ordained and established by the people of the United States. In the expressive language of Webster, the Union is, " the association of the people under a constitution of government, uniting their highest interests, cementing their present enjoyments, and blending in an indivisible mass all their hopes for the future."

Although reasoning with great skill and eloquence from the strict letter of the Constitution, it is evident that Webster's real power did not come from his constitutional arguments as such. The very question over which he and Calhoun fought was whether the Union should be regarded and interpreted from the standpoint of constitutional law or of international law. If the states were never sovereign or had yielded up their sovereignty, then Webster's contention, that secession is an unconstitutional act, was valid. But to Calhoun, who looked upon the Union as, in ultimate analysis at least, a treaty between sovereign states, secession could not be regarded as unconstitutional, but at the worst as a breach of international law. The discussion, as they carried it on, amounted to an argument over the legality of an act, with one of the parties denying the existence of the law under which such validity was contested. Webster wished to make a purely legal argument on the question of legal sovereignty. Calhoun declined to make it purely a legal question, but at the same time disregarded the matter of fact.

When we consider the social and economic forces on which political forms are based, Webster had the stronger position, and for this reason. Calhoun was continually looking backward to a state of things that once perhaps may have existed, and he failed to observe that every year was carrying him farther away from his premise.   The fatal flaw in his argument was that, even granting his cherished hypothesis that the states were originally sovereign, it did not follow that they would continue to possess that fulness of power forever.[1]   On the other hand, Webster's hypothesis was looking to the future tense, and every year of nationalizing conditions was therefore strengthening his contention.   The great weight of his argument was due to the fact that even if his interpretation of "We, the people" was denied, it did not follow that his conclusions were not sound.   His power as a controversialist really came, not from the strength of his constitutional arguments as such, but from the fact that he followed a great current of public sentiment, springing from the impulse of nationality. He had with him the reasoned and unreasoned forces of an ethnic and geographic unity struggling toward self-expression.

---

[1] Calhoun recognized this at times. In reply to a suggestion that the best policy for the South would be separation, he said (1838) : "That is a natural and common conclusion, but those who make it up do not think of the difficulty involved in the word; how many bleeding pores must be taken up in passing the knife of separation through a body politic (in order to make two of one) which has been so long bound together by so many ties, political, social, and commercial. . . . We must remember it is the most difficult process in the world to make two people of one; and that there is no example of it, if we except the Jews."   *Correspondence,* 391.

The political theory of the nationalist school was not fully stated until the events of the Civil War had shown the strength of the Union sentiment. In this great struggle the latent force of the national spirit was at last decisively manifested, and the nature of the American Union settled beyond question. At the close of the four years of war there could be no uncertainty whether the United States should be ranked as a confederation or as a nation. There was, perhaps, room for question as to the exact powers possessed respectively by central and by local governments, but the great problem of nationality was settled beyond dispute.

This nationalist tendency was marked not only in the United States, but also in European countries, where similar unifying influences were at work. The struggles of the Hungarians, the Poles, the Greeks, the profound movements preceding the establishment of German and Italian national unity — all gave evidence of the vitality of the national principle in world politics. The right of each nationality to organization as a separate state was strongly emphasized; the doctrine of nationality was, indeed, the most conspicuous political dogma of the time. It is a significant fact that, within one decade, three great peoples — the United States, Germany, and Italy — established by "blood and iron" the fact of their national unity.

u

The nationalist theory in its later form differed materially from that advanced by Webster and his school. The doctrine was, in the first place, less strictly legal and constitutional in form; it contained a larger element of the philosophy that calls attention to the organic elements in the state, and correspondingly less of the contract theory of the eighteenth century; and finally it emphasized more strongly the unity and indivisibility of the sovereignty, and consequently the wholly subordinate position of the states.

In the first place, the form of the national argument was radically changed. Webster and his school had relied almost entirely upon legal and constitutional proofs that the United States is a nation : "We, the people of the United States"; "the supreme law of the land"; the provisions concerning the "general welfare" and all "necessary and proper" powers — these were the foundations upon which the cause rested. The plain language of the Constitution, it was said, is amply sufficient to show the national character of that instrument. The Constitution was made the central figure in the discussion, strict adherence to its requirements was demanded, and argument was not carried beyond its boundaries. In the course of the war, however, the point of view changed. The stern necessities of that great conflict led to a certain disregard for strictly legal forms, and provoked the expression of a determination to maintain the Union at whatever cost, while the whole war brought into view the unexpected strength of the Union sentiment. Although not abandoning the claim that the Constitution is a distinctly national instrument, the new school was not satisfied to rest with the literal and legal proof. They asserted that whatever the correct interpretation of the Constitution may be, the United States is and must be recognized as a nation. The argument was carried back of governmental forms, back of the written Constitution, so long a popular idol, to the primary source of power, the creator of these forms, the American nation as it exists behind the Constitution. This idea was expressed by Lincoln, when he made the assertion that "measures otherwise unconstitutional might become lawful by becoming indispensable to the preservation of the Constitution, through the preservation of the Nation." [1] Evidence of the same spirit is given by the statement of Fisher that, "if *the* Union and *the* government cannot be saved out of this terrible shock of war constitutionally, *a* Union and *a* government must be saved unconstitutionally." [2] The fact that there is an unwritten constitution of the nation, in contrast to the written Constitution of the government, was frequently pointed out. Jameson, for example, distinguished constitutions as "organic growths" from constitutions as "instruments of evidence." The former are the product of various

[1] *Works*, II, 508. [2] *The Trial of the Constitution*, 199 (1862).

social and political forces; the latter, "the result of an attempt to express in technical language some particular constitution, existing as an organic growth."[1] Brownson distinguished between the Constitution of the state or nation on the one hand, and the Constitution of the government on the other. The Constitution of the nation, the "congenital" or "providential" Constitution, as it is variously termed, consists in "the genius, the character, the habits, customs and wants of the people"; and upon this the governmental Constitution must rest if it is to operate successfully.[2] Mulford distinguished between the historical and the enacted constitution, one the result of the nation's historical development, the other the formula prescribed for public order at any given time.[3] Still more striking was the argument of Hurd, who took the ground that the effort to determine from the Constitution itself, whether the states or the United States is sovereign, is wholly futile, and must be so in the nature of the case.[4] Sovereignty, said he, does not proceed from or depend upon constitution

[1] J. A. Jameson, *Constitutional Conventions*, Sec. 63 (1866).

[2] O. A. Brownson, *The American Republic*, Chap. VII (1866).

[3] Elisha Mulford, *The Nation*, Chap. IX. (1870). A writer decidedly under the influence of the German Transcendentalists.

[4] John C. Hurd, *The Law of Freedom and Bondage* (1858); *The Theory of our National Existence* (1881); *The Union State* (1890). "Sovereignty cannot be an attribute of law, because, by the nature of things, law must proceed from sovereignty. By the preëxistence of a sovereignty, law becomes possible." *The Theory of our National Existence*, 97.

or law, but itself makes constitutions and laws. It is the creator, not the creature. Sovereignty is a matter of fact rather than of law, and hence it is to the facts we must look for an answer to the question.

With this group of thinkers, dominated by the spirit of nationality, and influenced by the philosophy of such writers as De Maistre [1] and Lieber, the tendency was to go back to the power that makes and unmakes constitutions. They were no longer satisfied to construe the language of a written document, but claimed the right to make an examination of the political, social, and economic forces which are the life and spirit of a state. They were no longer interpreters of law, but observers of the forces that make and unmake law.

Among those entertaining such views there was little question as to whether the sovereignty belonged to the individual states or to the Union. Judged by all the canons of distinction, the states could not be regarded as nations; this attribute must be reserved for the United States as a whole. The sovereignty was unhesitatingly attributed to the people of the nation. " Back of all the states," said Jameson, "and of all forms of government for either the states or the Union, we are to conceive of the nation, a political body, one and indivisible." [2] Brownson thought that by the

---

[1] A conspicuous representative of the reaction against the French Revolution. See his *Essai sur le principe générateur des constitutions politiques*, 1807.

[2] *Op. cit.* Sec. 51. See Secs. 30–31 on definition of a nation.

unwritten constitution the sovereignty rests with
"the people as a whole or the collective body" in
the modified organic sense, although by the written
constitution there is in fact no sovereignty, the
governmental powers being divided between the
local and the general governments. Mulford denounced the confederate principle in the language
of German transcendentalism, and declared that
the supreme power in the United States rested
only in the nation at large, and not in any commonwealth. On every hand the supremacy of the
Union was asserted in the strongest terms, and
the dignity of the states disparaged. This was a
legitimate conclusion from the great demonstration
of strength exhibited in the maintenance of national
authority and the preservation of the Union.

Although the defenders of the Union agreed
in vesting the sovereignty in the nation as contrasted with the individual states, there was not
entire harmony of opinion as to what part the
states occupied in the Union. On the one hand, it
was held that the sovereignty of the United States
is constituted regardless of and independent of the
states. Thus Jameson maintained that the nation
is "a political body, one and indivisible, made up
of the citizens of the United States, without distinction of age, sex, color, or condition of life." [1]

[1] Cf. Joel Tiffany, *A Treatise on Government and Constitutional
Law* (1867); J. N. Pomeroy, *Constitutional Law* (1868). For a discussion of the various theories as to the status of the commonwealths

This is the ultimate source of political power, out of which all governmental authority flows. Generally and regularly the sovereignty is exercised, it is true, through the groups called states; but back of these states there is a power by which they may be limited and restrained; namely, the sovereignty of the nation.[1]

On the other hand, the necessity of recognizing the states as integral parts of the Union was not less strongly urged. Brownson, although defending the sovereignty of the nation, declared that the political or sovereign people of the United States existed as states united and only in this way.[2] The sovereign nation was, therefore, the people as organized in states. To the same end Hurd contended for the recognition of the "states united." "The people," he declared, "or the nation holding sovereignty as distinct from the states, or the politically organized people of the states, was not even a myth" (until the Civil War). The states alone were not sovereign, the people were not sovereign, but this attribute belonged exclusively to the *states in Union.* This view seems to have also the sanction of the Supreme Court in its declaration: "The

which passed ordinances of secession, see W. A. Dunning, *Essays on the Civil War and Reconstruction.*

[1] *Constitutional Conventions*, Sec. 57; also *Political Science Quarterly*, V, 193. In the first edition of the *Constitutional Conventions*, Jameson spoke of a "quasi-sovereignty" in the states. Cf. Mulford, Pomeroy, and others.

[2] *American Republic*, 219.

states disunited might exist. Without the states in union, there could be no such political body as the United States." [1]

In this discussion, however, there is no claim that the individual states are sovereign. The issue is one as to how the national sovereignty is organized, whether it rests with the people of the whole nation, or with an association or group of states. The whole controversy really arises from a failure to distinguish clearly between the legal and the political side of sovereignty — a lesson which the events of the Civil War might have made clear. [2]

The new view of the Union differed in another respect from that of Webster, namely, in regard to the genesis of the United States. Webster thought of the Union as formed, in accordance with the political philosophy of the Revolutionary era, by means of a social contract between individuals. In the new national school, the tendency was to disregard the doctrine of the social contract, and to emphasize strongly the instinctive forces whose action and interaction produces a state. This dis-

---

[1] Lane County *v.* Oregon, 7 Wallace, 76 (1868). The court still continued to speak of a divided sovereignty. See United States *v.* Cruikshank, 92 U. S., 550 (1875); *Ex parte* Siebold, 100 U. S., 384 (1879). With this some of the commentators agree. See Cooley, *Constitutional Limitations* (3d edition, 1874), 1; Black, *Constitutional Law*, 21.

[2] On the question as to just where the sovereignty in a state is located, see Woodrow Wilson, *An Old Master*, 95; Willoughby, *The Nature of the State*, 293–294, 307.

tinction was developed by Lieber, who held that the great difference between "people" and "nation" lies in the fact that the latter possesses organic unity. "People" signifies merely "the aggregate of the inhabitants of a territory without any additional idea, at least favorable idea." "Nation," on the other hand, implies a homogeneous population, inhabiting a coherent territory; a population having a common language, literature, institutions, and "an organic unity with one another, as well as being conscious of a common destiny." [1] In general, the new school thought of the Union as organic rather than contractual in nature. Though not in all cases clearly expressed, it was evident, nevertheless, that the contract philosophy was in general disrepute, and that the overwhelming tendency was to look upon the nation as an organic product, the result of an evolutionary process.[2] It would, of course, be a gross exaggeration to say that all those who maintained the supremacy of the Union repudiated the social-contract theory, but it is necessary to recognize the fact that the nation was something different in the popular mind and in the philosophic mind from the "people" of earlier days. Nation carried with it the idea of an ethnic and geographic unity, constituted without the con-

[1] *Miscellaneous Writings*, II, 128.

[2] See Jameson, Secs. 66–67; also Brownson, Hurd, Mulford, Woolsey to the same effect. John Draper, in *Thoughts on the Future Civil Policy of America* (1865), represents the extreme development of the organic theory.

sent of any one in particular; "people" was understood to be a body formed by a contract between
certain individuals.   The very fact that the Union
was "pinned together with bayonets" was enough
to show that the doctrine of voluntary contract
had faded into the background.   The general
idea was that the United States, by virtue of the
community of race, interests, and geographical
location, *ought to be* and is a nation; and ought to
be held together by force, if no other means would
avail.   This was the feeling that underlay the
great national movement of 1861–1865, and it
could not fail to be reflected in the philosophy of
that time and in the succeeding interpretations of
that event.

It is also to be observed that in the new school
the doctrine of sovereignty was subjected to important modifications.   In the contest over national
supremacy, the idea of a divided sovereignty was
laid aside, and the unity and indivisibility of the
supreme power strongly affirmed.[1]   As at an earlier
time Calhoun rejected the compromise doctrine, so
now the nationalistic school abandoned the idea,
declaring that the sovereignty is one and indivisible, and at the same time that it belonged to the
nation.   The idea of sovereignty was first strongly
stated and clearly expounded by Lieber, in his
Political Ethics and later received general support.   In the narrower and legal sense, the rights

[1] Webster spoke of the states as partly sovereign. *Works*, III, 321.

of the states were admitted, but in respect to
the ultimate political sovereignty dispute practically came to an end. The events of the Civil
War firmly established the fact that the one and
indivisible sovereignty belongs to the nation, or
the Union as a whole.[1] Calhoun's idea of the
nature of sovereignty was accepted, but it was
applied in a manner wholly different from what
he had expected or intended.

The nationalistic theory assumes its most complete and scientific form at the hands of J. W.
Burgess. The concepts of nation, sovereignty,
and the theory of the "federal state," are in his
works clearly and definitely stated, for almost the
first time. "Nation" is defined as "a population
of an ethnic unity, inhabiting a geographic unity,"
and the application of this is made to various
nationalities. The national state is presented as
the highest product of recent political development, and is shown to be "for the present and dis-
cernible future, the organ of interpretation in last
instance of the order of life for its subjects."[2]

[1] See Jameson, Brownson, Hurd, Woolsey, Burgess, in general
agreement on this point. Brownson insisted that by the written
Constitution, there is really no sovereignty in the United States, *op.
cit.* Chap. XI. Philemon Bliss, *Of Sovereignty* (1885), declared
that sovereignty has no application to a federal state; in fact is
inapplicable to any constitutional state. See Lectures VII–XII.

[2] *Political Science and Comparative Constitutional Law* (1891);
"The American Commonwealth" in the *Political Science Quarterly*,
Vol. I; review of Laband's *Staatsrecht*, *Ibid.* Vol. III, 123.

The doctrine of sovereignty is also strongly stated. It is conceived as the "original, absolute, unlimited, universal power over the individual subject, and all associations of subjects;"[1] an essential quality of the state, indeed the most indispensable mark of statehood. "Really the state cannot be conceived," says Burgess, "without sovereignty, *i.e.* without unlimited power over its subjects; that is its very essence." There is no other power, no association or organization which can be conceived as limiting the state in its control over its subjects, for the authority which could exercise such power would itself be sovereign. It is true that the state may abuse its unlimited power, and wrong the individual under its control, but the national state is after all "the human organ least likely to do wrong." Moreover, this unlimited power on the part of the state necessitates no apology to civil liberty for its existence, since this very power is the real guaranty of and security for individual liberty; and hence the more completely and really sovereign the state is, the more secure is the liberty of the individual.[2]

From the principle that sovereignty is a unit, it follows that the so-called "federal state" is an impossibility. What seems such, is either a number of sovereign states, having an equal number of local governments and a common central government, or one sovereign state having a central

[1] *Political Science*, I, 52.   Cf. review of Laband.
[2] *Ibid.* I, 57.

government and several local governments.[1] There may be a federal system of government in which the sovereign state allots certain powers to the central government, and others to the local governments. But in this case the sovereignty is in no way divided, and there is no federal state. Sovereignty, it is urged, "is entire or not at all," and what remains to the former states under such a system of government is only "the residuary powers of government," which are by no means equivalent to sovereignty or any portion thereof. The sovereignty remains with the central state, undivided and indivisible.

Applying these principles to the United States, it is seen that the characteristics of a nation have been clearly evident here from the beginning, although not always accorded full recognition. The political system of the United States is a dual government, with the ultimate sovereignty resting in the nation.[2] The nation has organized the central government, indicated a sphere of individual liberty, and given to the commonwealth residuary powers of government. The so-called "states" are not sovereign or semi-sovereign, but merely organs of government for the nation. "It is no longer proper," says Burgess, "to call them states at

---

[1] *Ibid.* I, 79 ff.; II, 10 ff.

[2] Cf. W. W. Willoughby, *The Nature of the State*, especially the interesting discussion in Chap. X on the nature of the composite state.

all. It is in fact only a title of honor, without any corresponding substance." The commonwealths are, strictly speaking, neither sovereign nor states, and to call them either is inaccurate and misleading. Attention is called to the diminishing importance of the "states" in our political system, in contrast with the rapidly increasing power and influence of the modern city, and serious doubt is raised as to the ability of the "state" to hold its place as a unit of government in our political system, if the influences operating during the last half century continue uninterrupted.[1]

The development of American political theory in relation to the nature of the Union may now be summarized as follows. At the time of the adoption of the Constitution, and for a considerable period thereafter, it was believed that the Union was of a peculiar and anomalous character, and that the sovereignty, so far as vested in government, was divided between the states and the United States. The real sovereign was thought to be the "people," but whether this meant the

[1] On the real place of the states see *Political Science Quarterly*, Vol. I, "The American Commonwealth." On the relation between civil liberty and nationality, see *Political Science*, I, 224. Woodrow Wilson maintains that the members of the Union are still genuine states, although their "sphere is limited by the presiding and sovereign powers of a State superordinated to them . . . they have dominion; it has sovereignty." *An Old Master and other Political Essays* (1893), 94.

people of the United States as a whole or the
people of the several states was left undetermined.
As the contest between nationalism and states-
rights became more acute, this middle position was
abandoned by both parties. Calhoun contended
that the sovereign people were the people of the
several states, and that the sovereignty was, moreover, essentially indivisible. The states were hence
sovereign communities, and the general government had only the powers delegated to it by them.

On the other hand, the nationalist position was
defended by Webster, who declared that the Constitution was adopted by the people of the United
States as a whole, by means of an agreement as
binding as the social contract. After the war had
settled the vexed question of secession, the new
school of nationalists developed and strengthened
the earlier doctrine. The argument from the letter of the law was less emphasized and the consideration of social and political facts made more
conspicuous. The nation was declared supreme,
but this differed from the earlier " people " in that
the contract idea was largely eliminated, and the
organic and evolutionary character of the nation
given greater attention. Calhoun's doctrine of the
indivisibility of sovereignty was accepted, but sovereignty was claimed for the Union to the exclusion of the states, which were relegated to the
position of organs of the nation. Differences of
opinion appeared as to the exact location of the

sovereignty, whether with the nation as an aggregation of individuals or as an aggregation of states;
but the sovereignty of the Union was undisputed.

Looking back over the development of the
United States, a great growth in national spirit
and sentiment is at once observed. In 1787, the
general attitude toward the central government
was that of suspicion and distrust, if not of open
hostility. Liberty was regarded as local in character, and the states as the great champions of
the individual. The greater the power of the central government, the greater the danger to the
freedom of the citizen. "Consolidated" government was considered as equivalent to tyranny and
oppression. A century of national development has
reversed this attitude. The states are now looked
upon with more suspicion than is the national government, and it is frequently considered a matter
of congratulation when a given subject falls under
federal administration. It is no longer generally
feared that human liberty is menaced by the federal government, and protected only by the states.
Denunciation of the United States as a "consolidated fabric" of "aristocratical tyranny" is seldom heard, but certain states are sometimes
denominated as "rotten boroughs." The state has
in fact in many cases become a less important unit,
economically, politically, and socially than the city,
and, on the whole, the tendency of this time is over-
whelmingly national, both in fact and in theory.

CHAPTER VIII

RECENT TENDENCIES

IN the last half of the nineteenth century there appeared in the United States a group of political theorists differing from the earlier thinkers in respect to method and upon many important doctrines of political science. The new method was more systematic and scientific than that which preceded it, while the results reached showed a pronounced reaction from the individualistic philosophy of the early years of the century.[1]

Much of the credit for the establishment of this new school belongs to Francis Lieber, a German scientist who came to this country in 1827, and, as an educator and author, left a deep impress on the political thought of America. His *Manual of Political Ethics* (1838–1839) and *Civil Liberty and Self-Government* (1853) were the first systematic treatises on political science that appeared in the United States, and their influence was widespread.[2]

[1] The discussion of the two preceding chapters has partly anticipated the doctrines here considered.

[2] See also the *Miscellaneous Writings of Lieber*, edited by D. C. Gilman, also *Legal and Political Hermeneutics* (1837). For an account of Lieber's life, see *The Life and Letters of Francis Lieber*, by T. S. Perry; also *Francis Lieber*, by L. R. Harley.

Following Lieber, came a line of American political scientists, many of whom were trained in German schools, and all of whom had acquired a scientific method of discussing political phenomena. Among the most conspicuous figures in the new school are Theodore Woolsey, whose *Political Science* appeared in 1877, and John W. Burgess, who wrote, in 1890, *Political Science and Comparative Constitutional Law*, and a number of others who have contributed materially to the development of the subject.[1]

The method of these authorities has already been indicated, and need not be discussed at length. The significant fact about it is the change from the rather haphazard style of discussing political theory in earlier days to a more scientific way of approaching the questions of politics. A far more thorough knowledge of history and a broader comparative view of political institutions are conspicuous in the new system.

[1] Among these should be mentioned those writers who were conspicuous at the close of the Civil War, such as Brownson, Jameson, Mulford, Hurd, and others. Somewhat later come A. L. Lowell, *Essays on Government* (1892); Woodrow Wilson, *The State* (1889), and *An Old Master and Other Political Essays* (1893); F. J. Goodnow, especially in *Politics and Administration* (1900); W. W. Willoughby, *The Nature of the State* (1896), and *Social Justice* (1900); see also the works later cited. In the *Political Science Quarterly*, the *Annals of the American Academy of Political and Social Science*, the *American Historical Review*, the *Yale Review*, and the *American Journal of Sociology* are found numerous contributions to the literature of political science.

The doctrines of these men differ in many important respects from those earlier entertained. The individualistic ideas of the "natural right" school of political theory, indorsed in the Revolution, are discredited and repudiated. The notion that political society and government are based upon a contract between independent individuals and that such a contract is the sole source of political obligation, is regarded as no longer tenable. Calhoun and his school had already abandoned this doctrine, while such men as Story had seen the need of extensive qualification of it. Objections to the social contract were strongly urged by Lieber,[1] and were later more fully and clearly stated by others. In Lieber's opinion, the "state of nature" has no basis in fact. Man is essentially a social creature, and hence no artificial means for bringing him into society need be devised. Lieber condemned the contract theory as generally held, on the ground that it was both artificial and inadequate. Such an explanation of the origin of the state can be regarded as true only in the sense that every political society is composed of individuals who recognize the existence of mutual rights and duties. Only in the sense that there is a general recognition of these reciprocal claims can we say that the state is founded on contract; and this, of course, is far from what the doctrine is ordinarily taken to mean. As a matter of fact,

---

[1] *Political Ethics*, I, 288 ff. (2d edition, 1890).

the state may originate, and has originated, Lieber said, in a variety of ways, as, for example, through force, fraud, consent, religion.

Still more strongly is the opposition to the social-contract theory stated by Burgess. The hypothesis of an original contract to form the state is, as he reasons, wholly contrary to our knowledge of the historical development of political institutions. The social-contract theory assumes that "the idea of the state with all its attributes is consciously present in the minds of the individuals proposing to constitute the state, and that the disposition to obey law is universally established." [1] These conditions, history shows, are not present at the beginning of the political development of a people, but are the result of long growth and experience. This theory therefore cannot account for the origin of the state. Its only possible application is in changing the form of the state, or in cases when a state is planted upon new territory by a population already politically educated.

In the refusal to accept the contract theory as the basis for government, practically all the political scientists of note agree. The old explanation no longer seems sufficient, and is with practical

[1] *Political Science*, I, 62. With Burgess compare Woolsey, Brownson, Jameson, Wilson, Mulford, Willoughby, to the same effect. See the comprehensive discussion in Willoughby, *The Nature of the State*, Chaps. II–VI.

unanimity discarded.[1] The doctrines of natural law and natural rights have met a similar fate. In Lieber's political philosophy, it is true, the concept of natural law was still defended. The law of nature he defined as "the body of rights which we deduce from the essential nature of man."[2] The great axiom of natural law is, "I exist as a human being; therefore, I have a right to exist as a human being." Under this natural law, there are certain natural rights, or as Lieber preferred to call them, "primordial rights,"[3] which are inherent in the individual and inalienable by him. But even Lieber, with his leaning toward the old theory, did not

[1] F. M. Taylor, in *The Right of the State to be* (1891), defends a concept of natural law.

[2] *Political Ethics*, I, 68.

[3] *Ibid.* I, 177. Cf. Woolsey, *Political Science*, Vol. I, Chap. I. In his *Civil Liberty and Self-Government* Lieber distinguished between what he called "Anglican" liberty and "Gallican" liberty. The Anglican idea of liberty is that of a sphere of immunity from interference, protected by guaranties "at certain points where the experience of the race has shown the individual to be most in danger of attack." The Gallican idea is that all must share equally in voting power, and that the authority of a government based on universal suffrage may be indefinite in extent. One idea is that men are free when they are protected in a certain sphere against all encroachment, private or public; the other idea is that freedom consists in equal suffrage, no matter what the character of the government so based may be. This he thought was the great difference between the English and the French idea of liberty. It is interesting to observe that Benj. Constant, a famous French publicist of the early part of the century, made the same comparison between the liberty of the ancients and that of the moderns, among whom he included, of course, the French.

interpret the doctrine of natural rights as the seventeenth and eighteenth century revolutionists understood it, and this he was very careful to point out.

By the later thinkers the idea that men possess inherent and inalienable rights of a political or quasi-political character which are independent of the state, has been generally given up. It is held that these natural rights can have no other than an ethical value, and have no proper place in politics. "There never was, and there never can be," says Burgess, "any liberty upon this earth and among human beings, outside of state organization." [1] In speaking of natural rights, therefore, it is essential to remember that these alleged rights have no political force whatever, unless recognized and enforced by the state. It is asserted by Willoughby that "natural rights" could not have even a moral value in the supposed "state of nature"; they would really be equivalent to force and hence have no ethical significance. [2]

In this connection it is interesting to notice the restatement of the theory of "natural rights" as made by Giddings. [3] Disclaiming any connection with the earlier forms of this theory, he under-

[1] *Political Science*, I, 88.

[2] See *The Nature of the State*, 109 ; see also *Social Justice*, Chap. VIII. Cf. C. G. Tiedeman, *The Unwritten Constitution of the United States*, Chap. VI ; Lyman Abbott, *The Rights of Man*.

[3] Franklin H. Giddings, *Principles of Sociology*, 418–419 (1st edition, 1896). Cf. Spencer, *Principles of Sociology ;* E. A. Ross, *Social Control*, 421.

stands by natural rights those which are natural in the scientific sense of the term. In this field " natural " means, "that which is, on the whole, in harmony with the conditions of existence." On this basis, Giddings defines natural rights as, " socially necessary norms of right, enforced by natural selection in the sphere of social relations." Natural rights, as thus defined, are the foundation of both political and moral rights, and ultimately determine the character of both. This definition, it will be observed, is as destructive of natural rights in the ethical sense as of natural rights in the political sense.

The present tendency, then, in American political theory is to disregard the once dominant ideas of natural rights and the social contract, although it must be admitted that the political scientists are more agreed upon this point than is the general public. The origin of the state is regarded, not as the result of a deliberate agreement among men, but as the result of historical development, instinctive rather than conscious; and rights are considered to have their source not in nature, but in law. This new point of view involves no disregard of or contempt for human liberty, but only a belief that the earlier explanation and philosophy of the state was not only false but dangerous and misleading.

The modern school has, indeed, formulated a new idea of liberty, widely different from that taught in the early years of the Republic. The

"Fathers" believed that in the original state of nature all men enjoy perfect liberty, that they surrender a part of this liberty in order that a government may be organized, and that therefore the stronger the government, the less the liberty remaining to the individual. Liberty is, in short, the natural and inherent right of all men; government the necessary limitation of this liberty. Calhoun and his school, as it has been shown, repudiated this idea, and maintained that liberty is not the natural right of all men, but only the reward of the races or individuals properly qualified for its possession. Upon this basis, slavery was defended against the charge that it was inconsistent with human freedom, and in this sense and so applied, the theory was not accepted outside the South. The mistaken application of the idea had the effect of delaying recognition of the truth in what had been said until the controversy over slavery was at an end.

The Revolutionary idea of the nature of liberty was never realized in actual practice, and recent political events and political philosophy have combined to show that another theory of liberty has been generally accepted. The new doctrine is best stated by Burgess. By liberty he understands "a domain in which the individual is referred to his own will, and upon which government shall neither encroach itself nor permit encroachments from any other quarter." Such a sphere of action is necessary for the welfare and progress both of state and of individual. It is of vital importance to notice, however, that liberty is not a natural right which belongs to every human being without regard to the state or society under which he lives. On the contrary, it is logically true and may be historically demonstrated that "the state is the source of individual liberty."[1] It is the state that makes liberty possible, determines what its limits shall be, guarantees and protects it. In Burgess's view, then, men do not begin with complete liberty and organize government by sacrificing certain parts of this liberty, but on the contrary they obtain liberty only through the organization of political institutions. The state does not take away from civil liberty, but is the creator of liberty — the power that makes it possible.

Liberty, moreover, is not a right equally enjoyed by all. It is dependent upon the degree of civilization reached by the given people, and increases as this advances. The idea that liberty is a natural right is abandoned, and the inseparable connection between political liberty and political capacity is strongly emphasized. After an examination of the principle of nationality, and the characteristic qualities of various nations or races, the conclusion is drawn that the Teutonic nations are particularly endowed with political capacity. Their mission in the world is the political civilization of mankind.

[1] *Political Science*, I, 175.

From this as a premise are deduced further conclusions of the utmost importance.[1]   The first of these is that in a state composed of several nationalities, the Teutonic element should never surrender the balance of power to the others.   Another is that the Teutonic race can never regard the exercise of political power as a right of man, but it must always be their policy to condition the exercise of political rights on the possession of political capacity.   A final conclusion is that the Teutonic races must civilize the politically uncivilized.   They must have a colonial policy.   Barbaric races, if incapable, may be swept away; and such action "violates no rights of these populations which are not petty and trifling in comparison with its transcendent right and duty to establish political and legal order everywhere."   On the same principle, interference with the affairs of states not wholly barbaric, but nevertheless incapable of effecting political organization for themselves, is fully justified.   Jurisdiction may be assumed over such a state, and political civilization worked out for those who are unable to accomplish this unaided.   This propaganda of political civilization, it is asserted, is not only the right and privilege, but the mission and duty, the very highest obligation incumbent on the Teutonic races, including the United States. Such action is not unwarrantable or unjustifiable interference with the affairs of those who should

[1] *Political Science*, I, 44 *et seq.*

rightly be left unmolested, but is the performance
of the part marked out for the Teutonic nations
in the world's development.[1]

Closely related to the theory of liberty is the
doctrine as to the purpose or function of the state.
In the days of the Revolution, it was thought that
the end of the political society is to protect the life,
liberty, and property of its citizens, and beyond this
nothing more. The duty of the state was summed
up in the protection of individual rights, in harmony
with the individualistic character of the philosophy
of that day. In the theory of Lieber, this idea was
broadened out, and, as he phrased it, the duty
of the state is to do for man : first, what he
cannot do alone ; second, what he ought not to do
alone ; and third, what he will not do alone.[2] In
more recent times there has been in America a decided tendency to react against the early " protection theory " of government, and to consider
that the aim of the state is not limited to the maintenance of law and order in the community and

[1] It is a striking fact that within less than a decade the United
States embarked on a colonial policy, invoking in justification the
very principles which have just been analyzed. In the extended
discussions of the colonial policy of the United States during the
past four years, there has been no clearer formulation of the dominant theory than this. Burgess himself believes that the United
States is not yet ready for the propaganda of political civilization,
but should devote itself to its own problems of government and
liberty. See *infra*, p. 318.

[2] *Political Ethics*, I, Chap. V.

defence against foreign foes. In the new view, the state acts not only for the individual as such, but in the interests of the community as a whole. It is not limited to the negative function of preventing certain kinds of action, but may positively advance the general welfare by means and measures expressly directed to that end. This opinion is shared by such authorities as Woolsey, Burgess, Wilson, Willoughby and others. To these thinkers it appears that the duty of the state is not and cannot be limited to the protection of individual interests, but must be regarded as extending to acts for the advancement of the general welfare in all cases where it can safely act, and that the only limitations on governmental action are those dictated by experience or the needs of the time.

Woolsey took the position that the state cannot be limited to restraining individuals from injuring each other, but may justly act positively for the general welfare. "The sphere of the state," he said, "*may* reach as far as the nature and needs of man and of men reach;" and this each people decides for itself in accordance with its own peculiar conditions. In general the action of the state falls under four groups: 1, the redress of wrongs; 2, the prevention of wrongs; 3, a degree of care for the outward welfare of the community, as in respect to industry, roads, and health; 4, the cultivation of the spiritual nature, "by educating the religious nature, the moral sense, the taste, the in-

tellect." [1] The general limitation on the power of
the state is that there shall be no act in restraint
of the individual, except where there is imperative
reason for such restriction. He also enumerates
a series of individual rights which no just government ought to take away.

Woodrow Wilson asserts that the objects of government are the objects of organized society. The
great end for which society exists is "mutual aid
to self-development," and this purpose, therefore, is
the proper function of government. With particular reference to modern industrial conditions, a
distinction is drawn between what is termed " interference" on the part of the state, and what is
called "regulation," by which is meant an " equali-
zation of conditions in all branches of endeavor."
The limit of state activity is that of "necessary
coöperation " — the point at which such enforced
coöperation becomes a convenience rather than an
imperative necessity. This line is difficult to
draw, but may nevertheless be drawn. In general, we may lay down the rule that " the state
should do nothing which is equally possible under
equitable conditions to optional associations." [2]

A still broader view is that taken by Burgess in
his discussion of the ends of the state. These may
be considered, he says, under three heads : the

[1] *Political Science*, Book II, Chap. IV, "Sphere and Ends of the
State."

[2] *The State*, Sec. 1273 ff.

primary, the secondary, and the ultimate. The ultimate end of the state is defined as the " perfection of humanity, the civilization of the world; the perfect development of the human reason and its attainment to universal command over individualism; the apotheosis of man." [1] This end can be realized, however, only when a world-state is organized, and for this, mankind is not yet ready. Men must first be organized into national states, based on the principle of nationality. The proximate ends of the state are the establishment of government and liberty. The state must first of all establish peace and order; and in the next place mark out a sphere of liberty for the individual and later for associations. These are then the great ends of the state; the establishment of government and of liberty, so that the national genius may find proper expression; and, finally, the perfection of humanity. These objects must be followed, moreover, in an historical order which cannot be successfully reversed. Government must precede liberty, government and liberty must precede the final purpose for which the state exists. In the present stage of development, only the realization of government and liberty through the national state are proper objects of state activity. Beyond this broad outline Burgess makes no other attempt to mark out the limits of the operation either of state or of government.

[1] *Political Science*, Vol. I, Book II, Chap. IV.

An interesting study in this direction has been made by Willoughby.[1] The functions of the state are classified into three groups, of which the first contains those powers which concern the life of the state and the preservation of internal order, the second those which are concerned with human liberty, and the third those which have to do with the general welfare. A second method of classifying the aims of the state is to divide them into the essential and the non-essential functions. The essential functions concern the protection of the state against foreign interference, the preservation of the national life, and the maintenance of internal order. The non-essential functions include the "economic, industrial, and moral interests of the people." They are assumed by the state not because they are necessary but because they are advisable. The non-essential functions are subdivided into the socialistic and the non-socialistic. The first class, the socialistic, includes only activities which could be exercised by the people if left to private initiative, as the ownership and operation of railroads, or telegraph and telephone systems. The non-socialistic functions are "those which, if not assumed by the state, would not be exercised at all;" as, for example, such work as that performed by educational and labor bureaus. It is denied that any limit can be set to governmental

[1] *The Nature of the State*, Chap. XII. See also *Social Justice*, Chap. IX.

activity, and the contention is made that "each function must rest on its own utilitarian basis." This specific determination belongs to the domain of government rather than of political theory. Willoughby predicts, however, that with the development of civilization and the increasing complexity of industrial interests, the activity of the state must continue to expand.

Among the authorities on political economy, the early idea of *laissez faire*, at least in its extreme form, has been subjected to severe criticism, and in general has been abandoned. The new position is a mean between socialism and extreme individualism. Francis A. Walker characterized the situation when he spoke of "those of us who discerned the coming of a storm and removed ourselves and our effects from the lower ground of an uncompromising individualism to positions somewhat more elevated and seemingly secure." [1] He declared, and this statement is typical of the general attitude of the economists, that he believed "a large practical gain to the order of society and the happiness of its constituent members would in the long result accrue from the interposition of the state." [2] Every proposal, however, for the ex-

[1] *Discussions in Economics and Statistics* (1899), I, 344.

[2] *Ibid.* II, 271. In the American Economic Association (1885) there was an interesting discussion on this point. Among other statements, that of Edmund J. James was significant : " We do not regard [the state] as a merely negative factor, the influence of which is most happy when it is smallest, but we recognize that some of

tension of the powers and duties of the state should be subjected to careful scrutiny, and the burden of proof should be thrown upon those who advocate the innovation. Furthermore, no changes should be made in the direction of state regulation for transient causes or doubtful objects. The principle of action would seem to be to consider each case on its own merits, without reference to the question of individualism or socialism. In cases where the economic principle of competition appears to be threatened, the interference of the state seems to be most cheerfully welcomed.[1]

From a consideration of these various opinions, it is evident that the modern idea as to what is the purpose of the state has radically changed since the most necessary functions of a civilized society can be performed only by the state, and some others most efficiently by the state; that the state, in a word, is a permanent category of economic life, and not merely a temporary crutch which may be cast away when society becomes more perfect." *Publications of the American Economic Association*, Vol. I, 26.

An interesting attempt to lay down definite principles respecting the function of government has been made by H. C. Adams, in *The Relation of the State to Industrial Activity* (1887). His fundamental proposition is that neither the English idea of the individual as supreme, nor the German idea of the state as supreme, is the correct one. Both state activity and individual activity are in reality functions of *society* — the "living and growing organism — the ultimate thing disclosed by analysis of human relations." The point of view in the discussions of the sphere and duty of government should be therefore that of the society, rather than that of the individual or the state.

[1] See in this connection Richard T. Ely, *Socialism and Social Reform* (1894).

Y

the days of the "Fathers." They thought of the function of the state in a purely individualistic way; this idea modern thinkers have abandoned, and while they have not reached the paternalistic or socialistic extreme, have taken the broader social point of view. The "protection" theory of the state is on the decline; that of the general welfare is in the ascendant. The exigencies of modern industrial and urban life have forced the state to intervene at so many points where an immediate individual interest is difficult to show, that the old doctrine has been given up for the theory that the state acts for the general welfare. It is not admitted that there are no limits to the action of the state, but on the other hand it is fully conceded that there are no "natural rights" which bar the way. The question is now one of expediency rather than of principle. In general it is believed that the state should not do for the individual what he can do as well for himself, but each specific question must be decided on its own merits, and each action of the state justified, if at all, by the relative advantages of the proposed line of conduct.

At yet another point the drift away from the Revolutionary theory is evident; namely, in relation to the division of governmental powers. The generally accepted theory since the eighteenth century has been that all governmental powers may be divided into the legislative, the executive, and the judicial; that in every free government these powers should be carefully separated and a distinct set of officers should administer each class of them. This has long been regarded as a "fundamental" of political theory and of constitutional law as well.[1] Viewing the situation from the standpoint of administrative law, however, a new line of division has been recently drawn by Goodnow.[2] In *Politics and Administration* Goodnow criticises the theory of the tripartite division of governmental powers as an "unworkable and unapplicable rule of law," and proposes to substitute another classification in its place. The primary functions of the state may be divided, he maintains, into politics, "the expression of the will of the state," and administration, "the execution of that will." "Politics" includes constitution-making, legislation, selection of governmental officers, and the control of the function of executing the will of the state. This function of politics is discharged by constitutional conventions, legislatures, the judiciary, and the political parties. "Administration," on the other hand, may be divided into two classes: the administration of justice, commonly called the judicial authority, and the administration of govern-

[1] See William Bondy, "The Separation of Governmental Powers," in *Columbia Studies in History, Economics, and Public Law*, Vol. V.

[2] Frank J. Goodnow, *Politics and Administration* (1900), *Comparative Administrative Law* (1893).

ment, which includes what is ordinarily termed the executive authority, together with other functions of a quasi-judicial or semi-scientific or statistical character.[1]

The method of control over the administration is discussed, and the highly decentralized system adopted in Revolutionary times is subjected to severe criticism. The conclusion drawn is that the present administrative system of the various states should be much more centralized and consolidated than at present; and in the second place that the political party should receive legal recognition as a governmental organ. The fear of centralization which our fathers entertained is, he holds, under modern conditions no longer reasonable. It is a " battle-cry suitable only to an age that has already passed away," [2] — " a bogie which has been conjured up by designing persons conscious that a proper organization of our administrative system will work to their disadvantage." [3]   The party, furthermore, must no longer be regarded as a purely voluntary association but as a political body subject to public regulation and control, constituting,

[1] *Politics and Administration*, Chaps. II, IV.

[2] *Ibid.* 261.

[3] *Ibid.* 130. Cf. Ernst Freund, "The Law of Administration in America," in the *Political Science Quarterly*, Vol. IX. See also "Public Administration in Massachusetts," by Robert H. Whitten, in *Columbia University Studies*, Vol. VIII, No. 4; "The Centralization of Administration in New York State," by John A. Fairlie, *Ibid.* Vol. IX, No. 3.

in fact, a part of the government. In this way the party may be made responsible, and the danger, that under a more centralized system party bosses would wield still greater power, may be averted.[1]

Another interesting phase of American political theory is the effort made by numerous thinkers to distinguish between "state" and "government." From the earliest days of the Republic, the difference between "people" and "government" has been emphasized, and the assertion made that sovereignty rests with the "people" as distinguished from the "government." This idea was more systematically stated by Lieber, who made a distinction between state and government. The state in his opinion is the jural or political society which the whole community constitutes. The government is the instrument through which the political society acts, when it does not act directly.[2]

In the theory of Burgess, this distinction has been made a cardinal principle of political science and of public law. The state is " a particular portion of mankind viewed as an organized unit." The government is a particular form of organization through which the state acts. In early times, he points out, there was no clear distinction made between the state and the government; they were,

---

[1] On the function of political parties, see H. J. Ford, *The Rise and Growth of American Politics*, Chaps. XXIII–XXV.

[2] *Political Ethics*, I, 238; Brownson, *op. cit.* 174–175.

in fact, blended in the person of the king; but in modern times the distinction has become clearly evident, and the government need not now be confused with the political society. In the United States, in particular, this has been recognized and embodied in our system of public law. Here we have a separate and distinct organization for state and government in their several capacities.

Burgess makes several important applications of this doctrine to political problems. In the classification of political systems, for example, the recognition of this distinction between state and government is of great advantage. The difficulty involved in democratic Cæsarism is on this basis easily explained, for such a system is really a combination of democratic state with monarchic government. In the same way we may have a democratic state with an aristocratic government, or an aristocratic state with a monarchic government. Since the state and the government are distinct, any combination of monarchic, aristocratic, and democratic elements is possible.

Application of this idea is also made by Burgess to the vexed question of sovereignty. The strongest objection to the recognition of the absoluteness of sovereignty arises, it is pointed out, from the general failure of publicists to distinguish clearly between "state" and "government." One fears to place unlimited power in the hands of the ordinary government, and failing to distinguish between this and the state, declares against supreme power in general. In strict analysis, however, the " government is not the sovereign organization of the state. Back of the government lies the constitution and back of the constitution the original sovereign state which ordains the constitution both of government and liberty." Recognizing the fact that the sovereignty belongs not with the ordinary government or administration, but with the state in supreme organization, the admission of the character of the ultimate power presents fewer and less formidable difficulties. This double organization is a feature in which American public law has advanced beyond that of the states of Europe, since here is to be found an organization of the government in its local and central branches, and then, above these governments, the organization of the state in its supreme and all-controlling capacity. Thus, in our political system, government and state are distinctly organized, and have distinct methods of action.[1]

The reflection of American political theorists on the problems of modern democracy has not up to the present time taken on scientific form. In fact,

[1] A similar distinction is made by Woodrow Wilson, although in his theory the line is drawn between " society " and " government," while the terms " state " and " government " are used interchangeably. Society, in his phrase, is termed an " organism," and government is characterized as an " organ." *The State*, Secs. 1160, 1269-1273. Cf. Willoughby, *The Nature of the State*, 8. Wil-

the two great studies of American democracy have
been made respectively by a Frenchman and an
Englishman : *Democracy in America* by De Tocqueville and *The American Commonwealth* by James
Bryce.   There has been no profound and compre-
hensive study of the facts and the philosophy of
modern democracy by an American thinker.   In
recent years, however, considerable attention has
been given to the nature and meaning of democratic institutions, and there have been numerous
discussions centering around the problems of
democracy.   The weakness of popular government
in our large cities has been considered by a number of thinkers ; among the most conspicuous is
Godkin, in his *Unforeseen Tendencies of Democracy*
and *Problems of Modern Democracy*.[1]   The relation
of democratic government to modern industrial com-
binations has been considered by Moses in his suggestive sketch on *Democracy and Social Growth*.[2]
The compatibility between democracy and colonial
government has been discussed, among others, by
Giddings in *Democracy and Empire*.   Eliot has
pointed out certain contributions made by Ameri-

loughby distinguishes between state and government on the ground
that, strictly speaking, state is "an abstract term," whereas government is "emphatically concrete" — a distinction corresponding, he
says, to that between a person and his bodily frame.   For his criticism of Burgess's theory, see *op. cit.* 206, note.

[1] E. L. Godkin, *Unforeseen Tendencies of Democracy* (1898),
Problems of Modern Democracy (1896).

[2] Bernard J. Moses, *Democracy and Social Growth* (1898).

can democracy to civilization,[1] and Lowell has shown the relation between democracy and the constitution.[2] Numerous other interesting and useful contributions have been made, but in none or all of them is there found that complete study of modern or American democracy which it is desirable to have.

Within the last few decades, no little attention has been given in America to the study of social forces in the general sense of the term. These investigations have been directed primarily to the observation and classification of social facts, but incidentally contributions have been made to the solution of certain problems of political theory. Attention has already been called to the restatement of the doctrine of natural rights at the hands of Giddings.[3] In his *Dynamic Sociology* (1883), Lester F. Ward[4] lays great emphasis on a more scientific direction of social forces. The science of society, he urges, should lead up to the art of society, which in his terminology is known as " collective telesis." There ought to be a transformation of

[1] Charles William Eliot, *American Contributions to Civilization* (1897).

[2] A. L. Lowell, *Essays on Government* (1892). See also Gamaliel Bradford, *The Lesson of Popular Government* (1899); Jane Addams, *Democracy and Social Ethics* (1902); J. H. Hyslop, *Democracy, A Study of Government* (1899); David Starr Jordan, *Imperial Democracy* (1899). [3] See *ante*, p. 310.

[4] See also "Collective Telesis," in the *American Journal of Sociology*, Vol. II.

government from its present unscientific and un-progressive methods to "a central academy of science which shall stand in the same relation to the control of men, in which a polytechnic insti-tute stands to the control of nature." Government would be then, in truth, "the legislative application of sociological principles," and this is what he understands by "sociocracy" — "the scientific control of social forces by the collective mind of society for its advantage."

Following the same general method, John R. Commons has worked out a somewhat elaborate account of the sociological view of sovereignty which he states, of course, in social rather than political terms.[1] The most suggestive of these contributions, however, is that made by Ross in his *Social Control*, 1901.[2] Believing that a study of social control should not be limited to an examina-tion of laws alone, Ross has instituted a compre-hensive study of all social forces that go to make up the control of the group over the individual. To this end the work is divided into a study of the *grounds* of control, the *means* of control, and the *system* of control. Under the grounds of control are discussed the rôle of sympathy, sociability, the sense of justice, and of individual reaction as bases of social order. Under the means of control, there

[1] *American Journal of Sociology*, Vol. V.

[2] E. A. Ross, *Social Control, A Survey of the Foundations of Order*.

is given a description and analysis of the various forces, by means of which the society obtains social obedience and effects social control. These instrumentalities are partly legal, as law, belief, ceremony, education, illusion; and partly ethical, as public opinion, suggestion, art, and social valuation. The complicated machinery for producing obedience on the part of the individual to the will of the group is subjected to careful examination, with results that are at times startling. Ross maintains, however, that the full understanding of these subtle methods need not lead to any such disastrous consequences as those drawn by the Anarchists. Simply because the "X-ray shows control in all social tissues and the spectroscope reveals the element of collective ascendancy in almost every culture product," it does not follow that all these tissues and products must be destroyed. A full comprehension of the facts of social control, while not wholly quieting to the individual thus controlled, need not lead to rebellion against this restraint.

Under the system of control are examined such topics as class control, the vicissitudes of social control, the limits and criteria of control. The assertion is made that in the future the control of society will be secured largely through the instrumentality of education — the best method of insurance against the spirit of disobedience in the individual. In the same connection an effort is made to lay down certain canons or principles of

social interference.   Of these the most significant
are : " Social interference should not be so pater-
nal as to check the self-extinction of the morally
ill-constituted ; " and, " Social interference should
not so limit the struggle for existence as to nullify
the selective process." [1]

In conclusion, it appears that recent political
theory in the United States shows a decided tendency away from many doctrines that were held by
the men of 1776.   The same forces that have led
to the general abandonment of the individualistic
philosophy of the eighteenth century by political
scientists elsewhere have been at work here and
with the same result.   The Revolutionary doctrines
of an original state of nature, natural rights, the
social contract, the idea that the function of the
government is limited to the protection of person
and property, — none of these finds wide acceptance
among the leaders in the development of political
science.   The great service rendered by these doctrines, under other and earlier conditions, is fully
recognized, and the presence of a certain element
of truth in them is freely admitted, but they are no
longer generally received as the best explanation
for political phenomena.   Nevertheless, it must be
said that thus far the rejection of these doctrines
is a scientific tendency rather than a popular
movement.   Probably these ideas continue to be

[1] Chap. XXX.

articles of the popular creed, although just how far they are seriously adhered to it is difficult to ascertain. As far as the theory of the function of government is concerned, it would seem that the public has gone beyond the political scientists, and is ready for assumption of extensive powers by the political authorities. The public, or at least a large portion of it, is ready for the extension of the functions of government in almost any direction where the general welfare may be advanced, regardless of whether individuals as such are benefited thereby or not. But in regard to the conception of natural right and the social-contract theory, the precise condition of public opinion is, at the present time, not easy to estimate.

CHAPTER IX

In conclusion of this study, a few words may be said upon the general characteristics of American political theory. It is evident from the preceding chapters that thus far there has been no remarkable development of political philosophy in the United States. Until recently, there has been no attempt at all at systematic discussion of the problems of politics, and, although the new school has accomplished much, it has not yet developed a body of typical American political theory. It would be putting it strongly to say that there is no American political theory, but it is certainly true that very few contributions to systematic politics have been made by the great republic of the New World. Many of the characteristic features even of our own political system have received comparatively little attention; as, for example, democracy as an all-pervading influence in society and state, the rule of the majority, written constitutions, the relation between church and state. These ideas seem to be so generally accepted that argument or discussion is regarded as superfluous. They are articles of political faith, received with implicit confidence and trust.

In general, American political theory has been struck off in connection with controversies over specific subjects. The rights of man, the consent of the governed, the right of revolution, were discussed in relation to the Revolution of 1776. The question of aristocracy, artificial and natural, was associated with the struggle between the Federalists and their opponents; the effort to restrict the spread of slavery led to the discussion of the proper relation between unequal races under conditions which render coexistence on the same soil necessary. The great problem of the character of the Union gave rise to the examination of the nature of federal government, the essential marks of sovereignty, and the elements of nationality. In recent days, the territorial expansion of the United States again raises the problem of the consent of the governed, and the right relation between races of widely different capacity. But in all these instances the constitutional or legal aspects of the problem have been most freely and most fully discussed, while the principles of political science have been the object of far less attention. The nature of the Union, for example, was much more thoroughly and ably treated from the constitutional point of view than from that of political science; or, to take another case, the constitutional phases of slavery extension were much more carefully studied than the question of human rights or of race relations.

The causes of this scarcity of political theory are various. It may be urged that the lack of theory is due to the tendency of the American or the Englishman toward action rather than reflection — to be practical rather than philosophical. In this connection it is well to remember, however, that it was an English thinker, John Locke, who worked out the fundamental principles of the English, American, and French revolutions of the seventeenth and eighteenth centuries. Another Englishman, Edmund Burke, was the author of the most effective work written against those principles, and yet another Englishman, Thomas Hobbes, framed one of the strongest theoretical arguments in favor of absolutism. A more plausible explanation than inability to think abstractly is found in the argument that the tendencies of modern democracy are not yet fully enough developed to make possible the formulation of political theory respecting these new conditions. From this point of view, the development of a typical American theory is yet to come.

It may further be questioned how far American political theory is dependent upon foreign sources for its inspiration, and to which of these sources we are especially indebted. Some reference has been made to this in the discussion of the various schools, but a summary of these influences may not be inappropriate at this point. The great reservoir from which the Fathers drew was the

English political theory of the preceding century —the ideas of Sydney, Locke, and the English Whig revolutionists. This was the origin of the fundamental doctrines to which the Patriots adhered. This body of ideas has had in the past, and still has, a great hold on the political thought of the American. Also of great influence on the course of American political speculation have been the individualistic theories of Mill and Spencer, which have been widely read and widely accepted. Among jurists, the theory of John Austin and the school of positive law has been the subject of frequent discussion, and has been very influential.

Of French thinkers by far the strongest influence exerted on American theory was that of Montesquieu, through the famous doctrine of the tripartite division of governmental powers. This proposition was readily taken up from the first, and remains to this day scarcely contested. The French Revolution gave a great impulse to the democratic movement in America, as did the revolutions of 1830 and 1848, yet few of the doctrines of that day took deep root in American soil. Destutt de Tracy was recommended by Jefferson, but never was highly influential. One of the reactionaries against the French Revolution, De Maistre, has been sometimes referred to in the controversy over the nature of the Union, because of his statement of the theory that constitutions can-

z

not be made offhand, but are the result of growth through long periods. The influence of Comte upon social and political science must be included in the summary of French influence upon American thought. Upon the whole, it is evident that American theory has pursued its course without much regard to the political ideas current among the French. Doubtless the Revolution of 1789 and the succeeding revolutions helped to strengthen the democratic impulse and tendency, for the influence of these movements was world-wide. But the immediate and direct effect of these events on American political thought, it is not easy to discover. The influence came in the form of a general stimulus rather than of particular doctrines or principles.

In recent years the influence of the German political scientists has been most pronounced. This influence began with the work of Francis Lieber as an instructor in American schools and an investigator in the field of political science. In the movement toward the study of politics during the last few decades, the leaders, almost without exception, have been men trained in German schools, familiar with German methods, and profoundly influenced by German ideas. The work of such publicists as Gneist, Stein, Ihering, Bluntschli, Jellinek, and Holtzendorff is clearly evident in the method and thought of present day political scientists. So far as particular doctrines are concerned, the influence of the German school is most obvious in relation to the contract theory of the origin of the state and the idea of the function of the state. The theory that the state originates in an agreement between men was assailed by the German thinkers and the historical, organic, evolutionary idea substituted for it. The purpose of the state they have expanded from the "police theory" to that of general care for the interests of the community. Changes of American theory in this direction cannot, however, be attributed exclusively to the influence of the German school, for the same tendencies have been conspicuous in English and French theory, and in the case of the contract had already been developed by Calhoun and Story. It is interesting to observe at this point that as between the idea of "natural rights" — the German *Naturrecht* — and the Austinian theory, the general tendency in the United States has been to accept the doctrine that there is a body of natural rights semi-ethical, semi-political in nature. The idea that there are inalienable rights of man, quasi-political in character, has taken firm hold of the popular mind, and has not been dislodged by any of the numerous attacks upon this theory since the French Revolution.

The chief foreign influences at work upon the American theory have been the English, the French, and the German. Of these it may be said that the French influence consists largely in the democratic impulse given during the days of the Revolution, the German contribution is chiefly in the direction of scientific method, and that the fundamental political ideas of the Americans have been deeply influenced only by the English thinkers, especially those of the seventeenth century. The present generation looks back to the Fathers and the Fathers looked back to the men of the preceding century.

From a consideration of outside influence upon American ideas, we turn to an examination of the effect of American theory on other peoples. The general influence of American institutions and ideas has been great, but examples of specific doctrines or particular men who have left their impress on the political ideas of other countries are not easy to find. Such instances, although infrequent, are not, however, wholly wanting. Thomas Paine in reply to Burke, Calhoun on the rights of minorities, Lieber on the idea of self-government, are cases in point. Of special importance also was the American theory of a federal union as expounded in the *Federalist* and by Webster and Calhoun. Particularly in connection with the German problem of national unity, these ideas were widely discussed. The *Federalist* theory of a double sovereignty was predominant in the school of which Waitz was the chief exponent, and Calhoun's doctrine of the indivisibility of sovereignty is accepted by Max Seydel and

those of his particularistic faith. American institutions and ideas as described in the brilliant study
of De Tocqueville (1835) were made familiar to
Europeans, and in this way left their impress
upon those peoples at a critical period in the
history of constitutional government. In more
recent times a like service has been rendered by
James Bryce in his classic work on the *American
Commonwealth*.

It goes without saying, that the mightiest influence exerted by the United States in the domain
of political science, has been due to the example
of a democracy successfully working on a large
scale. It would be a gross exaggeration to say
without qualification that the constitutional reforms of the nineteenth century were caused by
the developments in America; but, on the other
hand, it is clearly evident that the American
Republic has been a powerful factor in the
growth of constitutional democracy and of constitutional government in general. In Mexico and
the South American republics, this influence is
seen in institutions framed obviously after the
American type. In European countries, the influence is far less powerful, but even there it has
been remarkable. Not always, or even often, taking the shape of systematic theory, the democratic
spirit and practice of the United States have, nevertheless, made themselves felt in the development
of free institutions. What has been said of demo-

cratic government might also be said of federal government, for in this field the practical influence of the American system has been widespread. The systems of Germany, Canada, Australia, Mexico, and Brazil are sufficient evidence of this.

In conclusion, it may be profitable to notice what has been the broad tendency of American politics, including the theoretical and the practical. During the early period of our history the movement was steadily democratic. Using the suffrage as a standard, although this is not the only test that might be applied, it is evident that the Fathers were more democratic than the Puritans; the Jeffersonian democracy was more liberal than that of 1776; the Jacksonian democracy went far beyond the Jeffersonian school; the Abolitionists extended the boundary lines farther yet; and the advocates of women's suffrage have even surpassed this liberal provision. The political people were, roughly speaking, in the first stage the church-members, in the next the freeholders, in the third place the white male citizens, in the fourth period all adult males, and now tend to include the whole adult population.[1] Property qualifications have disappeared, religious restrictions have fallen into disuse, popular election of officers has displaced the system of legislative choice, constitutions are now usually adopted by popular vote, and

[1] The recent tendency to require educational or property tests is an exception to this uniform advance.

the referendum has been introduced upon many state and local issues.

Certain events in very recent times have been interpreted, however, as indicative of a decline in democratic faith. It is asserted that the rapid concentration of wealth is destroying the economic basis on which democracy rests, and that the substance of power has passed or is passing from the masses. The forms of power, it is said, cannot long remain in conflict with the actual forces and facts, and as the organization of industry has become undemocratic, the organization of government must soon follow in the same direction. It is further urged that the United States has acquired a vast domain lying outside of our geographical group, containing a population which can never be admitted to equal fellowship in the Union, but, if held at all, must be retained on terms of political inequality. The conclusion drawn is that the ideals of earlier days have been forgotten, and that the present tendency is away from democratic institutions.

Without attempting to discuss the future, for that lies outside the scope of an historical study, it may be said that down to the present time, at least, the tendency of American political theory and practice must be regarded as essentially democratic. There is little in either the industrial or the colonial situation to indicate a departure from the line of democratic progress. It is true that the concentration of wealth is increasing at a very rapid rate, and that the legal title to much property is passing into the hands of a few. But it must be remembered that under present conditions, the increase of private possessions does not necessarily signify that power is passing from the hands of the people. On the contrary, in many industries the greater the growth of individual or corporate control, the nearer is that control to becoming popular control. If, for example, a railroad combination should acquire all the railroad systems of the United States, it is highly probable that railroad operation would very soon become a government function or, at least, the situation would give rise to a very large measure of regulation by the people. What seems like the climax of individual or corporate control is likely to pass over into governmental control or regulation. The idea that property is an absolute and unassailable right of the individual and that government exists chiefly for the purpose of protecting this right, is no longer accepted as in the earlier days. On the contrary, the relation of property to the community is now emphasized, and the right of the state to defend its citizens against unfair competition is widely recognized. It is evident, then, that the concentration of wealth does not signify under present conditions the destruction of democratic government, but, on the contrary, is likely if continued to call out a greater extension of democratic activity. In any event, the permanent crystallization of enormous wealth in the hands of any class is not likely to occur, since the transmission of property from one generation to another is in the hands of the people, and may readily be controlled by the machinery of government if such a tendency becomes threatening. Inheritance is generally regarded as a social function, and the inheritance tax is a remedy which is capable of indefinite extension. This instrument may do for democracy what the law of entail did for the old aristocracies. We conclude, therefore, that from the industrial point of view there is little ground for believing that the present drift is away from democracy.

It is further urged, however, that the acquisition of territory unfit for admission into the Union, and without the consent of the population annexed, is an indication of a defection from the principles of the Fathers and the settled policy of the United States. Reasoning from precedent, however, it appears that the phrase "consent of the governed" was never applied in the literal, or anything approximating the literal, sense of the term. The Puritans disregarded the Indians altogether, and consulted the preferences of the church members, who were the political people. The Fathers disregarded the negroes and consulted the freeholders, to the exclusion of a large proportion of the male adults. Likewise the Jeffersonian and the Jacksonian democracy ignored the blacks as a political element, refusing them not only political but even the most rudimentary civil rights. The emancipation of the slaves was brought about in the course of a war that was fought in direct disregard of the principle of the consent of the governed. The eleven seceding states were simply held in the Union by force of arms, without their consent, and despite their most emphatic protest. From the point of view of the South, they were a separate people, and the war against them was one of conquest and subjugation.

Waiving the matter of precedent and considering the question as one of principle, it is evident that much depends on one's political theory. If we believe that government has no jurisdiction over men unless they have consented to it, and that every man is entitled to equal civil and political rights, regardless of his fitness for them, then it follows that to deprive any man of the suffrage for any cause, or any people of self-government for any cause, is a departure from democratic principles. On this basis it would be concluded that within the last four years democracy in the United States had received a decided setback. If, on the other hand, it is believed that liberty and rights are necessarily conditioned upon political capacity, and that the consent of the governed is a principle which, in the present state of affairs, cannot be perfectly realized, then the situation is altered.

From this point of view, the possession of full political rights by every man is an ideal which should, as far as possible, be realized. This was the contemporary interpretation of the Fathers who framed the Revolutionary state constitutions; this was the idea of Thomas Jefferson, of Calhoun, and of Lincoln, and it is the view taken by the overwhelming majority of modern political scientists. This position, it is submitted, is the only tenable one for modern democracy. Doubtless this doctrine may be perverted to despotic uses, but it is not so near despotism as is the opposite doctrine to anarchy; for the full application of the doctrine of the consent of the governed and of the absolute equality of all, in political as well as civil rights at the present day, would be equivalent to the dissolution of every political society now existing. Even with civilized peoples the democracy of the present day must of necessity be imperfect; there must be in every community some exceptions to the general law of political equality.

It appears, then, that whatever may be said of the opportuneness of the new movement in time or place, the charge that it is a departure from democratic ideas has no basis in the principles of political science. Democracy does not demand that barbarians be admitted to equal political rights with peoples long trained in the art of self-government, nor, on the other hand, does it require that democratic states leave the work of political civilization to countries where constitutional liberty is unknown, or to states possessing a less degree of constitutional liberty than their own. It cannot be an article of democratic faith that democratic states must stand by and allow the despotic states of the world to extend a despotic system over the weaker nations of the earth.

Our conclusion is, then, that the charge that democracy is on the decline in the United States is not proven. There are certain tendencies, which, if taken alone, might seem to point in such a direction; but when we consider as a whole the numerous tendencies of which democracy is made up, it is found that there are other and counter-balancing influences, equally important and significant. Hence, it cannot be said that the broad tendency of American political life is away from democracy.

BIBLIOGRAPHY

ABBOTT, LYMAN. The Rights of Man. Boston, 1901.

ADAMS, H. C. The Relation of the State to Industrial Action, 1887, in publications of the American Economic Association, Vol. I.

ADAMS, JOHN. Works, 10 vols., edited by C. F. Adams. Boston, 1856.

Novanglus. 1774–75.

Thoughts on Government. 1776.

A Defence of the Constitutions of Government of the United States, 1787–88.

Discourses on Davila, 1790.

ADAMS, NEHEMIAH. A South-Side View of Slavery. Boston, 1854.

ADAMS, SAMUEL. Life of, by W. V. Wells, 3 vols. Boston, 1865.

ADDAMS, JANE. Democracy and Social Ethics. New York, 1902.

BALDWIN, HENRY. A General View of the Origin and Nature of the Constitution and Government of the United States. Philadelphia, 1837.

BARLOW, JOEL. Advice to the Privileged Orders in the Several States of Europe. Paris, 1792.

Joel Barlow to his Fellow-Citizens in the United States. Philadelphia, 1801.

BARNES, ALBERT. Scriptural Views of Slavery. Philadelphia, 1846.

The Church and Slavery. Philadelphia, 1857.

BATEMAN, W. O. Political and Constitutional Law of the United States. St. Louis, 1876.

BLAND, RICHARD. An Enquiry into the Rights of the British
    Colonists. 1776.
BLEDSOE, A. T. An Essay on Liberty and Slavery. Phila-
    delphia, 1856.
BLISS, PHILEMON. Of Sovereignty. Boston, 1885.
Boston Orations in Niles's Principles and Acts of the Ameri-
    can Revolution.
BOUCHER, JONATHAN. A View of the Cause and Conse-
    quences of the American Revolution. London, 1797.
BRADFORD, GAMALIEL. The Lesson of Popular Govern-
    ment. New York, 1899.
BROWNSON, O. A. Constitutional Government. Boston,
    1842.
    Essays and Reviews. New York, 1852.
    The American Republic. New York, 1866.
BURGESS, JOHN W. Political Science and Comparative Con-
    stitutional Law. Boston, 1890.
CALHOUN, J. C. Works, edited by Richard K. Cralle. 6
    vols. New York, 1833.
    Correspondence of John C. Calhoun, edited by J. Frank-
    lin Jameson, in Annual Report of the American His-
    torical Association for 1899, Vol. II.
    A Disquisition on Government and A Discourse on the
    Constitution and Government of the United States in
    Vol. I of Works.
CAMPBELL, JOHN. Negromania. Philadelphia, 1851.
CHANNING, W. E. Essays on Slavery. Boston, 1835.
CHIPMAN, NATHANIEL. Principles of Government. Bur-
    lington, 1833. First edition, 1793.
COOLEY, T. N. A Treatise on the Constitutional Limita-
    tions which rest upon the Legislative Power of the
    States of the American Union. Boston, 1868.
COOPER, THOMAS. Political Essays. Philadelphia, 1800.
    Consolidation. Columbia, 1830. Second edition.
    Lectures on the Elements of Political Economy. Charles-
    ton, 1826.

COTTON, JOHN. Questions and Answers upon Church Government. 1634.

The Way of the Churches of New England. 1645.

The Bloudy Tenent Washed and Made White in the Bloud of the Lambe. 1647.

The Way of Congregational Churches Cleared. 1648.

DANE, NATHAN. General Abridgement and Digest of American Law. Boston, 1823–29.

DAVENPORT, JOHN. A Discourse about Civil Government. 1663.

DAVIS, JEFFERSON. The Rise and Fall of the Confederate Government. New York. 1881.

DE BOW, J. D. B. The Industrial Resources of the Southern and Western States, 3 vols. New Orleans, 1852–53.

DEW, F. R. An Essay on Slavery. Richmond, 1849.

Review of the Debates in the Virginia Legislature. Richmond, 1833.

DICKINSON, JOHN. Writings of, in Memoirs of the Historical Society of Pennsylvania, Vol. XIV.

DRAPER, JOHN. Thoughts on the Future Civil Policy of the United States. New York, 1865.

ELIOT, C. W. American Contributions to Civilization. New York, 1897.

ELIOT, JOHN. The Christian Commonwealth or the Civil Policy of the Rising Kingdom of Jesus Christ, 1659, in Massachusetts Historical Collections, third series, Vol. IX.

ELY, RICHARD. Socialism. New York and Boston, 1894.

The Federalist, 1787–88.

FISHER, SYDNEY G. The Trial of the Constitution. Philadelphia, 1862.

FITZ-HUGH, GEORGE. Sociology for the South, or the Failure of Free Society. Richmond, 1854.

Cannibals All, or Slaves without Masters. Richmond, 1857.

FLETCHER, JOHN.   Studies on Slavery in Easy Lessons. Natchez, 1852.

FORD, P. L.   Pamphlets on the Constitution.   Brooklyn, 1888.

GARRISON, W. L.   Life by his sons.   3 vols.   New York, 1889.

GIDDINGS, F. H.   The Principles of Sociology.   New York, 1896.

Democracy and Empire.   New York, 1900.

GODKIN, E. L.   Problems of Modern Democracy.   Boston, 1896.

Unforeseen Tendencies of Democracy.   Boston, 1898.

GODWIN, T. S.   The Natural History of Secession.   New York, 1865.

GOODELL, WILLIAM.   Slavery and Anti-Slavery.   New York, 1852.

GOODNOW, F. J.   Comparative Administrative Law.   New York, 1893.

Politics and Administration.   New York, 1900.

GOODWIN, D. R.   Southern Slavery in its Present Aspects. Philadelphia, 1864.

GRIMKE, F.   Considerations on the Nature and Tendency of Free Institutions.   Cincinnati, 1848.

HAMILTON, ALEXANDER.   Works in 7 vols., edited by J. C. Hamilton.   New York, 1850.

HAMMOND, J. H.   Two Letters on Slavery addressed to Thomas Clarkson.   Columbia, 1845.

HANDLIN, W. W.   American Politics.   New Orleans, 1864.

HARPER, WILLIAM.   The Remedy by State Interposition or Nullification.   Charleston, 1832.

Memoir on Negro Slavery.   Charleston, 1852.

HELPER, H. R.   The Impending Crisis.   New York, 1859.

HILDRETH, RICHARD.   The Theory of Politics.   New York 1853.

Despotism in America.   Boston, 1854.

HOOKER, THOMAS. A Survey of the Summe of Church Discipline. London, 1648.

HOPKINS, J. H. Bible View of Slavery. 1863.

HOPKINS, STEPHEN. The Rights of Colonies Examined. 1765. Reprinted in Rhode Island Records, Vol. VI., 416.

HOSMER, WILLIAM. The Higher Law in its Relation to Civil Government. Auburn, 1852.

HURD, JOHN C. The Theory of our National Existence, as shown by the Action of the Government of the United States since 1861. Boston, 1881.
The Union State. New York, 1890.

HYSLOP, J. H. Democracy. New York, 1899.

JAMESON, J. A. The Constitutional Convention. New York, 1866.

JAY, WILLIAM. Miscellaneous Writings on Slavery. Boston, 1853.

JEFFERSON, THOMAS. Works in 10 vols., edited by P. L. Ford. New York, 1892–99. Also an edition in 9 vols. by H. A. Washington. New York, 1861.
Summary View of the Rights of the Colonists. 1774.
Notes on Virginia. 1782.

JORDAN, DAVID STARR. Imperial Democracy. New York, 1899.

LIEBER, FRANCIS. Political Ethics. Boston, 1838–39.
Legal and Political Hermeneutics. Boston, 1839.
Civil Liberty and Self-Government. Philadelphia, 1853.
Miscellaneous Writings, edited by D. C. Gilman. 2 vols. Philadelphia, 1881.

LINCOLN, ABRAHAM. Works of, edited by Nicolay and Hay. 2 vols. New York, 1894.

LOWELL, A. L. Essays on Government. Boston, 1892.

MADISON, JAMES. Works in 4 vols. Philadelphia, 1865.

MANSFIELD, E. D. The Political Grammar of the United States. New York, 1834.

MATHER, COTTON. Magnalia. London, 1702.

MATHER, RICHARD. Church Government and Church Covenant Discussed. London, 1643.

Model of Church and Civil Power.

MOSES, BERNARD. Democracy and Social Growth in America. New York, 1898.

MULFORD, ELISHA. The Nation. New York, 1870.

OTIS, JAMES. A Vindication of the Conduct of the House of Representatives. 1762.

The Rights of British Colonists Asserted and Proved. 1764.

PAINE, THOMAS. Works of, edited by Moncure D. Conway. New York, 1894. Four volumes. Of especial importance are —

Common Sense. 1776.

The Forester's Letters. 1776.

The American Crisis. 1776–83.

The Rights of Man. 1792.

PARKER, JOEL. The Three Powers of Government. New York, 1869.

PAULDING, J. K. Slavery in the United States. New York, 1836.

PHILLIPS, WENDELL. Speeches, Letters, and Lectures. 2 vols. Boston, 1863–91.

POMEROY, J. N. An Introduction to the Constitutional Law of the United States. New York, 1868.

RAWLE, WILLIAM. A View of the Constitution of the United States of America. Philadelphia, 1825.

ROSS, E. A. Social Control. New York, 1901.

ROSS, F. A. Slavery Ordained of God. Philadelphia, 1859.

SAGE, BERNARD J. (Centz, P. C.) The Republic of Republics, or American Federal Liberty. England, 1865.

SAWYER, G. S. Southern Institutes. Philadelphia, 1859.

SEABURY, SAMUEL. American Slavery Justified. New York, 1861.

SIMMS, W. S. The Morals of Slavery. Charleston, 1837.

SMITH, W. A. Lectures on the Philosophy and Practice of Slavery. Nashville, 1857.

STEPHENS, A. H. A Constitutional View of the Late War between the States. Philadelphia, 1867.

Savannah Speech of March 21, 1861, in Moore's Rebellion Record, I., D, 44–48.

STORY, JOSEPH. Commentaries on the Constitution. Boston, 1833.

Miscellaneous Writings, edited by W. W. Story. Boston, 1852.

STRINGFELLOW, T. Scriptural and Statistical Views in Favor of Slavery. Richmond, 1856. Fourth edition.

TAYLOR, F. M. The Right of the State to Be. Ann Arbor, 1891.

TAYLOR, JOHN. An Enquiry into the Principles and Policy of the Government of the United States. Fredericksburg, 1814.

Construction Construed and the Constitution Vindicated, 1820.

Tyranny Unmasked. Washington, 1822.

New Views of the Constitution. Washington, 1823.

THOREAU, H. D. Civil Disobedience, 1849, in A Yankee in Canada. Boston, 1866.

THORNTON, J. W. The Pulpit of the American Revolution. Boston, 1860.

TIEDEMANN, C. G. The Unwritten Constitution of the United States. New York, 1890.

TIFFANY, JOEL. A Treatise on Government and Constitutional Law. Albany, 1867.

TUCKER, H. ST. GEORGE. Commentaries on Blackstone. Philadelphia, 1803. Of especial importance, Appendix to Vol. I.

UPSHUR, A. P. A Brief Inquiry into the True Nature and Character of our Federal Government. Petersburg, 1840.

VAN EVRIE, J. H. Negroes and Negro Slavery. New York, 1861.

WALKER, FRANCIS A. Discussions on Economics and Statistics. New York, 1899.

WARD, LESTER F.   Dynamic Sociology.   New York, 1883.
    Collective Telesis, in *American Journal of Sociology*,
    Vol. II.
WAYLAND, FRANCIS.   The Elements of Moral Science.
    New York, 1835.
WEBSTER, DANIEL.   Works of, in 6 vols.   Boston, 1851.
WILLIAMS, ROGER.   The Bloudy Tenent of Persecution for
    Cause of Conscience.   London, 1644.
    The Bloudy Tenent yet More Bloudy.   London, 1652.
WILLOUGHBY, W. W.   The Nature of the State.   New
    York, 1896.
    Social Justice.   New York, 1900.
WILSON, JAMES.   Works, edited by J. D. Andrews.   Chicago,
    1896.
WILSON, WOODROW.   The State.   Boston, 1889.
    An Old Master and Other Political Essays.   Boston, 1893.
WINTHROP, JOHN.   History of New England.   1630–49.
WISE, JOHN.   A Vindication of the Government of New
    England Churches.   Boston, 1772.
WOOLSEY, THEODORE D.   Political Science.   New York,
    1877.

INDEX

Abolitionism: premises in theory of, 207; typical platform of, 207; attitude toward slaveholders, 209; relation to no-government theory, 209; historical significance of, 216.

Adams, John: theory of, during the Revolution, 43, 48, 52, 69; basis of later theory, 124; criticism of pure democracy, 125 *seq.;* doctrine of aristocracy, 130 *seq.;* theory as to balance of powers, 136 *seq.;* comparison of, with Samuel Adams, 135; fundamental principle in creed of, 140; comparison of, with Jefferson, 162.

Adams, Samuel: on the right of revolution, 56; on purpose of the state, 62; on monarchy, 69; comparison of, with John Adams, 135.

Anti-slavery: radical Abolitionist theory, 206; the philosophical argument, 217; Lincoln's theory, 221; comparison with pro-slavery theory, 248. *See* Abolitionism.

Aristocracy: denunciation of, in 1776, 75; Adams's defence of, 130 *seq.;* principal features in aristocracy, 131; recognition of, in government, 132; hereditary nobility, 133; John and Samuel Adams on, 135; Jefferson on natural and artificial aristocracy, 155; decline of, during Jacksonian period, 184; Lincoln's criticism of, 224; pro-slavery theory of, 236.

Balance of powers: Paine's opposition to, 73; doctrine of, in 1776, 79; development of, in Revolutionary state constitutions, 80; *Federalist's* doctrine of, 107; John Adams's theory of, 136; readjustment of, during Jacksonian epoch, 184; criticism of tripartite division by Goodnow, 323.

Bledsoe, A. T.: on nature of liberty, 235.

Boucher, J.: on consent of the governed, 64; on equality, 65; indorsement of divine-right theory by, 65; on absoluteness of government, 66; opposition to right of revolution, 67.

Brownson, O. A.: on constitution of state and of government, 292; on location of sovereignty in the United States, 295.

Burgess, J. W.: theory of, as to national state, 299; theory of sovereignty, 300; criticism of doctrine of federal state, 300; criticism of theory as to state of nature, 308; criticism of theory of natural rights, 310; concept of liberty, 313; theory of relation of Teutonic races to political civilization, 313; doctrine as to function of the state, 317; distinction between state and government, 325; application of distinction to problem of sovereignty, 326.

Calhoun, J. C.: defence of legislative power, 181; repudiation of

THE CITIZEN'S LIBRARY OF ECONOMICS, POLITICS, AND SOCIOLOGY

UNDER THE GENERAL EDITORSHIP OF

RICHARD T. ELY, Ph.D., LL.D.

*Director of the School of Economics and Political Science; Professor
of Political Economy at the University of Wisconsin*

12mo. Half Leather. $1.25, net, each

Monopolies and Trusts. By RICHARD T. ELY, Ph.D., LL.D.

"It is admirable. It is the soundest contribution on the subject that has
appeared." — Professor JOHN R. COMMONS.

" By all odds the best written of Professor Ely's work." — Professor SIMON N.
PATTEN, *University of Pennsylvania.*

Outlines of Economics. By RICHARD T. ELY, Ph.D., LL.D.,
author of " Monopolies and Trusts," etc.

The Economics of Distribution. By JOHN A. HOBSON, author
of "The Evolution of Modern Capitalism," etc.

World Politics. By PAUL S. REINSCH, Ph.D., LL.B., Assistant
Professor of Political Science, University of Wisconsin.

Economic Crises. By EDWARD D. JONES, Ph.D., Instructor in
Economics and Statistics, University of Wisconsin.

Government in Switzerland. By JOHN MARTIN VINCENT, Ph.D.,
Associate Professor of History, Johns Hopkins University.

Political Parties in the United States, 1846-1861. By
JESSE MACY, LL.D., Professor of Political Science in Iowa College.

Essays on the Monetary History of the United States.
By CHARLES J. BULLOCK, Ph.D., Assistant Professor of Economics,
Williams College.

Social Control: A Survey of the Foundations of Order.
By EDWARD ALSWORTH ROSS, Ph.D.

THE MACMILLAN COMPANY

66 FIFTH AVENUE, NEW YORK

The Citizen's Library of Economics, Politics, and Sociology

Colonial Government. By PAUL S. REINSCH, Ph.D., LL.B., Assistant Professor of Political Science in the University of Wisconsin. Cloth, 12mo. *Now ready.* $1.25 net.

The main divisions of the book are as follows: 1. The Extant and Component Parts of Existing Colonial Empires. 2. Motives and Methods of Colonization. 3. Forms of Colonial Government. 4. Relations between the Mother Country and the Colonies. 5. Internal Government of the Colonies. 6. The Ethical Elements in Colonial Politics. 7. The Special Colonial Problems of the United States.

Democracy and Social Ethics. By JANE ADDAMS, head of " Hull House," Chicago; joint author of " Philanthropy and Social Progress." Cloth, 12mo. *Now ready.* $1.25 net.

Miss Addams's work as head of " Hull House " is known to all persons who are interested in social amelioration, and her writings in the best periodical literature have produced the impression that they proceed from a personality equally strong and gracious. This work will show the profound insight into social conditions and the practical wisdom which we all expect from Miss Addams. As the title implies, it will be occupied with the reciprocal relations of ethical progress and the growth of democratic thought, sentiment, and institutions.

Municipal Engineering and Sanitation. By M. N. BAKER, Ph.B., Associate Editor of *Engineering News ;* Editor of *A Manual of American Water Works.* Cloth, 12mo. $1.25 net.
[*Now ready.*]

This work will discuss in a general introduction the city and its needs, and the plan of the city, and then pass on to such practical questions as ways and means of communication, municipal supplies, collection and disposal of wastes, recreation and art, administration, finance, and public policy. Mr. Baker's work on the *Engineering News* and the annual *Manual of American Water Works* has made him known as one of the leading authorities on all questions of municipal policy. He has the important advantage of combining the technical knowledge of the engineer with long familiarity with economic discussions; and it is expected that this volume will appeal to all classes in any way concerned in municipal affairs.

American Municipal Progress. By CHARLES ZUEBLIN, B.D., Associate Professor of Sociology in the University of Chicago. Cloth, 12mo. *Now ready.* $1.25 net.

Professor Zueblin is well known as one of the most successful University extension lecturers of the country, and his favorite theme in recent years has been municipal progress. In the preparation of this work, he has repeatedly conducted personal investigations into the social life of the leading cities of Europe, especially England, and the United States. This work combines thoroughness with a popular and pleasing style. It takes up the problem of the so-called public utilities, public schools, libraries, children's playgrounds, public baths, public gymnasiums, etc. All these questions are discussed from the standpoint of public welfare.

Irrigation Institutions : A Discussion of the Economic and Legal Questions created by the Growth of Irrigated Agriculture in the West. By ELWOOD MEAD, C.E., M.S., Chief of Irrigation Investigations, Department of Agriculture; Professor of Institutions and Practice of Irrigation in the University of California, and Special Lecturer on Irrigation Engineering in Harvard University. Cloth. 12mo. $1.25, *net. Ready.*

This book is based on twenty years' experience in the development of irrigated agriculture in the arid West. This experience brought the author in contact with farmers, ditch builders, investors in irrigation securities, legislatures and jurists, who were shaping the legal principles which are to control the distribution and use of Western water supplies, and the social and economic fabric under which unnumbered millions of people must dwell. All phases of the subject have been dealt with. Irrigation laws are so ambiguous or contradictory that their meaning is not easy to interpret, and the water rights which govern the value of farms have many forms and are acquired by many methods.

THE MACMILLAN COMPANY
66 FIFTH AVENUE, NEW YORK